THE CAREFREE GETAWAY GUIDE FOR NEW YORKERS

DAY AND WEEKEND TRIPS WITHOUT A CAR

THEODORE W. SCULL
MAPS BY CHARLES BAHNE

THE HARVARD COMMON PRESS
Harvard and Boston, Massachusetts

The Harvard Common Press
535 Albany Street
Boston, Massachusetts 02118

Copyright © 1985 by The Harvard Common Press

All rights reserved. No part of this publication may be reproduced or transmitted in any form or by any means, electronic or mechanical, including photocopy, recording, or any information storage or retrieval system, without permission in writing from the publisher.

Printed in the United States of America.

LIBRARY OF CONGRESS CATALOGING IN PUBLICATION DATA
Scull, Theodore W., 1941–
The carefree getaway guide for New Yorkers.

Includes index.
1. New York (N.Y.)—Description—1981–
—Guide-books. 2. New York Region—Description and travel—Guide-books. I. Title.
F128.18.S36   1985   917.47'10443   85-840
ISBN 0-916782-68-9 (pbk.)

Cover design by Jackie Schuman
Book design by Joyce Weston

10 9 8 7 6 5 4 3 2 1

CONTENTS

INTRODUCTION   ix

NEW YORK CITY BOROUGHS

Upper Manhattan   3
Two Historic Houses in the Bronx   8
The New York Botanical Garden & The Bronx Zoo   13
City Island   18
Historic Flushing & Queens Botanical Garden   24
Brooklyn Heights   31
The Brooklyn Museum & Brooklyn Botanic Gardens   40
Jamaica Bay Wildlife Refuge   46
Brighton Beach, Sheepshead Bay & Coney Island   49

NEW YORK STATE

Staten Island   59
Port Jefferson & the Bridgeport Ferry   66
Bayard Cutting Arboretum   72
Hudson Valley Rail Route Guide   76
Sleepy Hollow Restorations   81
Cold Spring & Boscobel   88
Mohonk Mountain House   95

NEW JERSEY AND PENNSYLVANIA

Hoboken   103
Newark   109
Gladstone   116
A Day at the Beach   119
A Philadelphia Weekend   124

CONNECTICUT AND RHODE ISLAND

Shore Line Rail Route Guide   143
Waterbury   146
Essex   150
Island Destinations from New London   158
Mystic   166

APPENDIX: NEW YORK CITY TERMINALS   175
INDEX   189

ACKNOWLEDGMENTS

I wish to thank the following people for their knowledge, suggestions, and companionship during the preparation of this guide. Jim Feeney for helping me define the auto-free concept, Charles Bahne for his useful set of maps, Andrea Banks for her knowledge of exotic foods and for her companionship on several outings, Doug Bowen and Maureen Quinn for restaurant tips in Hoboken and Gladstone and information about the North Jersey Coast, Brad Hatry and Marilyn Riccitelli for their gustatory and historical knowledge of Brooklyn Heights and adjacent neighborhoods, John Henry for taking me to Block Island, Jim Kerner for help with New York City subway and bus data and procedures, and Faire Hart for sharing her deep affection for the Mohonk tradition. Finally, I thank four friends for accompanying me on the trips and sharing their opinions: Marguerite O'Neill, who brought a foreign point of view to the research as she is Irish, Anthony Perl, Sara Fargo, and George Herland.

Legend for all maps

————	————*	streets and roads*
～～～～	▨▨▨▨*	pedestrian paths*
····o^STATION····	▪▪▪▪▪▪▪▪	rapid transit lines
—■—■— stations	—■—■—	railroad lines
– – – –	▬ ▬ ▬ ▬	ferries
·············		bus routes

* - heavier lines indicate suggested walking route

INTRODUCTION

One-half the households in New York's five boroughs do not keep an automobile—because owning one is too expensive and because safe, affordable parking can be an unending hassle.

When I first moved to Manhattan in 1964, I sold my own car, and then began to wonder how on earth I would ever get out of and around this city without resorting to renting a replacement. In the ensuing twenty-one years, I *have* rented a car—once. I quickly discovered that the tri-state region offers this country's most comprehensive network of trains, buses, even ferries, and that with a little initiative I could learn how to make them all work for me. I found freedom from the burdens of car ownership, along with a new kind of freedom to travel and I do not think that I'll ever go back to those auto-dependent years before coming to New York.

The publication of this auto-free guide is a natural outgrowth of more than two decades of getting to know my city, Long Island, and adjacent states. This book also demonstrates a fervent desire to share my discoveries with others. It's the first guide ever designed for New Yorkers that exclusively advocates the use of safe, comfortable, and economical public transportation to reach the nearby seashore, wildlife sanctuaries, historic towns, country walks, ethnic neighborhoods, cozy inns, and unusual dining experiences.

Destinations that cannot be conveniently reached without a car have no place in this guide.

One of the most successful travel slogans of all time, and a personal favorite of mine, "Getting there is half the fun," comes through on these pages loud and clear. For some outings, the ride may be half the reason for taking the trip in the first place. There is no prettier train ride in this country, for instance, than the water-level route up the majestic Hudson River, on your way to a day spent enjoying the byways of nineteenth-century Cold Spring. On the way to a peaceful weekend on Block Island, for another example, the ferry from trainside in New London hugs the indented Connecticut shoreline before heading out across the open waters of Long Island Sound to berth virtually at the front steps of several historic island inns.

Introduction

All the day trips described here fall within the five boroughs or the tri-state (New York, Connecticut, New Jersey) area, and none are more than a hundred miles from Manhattan. The transportation expenses for each trip are surprisingly economical, often amounting to less than $15 per person. Within the city and immediate outlying districts the transportation costs may be no more than a couple of tokens.

The overnight and weekend escapes reach out to a maximum of 150 miles, including destinations in Rhode Island and Pennsylvania. Tickets both ways generally range upward from $15 to a maximum of $35.

The selection of eating places I have given allows you to decide how much you want to spend, and ranges from simple restaurants with a special local flavor to find dining in well-known country inns. For some outings, I will tell you whether it is advisable to take along some food, or if you can buy locally the ingredients for a picnic to enjoy in a choice spot.

For weekend trips, the book's inns and hotels cater to the budget traveler as well as to those who desire the best, but not necessarily the most expensive, accommodations.

All transportation fares, entry fees, meal prices, and rates for the night are the most up-to-date available at the time of writing, but in our rapidly changing word, they are subject to constant fluctuation—unfortunately mostly upward. Using the specific costs listed here does give you a good approximation of what you can expect to spend.

The destinations are arranged geographically, beginning with the five boroughs, then branching out to Long Island, north up the Hudson, into Connecticut and Rhode Island, then across the Hudson to New Jersey and Pennsylvania.

"Getting There and Back" picks for each trip the best route and the most convenient means of transportation, and tells you in some detail the frequency of departures, the length of the journey, how much it will cost, and what you will see out the train or bus window or beyond the ship's railing. Before heading out for the suburban rail trip to Gladstone, New Jersey, for Sunday brunch at a country inn, for instance, you can read something first here about the landmark Beaux Arts Hoboken Terminal you'll pass through before boarding your train. When the view outside is especially appealing, you will know whether to sit on the left-hand or right-hand side of the train or bus.

You can follow your progress, too, on one of the route maps that are included throughout the guide. Two separate rail route guides accompany several of the outings. One of these is devoted to the scenic seventy-two-mile train trip up the Hudson Valley as far north as Poughkeepsie and the other to the 135-mile route along the Connecticut coast from Penn Station to Mystic.

Upon arrival at the station, depot, or landing it's reassuring to know that in nearly every case you will be within walking distance of the suggested sights and places to eat and stay. One exception to this standard approach is the Essex weekend, where you need to take a short taxi ride from the Old Saybrook Station—but here the experience awaiting you is well worth the small extra expense.

By reading the short keynote paragraphs for each chapters, you will first of all find out whether you want to read on to find out more; you'll also often discover the preferred season to take the trip, and how to make your outing coincide with a special annual event. While the beach at Spring Lake is obviously best in the summer, you might like to be reminded that the out-of-doors can also be enjoyed in the colder months—such as when the birds are stopping over to nest and feed at Jamaica Bay Wildlife Refuge in Queens, just a subway ride away on the A train. Some outings, such as antiquing along Atlantic Avenue in Brooklyn and dining at a neighborhood Middle Eastern or French restaurant, can be enjoyed at any time of the year. You will find that the popular sea chanty festival in Mystic, Connecticut, takes place on a special weekend in June, and that Sunday is the only day to consider visiting the little-known historic houses and Quaker meeting in Flushing.

Many destinations. such as the Hudson Valley's Sleepy Hollow Restorations and Riverdale's Wave Hill Estate, publish a calendar of events for special lectures, demonstrations of cooking, nature hikes, and photographic workshops, to name a few. Specific details, addresses, and phone numbers for more information are included in the keynote paragraphs.

There are apt to be some surprises in store. Unless you have already made a study of the subject, how would you know that Waterbury, Connecticut, would be a fine day's outing, combining a branch line rail ride up the Housatonic and Naugatuck Valleys into the heartland of America's great Industrial Revolution era with a visit to see the Brass City's products in the Mattatuck Museum *and* with a walk through a hillside neighborhood of preserved nineteenth-century mansions? Or that Jamaica Bay's East and West

Ponds are artificial creations that resulted from one of Robert Moses' brilliant suggestions during a subway construction project? Or that, for seventy-five cents, you can cross the Hudson in a matter of minutes and be in the midst of a happily bewildering choice of Italian, French, German, traditional seafood, and trendy gourmet restaurants in Hoboken, New Jersey?

Consult the "New York Area Transportation Operators" appendix for questions you might have about how to get schedules for Amtrak's fast "clockers" to Philadelphia; where to call to find out about the Long Island Rail Road's bicycle permits; how to find information on Metro-North's off-peak one-way fares to Philipse Manor; and about the city's relaxed requirements to secure senior citizen half-fare cards.

If you, as most people, are unfamiliar with the train and bus services off your regular routes, refer to this section to begin to understand how simple public transportation can be. Special area maps in "New York Area Transportation Operators" show the location of the major transportation terminals and how they tie in with your destination.

When you set out, you'll be surprised how pleasant getting there can be if you ride on one of the new subway cars on the IRT line to The Brooklyn Museum or on the freshly painted "Silver Fox" cars on the elevated Flushing Line to the Queens Botanical Garden. You can gain no better lesson of Manhattan geography than on a fascinating ride north to The Cloisters on the M4 bus through the Upper East Side, Harlem, and the Upper West Side. Most of the area commuter lines offer better service than in years past, and others are currently undergoing major improvements to their tracks, stations, and equipment.

Above all, it is hoped that this guide will give you the complete freedom you want when the urge rises to break away from your routine and head for the hills or the beach, to do something cultural, explore another city—and, of course, to have fun getting there. After a few trips you will no doubt make some of your own discoveries. Be sure to share them with others as I have mine with you, and happy auto-free traveling.

Theodore W. Scull
Manhattan, February 1985

NEW YORK CITY BOROUGHS

UPPER MANHATTAN
The Cloisters & Fort Tryon Park
Dyckman House & Inwood Hill Park

The Cloisters, Fort Tryon Park, New York, NY 10040. (212) 923-3700. Open Tuesday–Sunday 9:30 a.m.–5:15 p.m. Closed Monday. Suggested admission $4.

Dyckman House, Broadway and 204th Street, New York, NY 10040. (212) 755-4100. Open Tuesday–Sunday 11 a.m.–5 p.m. Closed Monday. Admission free.

The Metropolitan Museum's outstanding medieval art collection at the Cloisters features the world-famous Unicorn Tapestries and fine examples of religious frescos, illuminated manuscripts, and metal art objects in a peaceful setting of intimate rooms, small chapels, and open courtyards. Located high atop the Hudson Palisades, the Cloisters opened in 1938 thanks to generous funding from John D. Rockefeller, Jr.

To reach the museum, climb aboard a city bus for an absorbing ride through nearly the full gamut of New York neighborhoods to the very northern tip of Manhattan. Get off at the entrance to Fort Tryon Park, and enjoy a twenty-minute stroll through the beautifully landscaped grounds, with glorious views of the Hudson River from parapets and through breaks in the trees.

On a fine day, serious walkers might wish to add to their outing with a visit to the little-known Dyckman House on Upper Broadway, which is Manhattan's only surviving example of a Dutch Colonial-style farmhouse. On a small hill overlooking the commercial hubbub of Broadway, the period house seems curiously out of place.

Two blocks west, 196-acre Inwood Hill Park offers a three-quarter-mile scenic waterfront path running north to the meeting point of the Harlem and Hudson Rivers. If you intend to cover all the parts of the Upper Manhattan outing in one day, be sure to get an early start, and pack a picnic for a lunch break down by the river.

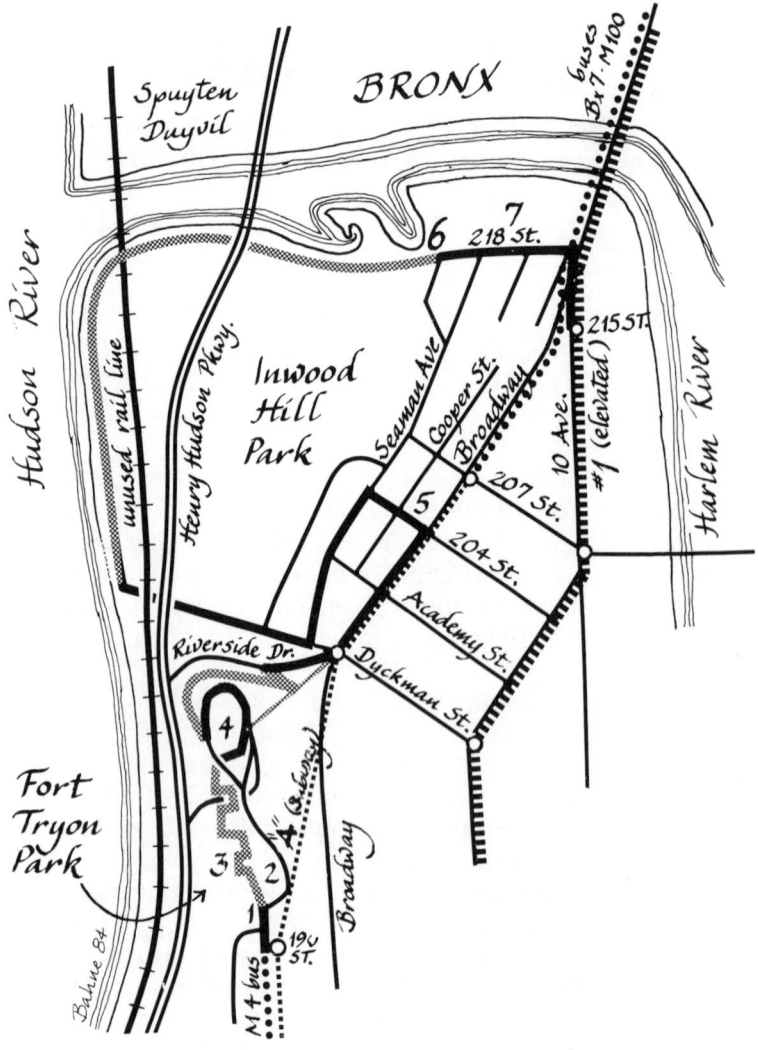

Upper Manhattan

1. Margaret Corbin Plaza
2. Cafeteria
3. Fort Tryon
4. The Cloisters
5. Dyckman House
6. Columbia University Boat House
7. Baker Field

Getting There and Back: From the West Side, by bus, take the M5 northbound along Broadway and Riverside Drive to any stop between 110th and 168th Streets, and transfer to the M4 marked variously "193 Street," "Fort Washington Ave.," "Fort Tryon Park," or "The Cloisters." By subway, take the IND A train to 190th Street, where an elevator will carry you up to Fort Washington Avenue at a point just a five-minute walk from the entrance to Fort Tryon Park.

From the East Side, take the M4, one of the city's most interesting bus routes (it's proudly featured on the front cover of the Manhattan bus map). The long ride, about one and one-half hours for the complete run, gives you an excellent overview of some of the richest as well as the poorest parts of the city, and of the solid middle-class neighborhoods of Washington Heights. The M4 begins opposite Penn Station on 32nd Street and turns north on Madison Avenue, lined for nearly three miles with exclusive shops that come to an abrupt end at 98th Street, the unofficial entrance to Spanish Harlem.

The bus turns left on 110th Street and heads west along the top boundary of Central Park, passing pockets of many abandoned yet substantial buildings, ripe for restoration, then climbs past the Cathedral Church of St. John the Divine, and crosses Broadway to reach Riverside Drive. To the left is wooded Riverside Park, and beyond through the trees the majestic Hudson River. To the right stand some fine older Upper West Side apartment houses.

At 135th Street, the M4 cuts back to Broadway and traverses a largely Spanish-speaking neighborhood with homogeneous six-story commercial and residential buildings lining the busy street for the next mile. At 155th Street, you pass Trinity Church's uptown cemetery and the Gothic Revival-style Episcopal Church of the Intercession. Next, on the left, in the stark surroundings of Audubon Terrace, a complex of classically styled buildings houses several organizations, including the American Geographical Society and the Museum of the American Indian. Columbia-Presbyterian Medical Center dominates the neighborhood around 165th Street, and at 168th Street the bus makes a left and then a right onto Fort Washington Avenue. The area is quietly residential again. At 178th Street, the bus passes beneath the approaches to the George Washington Bridge and the main uptown bus station, while brief glimpses of the bridge can be seen to the left.

The neighborhood includes many Tudor-style apartment houses, and little Bennett Park, on the left side between 183rd and 185th Streets, marks the highest spot in Manhattan, 268 feet above sea level. Just ahead now is the sixty-six-acre Fort Tryon Park, where the ride may end, unless the bus is marked "The Cloisters."

If this is the end of the line (or even if it isn't and you'd like a short walk), get off here at Margaret Corbin Plaza, stretch your legs, and stroll through the inviting park directly ahead to reach The Cloisters.

On the right side of the central walkway are isolated benches set in the shrubbery. On the left, narrow paths wind through reasonably looked-after flower gardens, at their best in the spring and early summer. On warm weekends, many local residents flock here for a chat or quiet read. Further along, a lovely vista point, 250 feet above the river and set on a terrace once occupied by Fort Tryon, gives sweeping views to the south toward the George Washington Bridge, across the river to the New Jersey Palisades, and north up the Hudson between the city of Yonkers and its towering cliffs. Rising from the treeline just before you is The Cloisters, to be reached in ten more minutes by descending the footpaths that twist away to the left and the right.

The museum's main entrance is found by approaching the building's right side, opposite the bus stop and car park. Be sure to pick up the useful little guide at the door, and follow the plan by keeping to the right to make a complete circuit of the two levels. Also, you may want to phone ahead for the schedule of conducted tours and special concerts of medieval music.

The museum is housed in an elaborate medieval-style building incorporating original sections from twelfth- to fifteenth-century chapels and cloisters from Spain and France. The settings are architecturally intriguing, an eclectic mix of styles that forms a varied string of galleries. The rooms, many of which open onto terraces overlooking the Hudson or surround peaceful little courtyards, are filled with religious paintings, sculpture, beautifully worked objects, jewels, and stained glass. Probably best known are the Franco-Flemish fifteenth- and sixteenth-century Unicorn Tapestries, showing the hunting-down and capture of the legendary beast. Allow two or three hours to tour the entire collection and to rest amidst the tranquil atmosphere of the courtyards, which contain examples of flowers, herbs, and plants grown during the Middle Ages.

At the end of the visit, you may wish to board the M4 bus right outside the door, or continue on to the Dyckman House and take a riverside walk through Inwood Hill Park. If you did not bring a picnic lunch, there is a cafeteria near the south end of Fort Tryon Park as well as simple coffee shops and fast food places along Broadway.

To reach the Dyckman House, leave the Cloisters at the north end, and follow one of the winding paths down through the woods to Riverside Drive. The park gradually becomes less well-maintained as you return to urban civilization. Riverside Drive leads into Broadway, where you make a left and walk up to 204th Street.

High on the northwest corner, the Dyckman House sits incongruously, with its front porch looking out over a changed modern world of shabby apartment houses and gas stations.

The fieldstone, brick, and wood Dyckman House, a Dutch Colonial-style farmhouse dating from 1783, offers us the only glimpse left in Manhattan of how a prosperous middle-class family might have lived in the countryside that once formed a large part of the island.

The Dyckmans established their farm near the northern tip of Manhattan as early as 1661, and eventually the family holdings totalled nearly three hundred acres. The original house was occupied both by the Continental Army and by the British occupation forces during the Revolutionary War. When the British withdrew in 1783, they burned it to the ground.

The present house is constructed from some of the salvaged materials, and its land was farmed until 1868. When the house was slated for demolition in 1915 to make way for an apartment building, Dyckman family descendents bought the place, furnished it with family heirlooms, and donated the property to the City of New York.

Enter the grounds through a side gate, and follow the walk up to the front porch, covered by part of the gambrel-style double-pitched roof. While there is no official guide, the caretaker at the door can answer your questions.

On the main floor, the smallish parlors are crowded with examples of late eighteenth-century upholstered and wooden furniture. Upstairs, the family bedrooms, located under the eaves, each have beds appearing absurdly short to us today, as well as those curious commodes that predated indoor plumbing. A narrow staircase from the ground floor leads down to the basement kitchen with its large cooking fireplace, and to the dining room with a table set seemingly for the next family meal.

In back the yard, surrounded by the kind of apartment houses once meant to replace this property, contains a garden, smokehouse, and a small hut used in the eighteenth century by the occupying British forces.

After your visit, the best return route is to walk to the end of Dyckman Street, where on warm, sunny weekends local residents wash their cars beneath the concrete arches of the Henry Hudson Parkway. Near the river, there is an opening onto a series of playing fields spread over a long strip of narrow land between the woods and the Hudson. A footpath parallels the river for about three-quarters of a mile with good views of the Palisades and the waterborne commerce. At the edge of an abandoned railroad line, turn around and head back the way you came to Broadway for the bus or subway.

TWO HISTORIC HOUSES IN THE BRONX
Van Cortlandt Mansion & Wave Hill Estate

Van Cortlandt Mansion, Broadway and 246th Street, Van Cortlandt Park, Bronx, NY 10471. (212) 543-3344. Open Tuesday–Saturday 10 a.m.–4:45 p.m., Sunday 12–4:45 p.m. Closed Monday and certain holidays. Admission adults $1.50, seniors $1, children free.

Wave Hill Estate, Independence Avenue and West 249th Street, Bronx, NY 10471. (212) 549-2055. Open daily 10 a.m.–4:30 p.m.; hours may vary with the season and are extended in the summer. Admission on weekdays free. On weekends and holidays, adults $2, seniors $1, children under 14 and members free.

Two quite different historic estates, within walking distance of each other, await visitors to the Bronx.

Van Cortlandt Mansion dates from 1748, which makes it the oldest surviving structure in the borough. The house is set in a

Two Historic Houses in the Bronx   9

grove of trees at the southern end of Van Cortlandt Park; its interior, furnished in seventeenth- and eighteenth-century American, Dutch, and English antiques, gives an idea of how a prosperous Dutch-English family would have lived around the time of the American Revolution.

Wave Hill, a half-hour's walk through leafy suburban Riverdale, is a lovely country garden estate overlooking the Hudson. Neighborhood people use the grounds as their own public park, and so can you. Spend a quiet afternoon in luxuriant surroundings, go on a nature walk, or take in a musical concert.

Allow a leisurely full day to visit both places, including travel time.

 Getting There: (See the end of the tour for *Getting Back.*) You have a choice of traveling by subway, city bus, express bus—or foot.

The tour described here first goes to Van Cortlandt Mansion and then to Wave Hill. Take a picnic lunch unless you would prefer to eat at a fast food restaurant on Upper Broadway. There are no eating facilities near or on the grounds of Wave Hill.

The most direct, if not the most pleasant route from the West Side, is to take the IRT #1 Broadway Local to the end of the line at 242nd Street, Van Cortlandt Park. This line, one of the grubbiest in the city, is very slow but safe during the day. The train runs underground, coming up for air briefly over a high trestle at 125th Street, going below again, and rising finally to an elevated line in Upper Manhattan. Look up to the left for The Cloisters and Inwood Hill Park (see the previous entry). After the 215th Street Station, the line crosses the Harlem River on the upper level of a road and rail bridge entering the Bronx at Marble Hill. A brief look to the left will show the Harlem River leading into the Hudson. The train rattles above Broadway until reaching the ancient terminus at 242nd Street, completed just after the turn of the century.

From the East Side, by subway, take your nearest cross-town bus to the IRT #1 Broadway local and follow the above West Side itinerary. Liberty Lines (212-881-1000) runs air-conditioned express bus BxM 3 every half-hour from stops between 26th Street, just west of Madison Avenue, and from 98th Street and Madison Avenue directly to 244th Street and Broadway at the edge of Van Cortlandt Park. Travel time from 82nd Street, for instance, is about thirty minutes. Fare is $3, and you need exact change.

From the subway or bus stop, walk north along Broadway to the Van Cortlandt Park Visitors Center. Pick up a map of the park at the Visitors Center, or, if closed, at the urban park rangers' office one flight down at the back of the building.

Van Cortlandt Park, once part of the large crop and sheep farm owned by the Van Cortlandt family, today comprises nearly two square miles of open spaces, woods, a lake, wildlife refuge and bird sanctuary, Indian burial grounds, playing fields, the oldest municipal golf course in the country, an 1842 aqueduct, and a local railroad freight line. The park is very popular on weekends and sometimes shows it.

Van Cortlandt Mansion is found just inside the park nestled in a grove of trees and surrounded by a protective iron fence. A guided tour, operating on demand, is usually available. Unless you are particularly familiar with this historical period, waiting for a guide is recommended over wandering on your own. There are summer concerts you might want to ask about.

The house, a simple yet stately square Georgian-style mansion, was built of rough fieldstone with brick window trim by Frederick Van Cortlandt in 1748. George Washington used the house on several occasions in 1781 to plan Revolutionary War strategy with French commander Comte de Rochambeau.

In 1889 the Van Cortlandt family deeded the estate to the City of New York, and in 1968 the house was declared a National Historic Landmark. Today the National Society of Colonial Dames (with headquarters at 215 East 71st Street, Manhattan) has custody of the house and grounds.

Inside the house, the four floors of painstakingly restored rooms are furnished with seventeenth- and eighteenth-century American, Dutch, and English antiques, hinting at the comfortable living standard enjoyed by this wealthy New York family.

In the basement, the open-hearth kitchen has a good collection of iron cooking utensils, and the adjacent preparation room is still used for drying herbs gathered from the garden. The room is also set up to show a slide-illustrated program of the Van Cortlandt's family history to small groups.

The sumptuously furnished parlors and dining room, set as if for the next meal, once received many important dinner and overnight guests. Upstairs, canopied beds, handsome chests of drawers, and wool carpets provided warm elegance.

One of the oldest doll houses in the country as well as other children's toys, toilet articles, and clothing fill the attic and former nursery.

To get from Van Cortlandt Mansion to Wave Hill, a half-hour walk, mostly through one of the most attractive residential neighborhoods in the entire city, is highly recommended, and not only because the bus routing is circuitous. One note of warning—there are no food facilities after you leave Broadway.

Leave the park the way you entered, cross Broadway, take the unnamed street staight ahead one short block to Post Road, and turn right. Walk up another block to the start of West 246th Street, where you make a left. Keep climbing past the grounds and buildings of Horace Mann, an academically challenging private school, which are on the right. The winding road weaves through a prosperous section of large and very expensive Riverdale homes.

Use the short road bridge to cross the Henry Hudson Parkway, and turn right onto the parallel service road for three blocks to West 249th Street. Turn left, and follow the road in an arc around to the entrance gates of Wave Hill.

Wave Hill, a twenty-eight-acre public garden estate overlooking the Hudson, has had many owners and rental tenants since the oldest section of the main house was completed in 1843–44 in Greek Revival style. Theodore Roosevelt, Mark Twain, and Arturo Toscanini were among the better-known people who found the place enchanting enough to rent for the summer.

Owned by the City of New York since 1960, the place rapidly fell into disrepair during the financial crisis. In the last few years, a major effort has returned much of the property, the main house, the greenhouses, and the grounds to their original condition. In some areas, the present gardeners are developing their own less formal styles, more suited to today's public use.

Many Riverdale residents come regularly to Wave Hill, and on a nice day in the warm months you are likely to see people contentedly seated in high-back wooden chairs scattered about the manicured lawns and beneath the expansive copper beeches reading, conversing, and dozing. Picnicking, however, is not permitted at Wave Hill.

The main house has an environmental learning center in the basement, small-scale art and botanical exhibits, an Alpine-beamed auditorium for lectures, and musical concerts that naturally feature

Toscanini's performances and broadcasts. To the left of the front door, there is a small gift shop. While the mansion beautifully fits the formal garden setting, its interior is only of modest interest.

Guided weekend walks and bird talks take visitors through the rose, herb, and English wild gardens, as well as the woodlands and greenhouses, where a variety of plants are for sale. Call ahead for special events, as the schedules vary from week to week. There are family photographic workshops, choral society concerts, historical talks on Wave Hill's architecture and famous summer residents, and a spring clean-up work day. But even if there is nothing organized on the day you come, the beautifully serene surroundings are worth the long trip north.

If you have not had enough walking, and would like to see the nearby Hudson River close up, leave Wave Hill by turning right down Independence Avenue, then right again down West 248th Street and across Palisade Avenue to the ninety-seven-acre Riverdale Park. Still largely undeveloped, the linear wooded space stretches for over a mile north and south, paralleling the river and the railroad line.

By walking north to where West 254th Street comes down to the river, you can return to Grand Central in twenty-eight minutes on a Metro-North train from Riverdale Station. Southbound service on weekends and holidays runs about every two hours from 10:07 a.m. Consult a green Hudson Line timetable before you choose to return this way. The one-way fare of $2.90 ($1.90 for seniors) is payable on the train.

Getting Back: to Manhattan from Wave Hill. Leave the way you came, and walk to 249th Street and Henry Hudson Parkway. For the West Side, take the M100 or Bx7 bus to West 225th Street and Broadway, and from there the IRT #1 line southbound. For a bus-only return, take the M100 to 168th Street and Broadway with a free transfer to the southbound M5. For the East Side, take the Bx24 bus to Fordham Road and Jerome Avenue and switch to the elevated IRT #4 southbound express. For a bus-only routing, take the M100 to 168th Street and Broadway, with a free transfer to the M3, or take the M100 to 160th Street and Amsterdam Avenue, where you transfer to the M101.

You can also return by express bus. Liberty Lines (212-881-1000) runs express routes from the corners of West 252nd and West 246th

Streets and from the Henry Hudson Parkway south into Manhattan about every half-hour. The BxM 1 goes to the East Side as far as Lexington Avenue and 32nd Street, and the BxM 2 goes down the West Side to Broadway and 34th Street. Call for a timetable for the schedule and exact stops. Fare is $3 in exact change.

THE NEW YORK BOTANICAL GARDEN & THE BRONX ZOO

The New York Botanical Garden, Bronx, NY 10458. (212) 220-8700. Grounds open daily dawn–dusk. The Enid A. Haupt Conservatory open Tuesday–Sunday 10 a.m.–5 p.m. Admission adults $2.50, seniors, students, and children 6–16 $1.25.

The Bronx Zoo, New York Zoological Society, Bronx, NY 10460. (212) 367-1010. Open daily 10 a.m.–5 p.m., Sunday and holidays 10 a.m.–5:30 p.m. November, December, and January, closing is 4:30 p.m. daily. Admission free Tuesday–Thursday; Friday–Monday adults $2.50, children 2–12 $1, seniors always free.

For a full day, mostly out-of-doors, at two of the city's most famous attractions, go north to the Bronx for a walk through The New York Botanical Garden and The Bronx Zoo.

While The Enid A. Haupt Conservatory with its seasonal and perennial indoor displays of native and foreign plants and flowers may be enjoyed at any time of the year, the wooded trails, formal gardens, and great open spaces are best saved for a spring, summer, or early fall hike.

To the south across Fordham Road, The Bronx Zoo features America's largest urban collection of animals and birds of 561 different species. Wild Asia provides a natural setting of hillsides, woods, and ponds for roaming tigers, elephants, and rhinos. The World of Birds is a tropical rain forest allowing multi-colored flyers the freedom to go from treetop to treetop. The pocket guide available at the gate lists feeding times for the animals, something that children will not want to miss.

Visitors with specific interests may wish to explore more thoroughly only one of these two destinations in a single trip.

14 New York City Boroughs

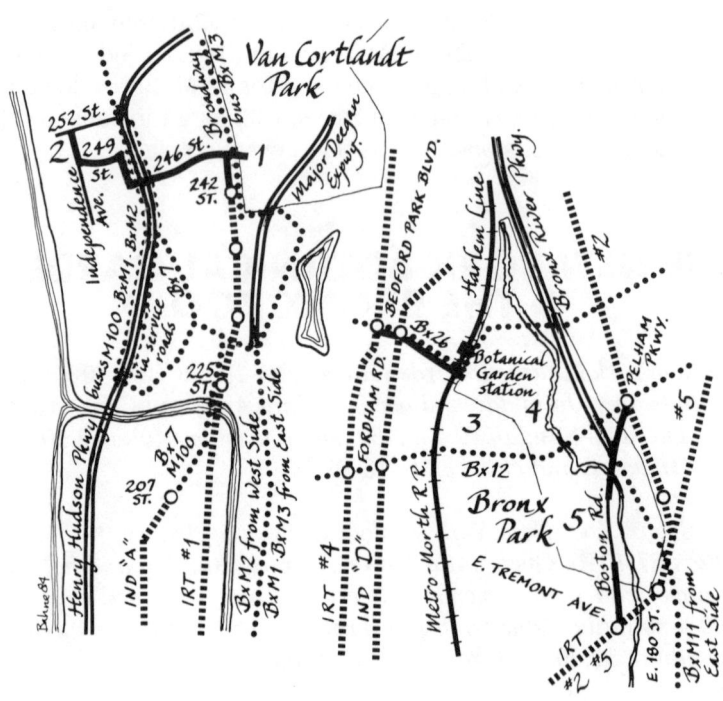

The Bronx

1. Van Cortlandt Mansion
2. Wave Hill
3. Fordham University
4. New York Botanical Garden
5. Bronx Zoo

Getting There and Back: From Grand Central, take the Metro-North commuter train on the Harlem Line (212-532-4900). Trains leave every hour on the half-hour on weekdays and weekends, taking twenty minutes for the ten miles to Botanical Garden Station, located directly across Southern Boulevard from the main pedestrian entrance. Off-peak one-way fare is $2.60, seniors $1.70. Metro-North offers a seasonal combination ticket that includes a round-trip rail ticket and entrance fee to the Conservatory. Adults $5.80, seniors $4.40, children under 12 $2.65.

From the West Side, by subway, take the IND D train marked "205 Street" to Bedford Park Boulevard, and walk east for eight blocks (fifteen minutes) along the road to the entrance. The neighborhood is quite safe.

From the East Side, by subway, take the IRT #4 Lexington Avenue express marked "Woodlawn-Jerome Ave" to Bedford Park Boulevard and walk about ten blocks east (twenty minutes).

The connecting Bx26 bus also runs along Bedford Park Boulevard to the Botanical Garden entrance, for those who do not wish to walk.

For first-timers entering the 250-acre botanical garden, the beauty and expanse of the place is absolutely staggering. And no public park in New York is so well-kept. While spring, summer, and early fall offer the greatest variety of flowering trees, shrubs, and plants, a walk among the pines and hemlocks on a warm winter's day is an equally refreshing tonic.

Most visitors will want to head directly for The Enid A. Haupt Conservatory, a wonderful Victorian crystal palace where a show of horticultural excellence is put on regardless the season or weather.

Every one of the interconnected glass pavilions offers a special display, some year-round and others according to the season. A towering variety of palm trees, bathed in natural light, fills the ninety-foot high central dome. Feel the heat and humidity of the Amazon jungle as you walk through a tropical rain forest of exotic plants, and, as a contrast, experience the hot and dry climate of the desert pavilion with its floor covered in small and tall cacti and other succulents. The more formal English and French gardens are a cool combination of clipped green shrubbery and bright seasonal floral displays. Kids will enjoy identifying the various animals shaped from English ivy.

Tours, included in the entrance fee, begin at frequent intervals, and are recommended for those who would like a deeper understanding of plants and flowers than may be gained from merely strolling through the elaborate displays or even reading the informative labels.

The Conservatory has a simple snack bar offering sandwiches and drinks, with tables for eating and a bit of a rest, before tackling the myriad of paths that winds among the outdoor floral displays and natural wooded settings. One route that covers most of the park heads in the direction of the Rock Garden to Rhododendron Hill and Magnolia Dell, then along one side of the Bronx River. Walk as far as Snuff Mill, an historic eighteenth-century stone building that now serves as public cafeteria and restaurant for special functions. The self-service section, open year-round weekdays 9 a.m.–4 p.m. and weekends 9 a.m.–5 p.m., is on the lower level, and offers full meals and lighter fare at very reasonable prices. After making your choice, take your food, on warm days, outside to a wide terrace among tall trees overlooking the tumbling little Bronx River. It's not hard to imagine here that you are deep in the Massachusetts Berkshires near the source of the Housatonic River, rather than in the heart of a great urban metropolis.

To the east of Snuff Mill are lilacs and rose gardens covering a full acre and displaying hundreds of varieties. To the south is the Pine Grove and the River Gate exit to Pelham Parkway and, across the street, The Bronx Zoo's Rainey Gate.

If you are not visiting the zoo, swing back through Azalea Glen and Daffodil Hill, two areas that border Southern Boulevard. If you have any energy left, consider visiting the botanical garden's museum, close to the entrance through which you passed. Besides changing exhibits featuring ecological and environmental studies relating to horticulture, there is a garden center that sells all sorts of plants, bulbs, seeds, and gardening tools, as well as gift items with plant and flower motifs.

If your day wouldn't be complete without a trip to The Bronx Zoo, read on.

Getting There and Back: A word of caution regarding the trip to the zoo. Both the West Side and East Side subway lines pass through a devastated area of the South Bronx on elevated trestles. Consider taking the Liberty Lines BxM 11 express bus from the East Side.

From the West Side, take the IRT #2 express marked "241 Street-White Plains Road" to the East Tremont Avenue Station (elevated). Walk down to the street and continue, at first under the elevated line, along Boston Road to the zoo's Asia Gate. The neighborhood is not a pleasant one. An alternate IRT #2 station, with a more attractive approach to the zoo, is Pelham Parkway elevated station three stops further along. The zoo's Bronxdale Gate is just west along the parkway.

From the East Side, take the IRT #5 express marked "Dyre Ave" to East Tremont Avenue, or, at East 180th Street, switch from the #5 to the #2 and get off at Pelham Parkway, and follow the above walking instructions.

The New York Botanical Garden & The Bronx Zoo

An alternate route that avoids the elevated subway line through the South Bronx is a subway-bus route involving two fares each way. From the West Side: take the IND D train marked "205 Street" to Fordham Road subway station and connect with the Bx12 bus marked "Pelham Bay" to The Bronx Zoo's Rainey Gate or the nearby Bronxdale Gate. From the East Side: take the IRT #4 express marked "Woodlawn-Jerome Ave" to Fordham Road elevated station and connect with the Bx12 as above.

If you prefer to go by express bus, Liberty Lines (212-881-1000) operates regular interval air-conditioned express bus BxM 11 from 26th Street, up Madison Avenue to the Bronxdale parking lot. Fare is $3, and well worth it in this case.

The 252-acre Bronx Zoo shares the southern half of Bronx Park with The New York Botanical Garden. If you are first visiting the garden, enter the zoo through the Rainey Gate, located across Fordham Road-Pelham Parkway from the garden's River Gate.

Pick up a map at the gate, then find a seat and allow some time to plan your visit. It's rewarding to follow several of the theme walks that include the Bird Valley's lakes, ponds, and aviaries, the Zoo Court, with its variety of animals housed in beautiful early twentieth-century buildings, and the Africa Trail, where, in the warmer months, the animals freely roam the open grasslands separated from you by dry moats rather than restricting fences.

The additional admission fee to see the World of Darkness is worth every penny. An eerie setting allows such nocturnal creatures as bats, owls, sloths, and sugar gliders to flap and slink about as they would in the natural forest at night.

In the spring, summer, and early fall, several completely different forms of conveyance can save you a great deal of walking, while giving a special vantage point. All charge small fees. The Bengali Express Monorail, with commentary, makes an aerial loop of Wild Asia. Skysafari, an aerial tramway, runs for nearly the zoo's entire width from Wild Asia, alongside Africa Trail, and over the South American Trail to a point next to the Children's Zoo. A Safari Tour Train operating on rubber tires gives a good orientation of the entire collection with its 3600 animals of 561 species, making it the largest urban zoo in the United States. Even elephants, those exotic beasts from Thailand, India, and Burma, and camels, the lumbering form of transportation in the Arab World, are pressed into service, and can be ridden in front of the old Elephant House in the Zoo Court.

For food, the indoor-outdoor cafeteria in an attractive setting overlooking the Wildfowl Pond has the largest in-zoo selection of hot meals and lighter fare. The Flamingo Pub, somewhat removed from the mainstream of pedestrian traffic and next to the pond of the same name, offers chicken, roast beef, shrimp, hamburgers, and pizza, with a bar licensed to sell beer and wine. For quick hot dogs and hamburgers, the Zoobar, near the Children's Zoo, has an outdoor eating area.

By consulting the zoo's guide you will find the schedules of morning and afternoon feeding times for crocodiles, sea lions, pelicans, penguins, and the big cats, flyway demonstrations in the World of Darkness, drenching rainstorms in the Reptile House, and loud thunder and lightning displays in the Rain Forest section of the World of Birds. The Bronx Zoo has so many dimensions that an entire day could easily be spent within the boundaries.

CITY ISLAND
A World Apart in the Bronx

City Island, an isolated residential seaside community linked by a short bridge to the northeast Bronx, features some of the best seafood restaurants in the East, and from its water's edge visitors may gawk at hundreds of private yachts under construction, being repaired, or simply moored, and even arrange for sailing lessons.

City Island Avenue, the village's one and one-half-mile main thoroughfare, is worth exploring from end to end to check out the restaurants and to poke around the antique and collectible stores clustered near the island's center. On the quiet side streets, rows of closely packed plain and fancy Victorian houses reveal a way of life that one would not expect to find so close to a great metropolitan area.

While urban decay, declining population, and high crime rates have crippled large areas of the Bronx mainland, City Island has held onto its reputation as a safe community in which to live; as a consequence, even its most ordinary houses now command relatively high prices. It's also a fine place to visit at any time of the year.

Originally, in the middle of the eighteenth century, City Island was settled with an eye to its becoming a rival port to Manhattan. That grand idea never came to pass, though, and the island, which was ultimately absorbed by New York City in 1895, established itself as a relatively quiet oystering and boat building center.

 Getting There and Back: You'll need to take a combination of subway and bus, at a total cost of four transit fares, and plan to have lunch or early dinner on the island. Most visitors will wish to make the return subway trip before dark.

There are several subway lines from both the East and West Sides that connect with the Bx12 bus to City Island.

From the East Side, take the Lexington Avenue IRT #6 local marked "Pelham Bay Park" to the northern end of the line, a forty-five-minute ride from midtown and the Upper East Side. There are pre-World War II decorative tiles and mosaics to be seen in the underground stations, and after Hunts Point Avenue and the unseen devastation of the South Bronx, the line rises to an elevated structure for the remainder of the trip. Shortly after crossing the Hutchinson River Parkway, the #6 comes to the end of the line at the edge of Pelham Bay Park and Bruckner Boulevard.

Follow signs indicating City Island buses downstairs and out to the street. Bus Bx12, marked "Rochelle Street-City Island Ave," leaves from in front of the Grand China Restaurant.

The most convenient route from the West Side uses the IND D train marked "205 Street," which runs underground all the way to Fordham Road, where you surface to connect with the eastbound Bx12 bus. This bus may be marked "Pelham Bay Park," meaning that you've got to ask for a free transfer for the continuation of the route to City Island. Alternate routes use the IND A train, which is underground to the end of the line at 207th Street, Washington Heights, or the IRT #1 Broadway local, mostly underground with some elevated sections, to 207th Street, where you connect with the Bx12 running the full width of the Bronx to City Island. A route description of the bus line follows below. Not recommended are the IRT #2 and #5, because they run elevated through some of the very worst sections of the South Bronx.

The complete west to east route of the Bx12 bus gives an interesting overview of some of the Bronx's more prosperous neighborhoods, and conveniently connects with all the above subway lines.

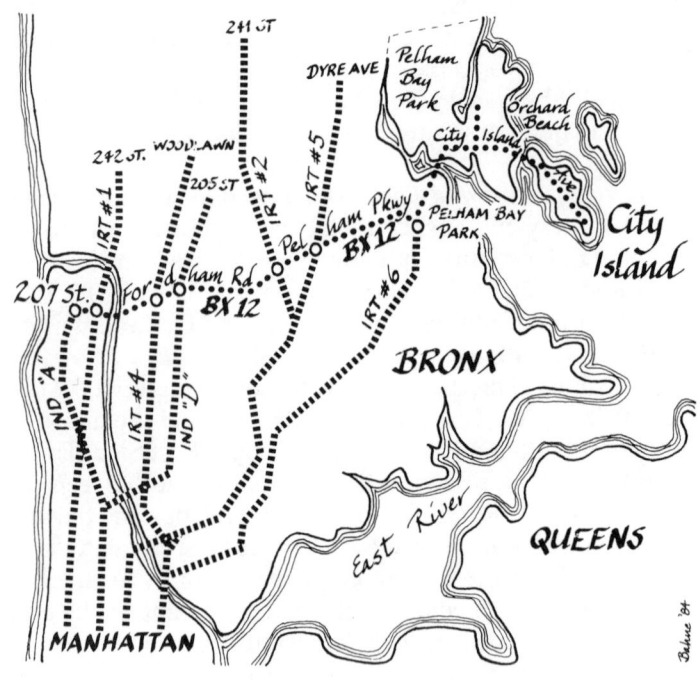

City Island

Beginning at its western end, which is the terminus for the IND A train in Upper Manhattan, the Bx12 crosses the Harlem River and the Major Deegan Expressway via the University Avenue Bridge, and enters the Bronx with a steep climb up West Fordham Road. After passing through the major Fordham shopping district and across the Grand Concourse, the attractive campus and Gothic buildings of Fordham University appear through the trees to the left. To the right, Arthur Avenue cuts into the heavily Italian neighborhood of Belmont, noted for its excellent Italian restaurants.

The bus runs between The New York Botanical Garden on the left and The Bronx Zoo on the right. After passing over the Bronx River Parkway, it uses Pelham Parkway, an attractive boulevard bordered by green open parkland, small apartment buildings, and single-family houses.

At the Pelham Bay subway (elevated here) station, the bus run may terminate. If so, there will be a free transfer to the City Island shuttle bus. The Bx12 route continues into Pelham Bay Park, the borough's largest, with some 2,117 acres of woodlands, open spaces, walking, cycling, and bridle paths, and a golf course. While crossing the Hutchinson River, the huge and somewhat forbidding Coop City complex rises to the left beyond the parallel Hell Gate rail line that carries Amtrak trains to and from Boston.

Deep into the park, the views are now of woods and marshlands and of the vast expanse of Long Island Sound stretching away to the north and south. To the left, the white crescent of Orchard Beach appears as the bus approaches the low bridge over to City Island. City Island Avenue, serving as the community's main street and running the full length of the 230-acre island to Belden Point, now begins.

Leave the bus at the first stop after crossing the bridge to avoid heavy traffic, and begin the island tour on foot.

City Island is a seafood lover's paradise, with its eating establishments ranging from open-air cafeterias, to simple diners, to large restaurants with studied decor and outdoor gardens. Some eating places have a distinctly Italian flavor, beginning with their names. Unless you have a restaurant already in mind, make your own survey by checking the menus of each place (most post their lunch and dinner cards in the front window) while strolling along the one and one-half-mile length of City Island Avenue. A good hour can be consumed by this delightful exercise, with allowance for an occasional detour down one of the residential side streets.

There is an especially large concentration of restaurants at the bridge end of City Island adjacent to some of the island's yacht marinas. Perhaps most famous of all is Thwaites Inn, a landmark eatery for islanders and visitors since 1870. At this large family-style restaurant, you cannot go wrong by ordering the fresh Maine broiled lobster with drawn butter. After touring the island and before you head home, you might also consider stopping in here for a drink in the popular piano bar. Phone (212) 885-1023 for reservations, which are recommended on weekends for lunch or dinner.

Near the middle of the island, you'll find a group of smaller, less distinguished restaurants, shops, collectible dealers, and the island's post office and public school.

At the far end, another cluster of restaurants offers even further choice. In this grouping, the Lobster Box, an up-market establishment that has been around since 1945, boasts seventeen ways to serve shrimp and twenty-two ways of dealing with lobster. The variety, somewhat bewildering for first-timers, ranges from simple butter and garlic sauces to rich casserole dishes. If your companions choose differently, you can sample around the table. The Lobster Box is closed on Mondays.

On a bright sunny day, for those not wishing to indulge in a large meal, Johnny's Reef Restaurant is a very popular cafeteria-style operation offering a great variety of fresh seafood at reasonable prices in a no-nonsense Long Island Sound setting. Johnny's is on the left just beyond Rochelle Street, the terminus for the Bx12 bus. A menu posted above the Fry Section offers ready-to-serve fried shrimp in a basket, with french fries and a dollop of cole slaw, for $10 including tax. There's no tipping. At the Steam Section, $9 buys bay scallops in a butter or garlic sauce, with fresh-baked bread to soak up the remaining liquid. At other counters, you can order a dozen littlenecks on the half shell for $7, and make your choice of alcoholic or non-alcoholic drink.

While there's indoor seating opposite the serving counters, the best location for your picnic is one of the several dozen tables available on the patio overlooking the stretch of water separating City Island from the North Shore of Long Island. From a choice spot near the railing, you can watch sail and motor boats cruising the Sound. Johnny's is plain and simple outdoor seafood dining at its best. Don't be put off by the sight of large numbers of families encountered here. Service is fast and efficient, and the dining areas are rapidly cleared and kept remarkably clean.

Eating is not the only possible pastime for visitors to City Island. Antique and knickknack browsers will find small shops, mostly open in the evenings and sometimes in the daytime, scattered along City Island Avenue. Most of them are concentrated in the 200s on City Island Avenue between Schofield and Fordham Streets. Nautical Antiques is crammed with brass fittings from ships, while Grandad's Barn, one of the largest stores, has room for furniture, lots of old china sets, and endless tables of knickknacks.

Boating is a great pastime on the island, and to reach the pockets of activity, walk down one of the side streets that end at the water's edge. Local residents claim that boats outnumber the island's population, and there is much evidence about to support the claim.

Boatbuilding, sales, repairs, docking, and related businesses such as sailmaking are the island's main industries. *Courageous* and *Intrepid*, the famous America's Cup winners, came out of the Minnieford Yacht Yard. Today, the owner Henry Sayers handles mostly smaller boats made of fiberglass.

If you would like to learn to sail, there are practical courses that can teach you the ropes in about twenty hours, either on two back-to-back weekends or on consecutive days during the week. The instruction combines classroom and over-the-water training on an individual or small group basis. Phone the Offshore Sailing School, East Schofield Street, at (212) 885-3200, or the New York Sailing School, 560 Minnieford Avenue, at (212) 885-3103. The price ranges from about $275 for one, with slightly lower rates for two or more.

At the east end of Fordham Street, at about the middle of the island, the city maintains the ferry *Michael Cosgrove* for transporting the coffins of the indigent and unknown for burial in Potter's Field on nearby Hart Island. Rikers Island prisoners do most of the work, and the general public is kept behind a fence and not allowed aboard the ferry.

On the same road that runs at a right angle to City Island Avenue, a former schoolhouse now serves as the home for the City Island Historical and Nautical Museum, housing an assemblage of items that reflects the island's history and connection to the sea, with special exhibits on the Hell Gate ship pilots and the racing yachts built here for America's Cup competition. Opening hours are limited to Sunday only from 2 to 4 p.m., and the telephone is (212) 885-1616.

The island's residential housing is a homogeneous or heterogeneous mix, depending on the street, of modest single-family houses, stylish Victorians, and experimental new condominiums. Pick Minnieford Avenue, a narrow lane that parallels City Island Avenue, or one of the many other side streets, to get the feel of how peaceful and isolated life in this little community can be. The bustle of the main street, with its bumper-to-bumper traffic on warm weather weekends, can seem miles away within one short block.

Of particular interest are the Grace Episcopal Church and its rectory on City Island Avenue at Pilot Street. Built in 1862, the wooden church is Gothic Revival style, with a steep peaked roof and tall slim tower, while the rectory is reminiscent of a modest Italian villa. A nearby house, at 141 Pilot Street and also built in about 1862, has similar features in its wooden-work porch and window design.

HISTORIC FLUSHING & QUEENS BOTANICAL GARDEN

Queens Botanical Garden, 43–45 Main Street, Flushing, NY 11355. (718) 886-3800. Open daily 9 a.m.–dusk. Admission free.

Queens Museum, New York City Building, Flushing Meadow Corona Park, Flushing, NY 11368. (718) 592-5555. Open Tuesday–Saturday 10 a.m.–5 p.m., Sunday 1–5 p.m. Closed Monday. Admission adults $1, students and seniors 50 cents.

In a conveniently compact section of Flushing in Northern Queens, several of New York's most historic buildings can be found, including the city's oldest house of worship.

The 1661 Bowne House served as an early clandestine Quaker meeting house until 1694, when the British government agreed to certain religious freedom in the colonies, and the Friends Meeting House was allowed to be built nearby. Except for a brief period during the Revolutionary War, this Flushing Meeting has maintained continuous weekly meetings, which outsiders are most welcome to attend.

Nearby, the Kingsland Homestead of 1774 is a fine example of a Dutch-English-style farmhouse. Adjacent to the house in a small park, the 1847 Weeping Beech Tree has the distinction of being one of the only living landmarks in New York City.

Within easy walking distance, the thirty-eight-acre Queens Botanical Garden boasts a wide variety of plants and flowers, with over four hundred species of roses, many of them still experimental and unnamed, and a charming Victorian wedding garden that has been the site for many outdoor marriage ceremonies.

An optional side trip for energetic walkers to Flushing Meadow Park visits the elaborately detailed panorama model of New York City, constructed for the 1964 World's Fair. For children, there is a small-scale zoo where the animals may be hand-fed, a realistic farm site, and a traditional carousel. Everything is within a short distance on foot.

The best time for a visit to historic Flushing is on any weekend year-round when the houses are open, or, if you wish to attend a Quaker Meeting, on Sunday. For the floral displays in the Queens Botanical Garden, choose any fine day in the spring or summer, the latter season if you want the roses to be at their best.

Getting There and Back: By subway, the IRT #7 Flushing Line, operating on an elevated structure in Queens, offers an interesting above-ground view of the borough. The line offers frequent service from Times Square to Main Street Flushing, where it is a walk of only a few minutes to the historic district and the botanical garden. Be warned that the line is slow going, especially during the lengthy reconstruction period. The work-related delays may add another five to fifteen minutes to the thirty-minute journey from midtown. The fare is ninety cents each way.

Or, go by Long Island Rail Road. The LIRR runs trains from Penn Station, at intervals of every half-hour or every hour, depending on the time of day, taking seventeen minutes to reach Flushing station, within a block of the subway stop. The one-way off-peak fare from Penn Station is $2.90, $1.90 for seniors, and double for the round trip. For information, (212) 739-4200.

The route guide will assume that you are taking the IRT #7 Flushing Line from Manhattan to the end of the line at Main Street, Flushing.

Although under reconstruction, the Flushing Line, opened to Main Street in 1928, is one of the city's more interesting rapid transit lines to ride. The IRT trains come in two color schemes, white or what is known as "silver fox." When Transit Authority President David Gunn took office in 1984, he set out to rid the system of rampant graffiti vandalism, and the Flushing Line became his first test case. The "Silver Fox" trains are painted maroon with a silver roof and a black top band across the front and rear of the cars. They are handsome to look at, more so in the daylight than in the tunnels.

The line begins at Times Square, with stops at Fifth Avenue and Grand Central for connections, before diving under the East River. At Hunters Point Avenue, the second stop in Queens, the line rises to an elevated structure and passes the LIRR's Hunterspoint Avenue platforms to the right. The train then makes several very sharp turns, squealing in the process, then pauses at Queensboro Plaza, a "spaghetti junction" interchange with the BMT R Line. The outbound station is one level above the inbound station.

26 New York City Boroughs

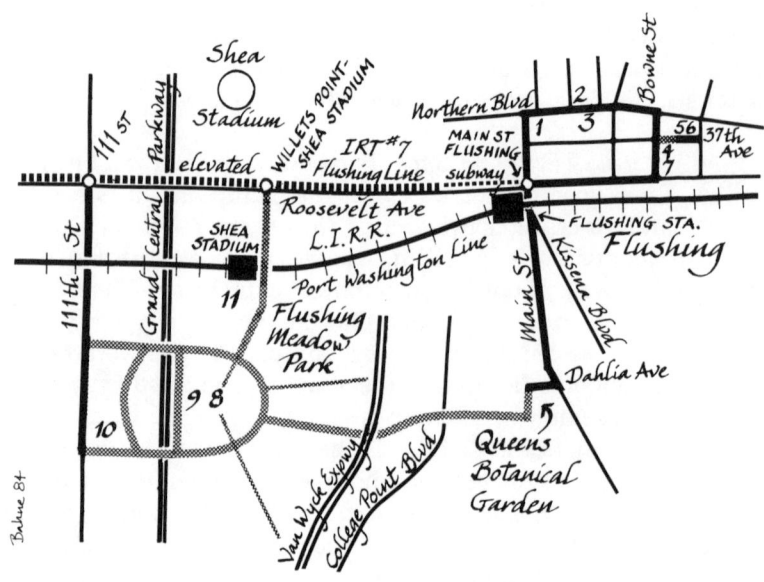

Flushing

HISTORIC FLUSHING
1. Quaker Meeting House
2. Flushing Town Hall
3. Armory
4. Bowne House
5. Kingsland House
6. Weeping Beech Park
7. Bowne Street Community Church

FLUSHING MEADOW PARK
8. Unisphere
9. Queens Museum
10. Flushing Meadow Zoo
11. National Tennis Center

The elevated tracks pass over the Sunnyside freight and passenger car yards, where Amtrak and New Jersey Transit trains are washed, cleaned, and prepared for their next trips, and over the Long Island Rail Road's main line and Amtrak's Hell Gate Route to New England.

The Flushing Line now becomes three tracks, with the center rails used for rush-hour express service inbound in the morning and outbound in the afternoon. At Woodside, the #7 interchanges with the LIRR, and, at 74th Street-Broadway, with the IND E and F and the BMT G and N trains. Be sure to note, especially at the Junction Boulevard Station, the fanciful light fixtures and stanchions evoking another era.

The neighborhoods below consist mostly of small brick apartment buildings and single-family row houses.

Near the end of the line, the train crosses the Grand Central Parkway, then passes Shea Stadium on the left, and on the right the Corona subway yards, Flushing Meadow Park, and several of the buildings left over from the 1964 World's Fair, before finally crossing the Van Wyck Expressway and Flushing Creek. In the final few hundred yards the train becomes a subway again, terminating underground at Main Street. Note the station's colorful tiles, a common feature of the IRT system.

The junction of Main Street and Roosevelt Avenue marks the commercial heart of Flushing, anchored by the Chase Manhattan Bank, Alexander's Department Store, Stern's, and Woolworth's. The recent influx of Koreans, Chinese, Southeast Asians, and Indians, now making up half the population, is responsible for Flushing's new name, "Little Asia."

Originally an English settlement called Vlissingen, after a city in the Flemish part of the Netherlands, Flushing, incorporated into New York City in 1900, remained a geographically separate community until the coming of the railroad, the subway, and the bridges at the beginning of this century.

Today, the place is part of the urban sprawl that characterizes Queens, and, at first glance, one wonders how anything historic could survive here. Begin the hunt by walking north along Main Street to Northern Boulevard, opposite the old movie palace, and turning right.

One block down Northern Boulevard on the right stands, quite inconspicuously, the oldest religious building in New York City. Built in 1694, and enlarged in 1717, the gray-shingled Quaker Meeting House has provided a place of worship for nearly three hundred years, apart from several years of British occupation in the Revolutionary War.

Walk around to the back, and, if it is Sunday morning, you are apt to find a small group of Friends meeting here or in discussion following the meeting. You are most welcome to join them in prayer. There are no ministers or priests, and therefore no order or ceremony to the meeting. At first, it is mostly a silent service, and then anyone who feels inspired may speak out on any subject by merely standing up. The topic does not necessarily need to be religious, but may address an issue of peace, human suffering, or a phenomenon of nature. Generally, the meeting concludes after about an hour, at which time those who wish to stay behind gather in an outer room to have an open discussion. The interior, characteristic of the Quakers, is quite plain, with heavy timber beams, plastered walls, and simple wooden benches. The small graveyard has some inscribed stones; those that are unmarked date from before 1835.

Practically across the busy boulevard stands the former Flushing Town Hall and Municipal Court House, a Romanesque Revival style brick building first built in 1862 and now the site for local public events. On the same side of the street as the Quaker Meeting House, the smallish crenellated red brick medieval style fortress is a National Guard Armory Building, completed in 1905, although it looks much older.

Turn right on Bowne Street, one block after Union, and walk one block to 37th Avenue, also known as Congressman Rosenthal Place. Just beyond the playground and park on the left is the shingled and painted Bowne House, built in 1661, with additions in 1680, 1696, and 1830.

A small plaque indentifies the site as a national shrine to religious freedom. Before the permanent Quaker Meeting was built nearby, Englishman John Bowne and others met here, until Bowne was arrested, sent to prison, and then exiled by the Dutch Government. Later in Amsterdam, he won his case, and the Quakers were allowed to worship in peace, now under English rule. The Bowne family lived here until 1946.

The house, furnished with colonial American antiques from nine generations of Bowne descendants, is open Tuesday, Saturday, and Sunday from 2 to 4:30 p.m. for an admission charge of $1, twenty-five cents for children. During the tour, the guide can tell you more details about John Bowne's fight for religious freedom.

Pass through the little park that interrupts 37th Avenue, and on the other side, opposite a playground, is Kingsland Homestead, a typical Dutch-English-style farmhouse, built in 1774, with pale yellow shingles and green shutters. In 1965 the house, at a site about one and one-half miles to the east, was threatened with demolition to make way for a shopping center. After a complex series of negotiations, in 1968 the house was moved to its present location. Volunteers will show you about the exhibits of early Queens life, mounted by the Queens County Historical Society, for free, during the same hours as for the Bowne House. Ask the guide to tell the complete story of how the house was saved from the wrecker's ball.

Next door, in a small enclosure, the Weeping Beech Tree stands as one of the city's only living landmarks. Planted as a cutting in 1847 by Samuel Parsons, a nurseryman who supplied the original trees for Prospect and Central Parks, the great old tree envelops the entire park, stands sixty-five feet high, and has a circumference of fourteen feet.

Return through the park to Bowne Street, turn left, and walk two blocks to Roosevelt Avenue. On the corner, the handsome Romanesque brick Bowne Street Community Congregational and Reformed Church, built in 1892, with some intricate detail and a tall Bohemian tower, now serves as well as the Korean Church of Queens.

Turn right on Roosevelt, walk two blocks back to Main Street, and turn left for the Queens Botanical Garden.

The fifteen-minute walk begins by passing under the LIRR overpass along Main Street to Dahlia Avenue. The sign for the Queens Botanical Garden points to the right. Ignore it. Pedestrians will find the entrance across Dahlia Avenue and to the right to be more pleasing than the one that passes through the parking lot.

Built on what was once a coal ash dump, the thirty-eight-acre Queens Botanical Garden is a quiet haven for flowers, plants, and people. On sunny days, local residents bring along their own chairs to share the natural beauty and each other's company. Senior citizens with a green thumb are encouraged to look after their own small garden plot, and every year thousands of pounds of vegetables are harvested.

Best begin the visit by walking around to the left through the Cherry Tree Circle, the evergreen collection, and the All-America Garden, where new varieties are continually being tested. In the spring, more than fifty thousand tulips and other flowering bulbs provide a rainbow of color. The Bee Garden supplies the gift shop with natural honey for sale, and the Bird Garden features plants that give food or shelter to birds. The Rose Garden is the outstanding section, with more than 250 varieties, not including another two hundred "test" roses. Spring and summer are the best times to see them in full bloom.

The Wedding Garden, in almost constant use on summer weekends, offers a splendid Victorian setting of streams, a gazebo, and weeping willows for the happy occasion. You can watch the ceremony in progress from behind a white picket fence, and wish the newlyweds a long life of happiness as they pass through the gate.

At the opposite end from where you entered, the Arboretum is a fine place to have a picnic amidst crab apple and flowering cherry trees.

If time and energy permit, you might consider walking through Flushing Meadow Park to Queens Museum to see the elaborate model of New York City. Allow about forty-five more minutes of walking, not including the visit to the museum and any other diversion that might crop up.

Leave the orchard by keeping left below the slight rise, and use the wide footbridge to cross over College Point Boulevard and to pass under the Van Wyck Expressway. Flushing Meadow Park, the sites for the 1939-1940 and 1964-1965 World's Fairs, has seen better days, and you will want to pass through it as quickly as possible.

Follow the formal path with the Unisphere and its fountain directly ahead to the building marked "The Panorama of New York City." The entrance is around to the right.

While there are always rotating exhibits in the galleries, occasionally featuring Queens artists and their achievements, it is the city panorama that most people come to see on their first visit. Take the elevator up to the second floor and turn right. Behind glass you look down upon the five boroughs as if you were flying around the city's perimeter at a height of several miles. The detail is good and generally up-to-date, but you can make it a "trivial pursuit" to pick out the location of not-yet-added new buildings or Manhattan piers that have burned down.

Take your time to locate other destinations mentioned in this book by walking around to the other side. About every minute the urban setting goes through a night cycle, but daylight lingers longer.

Getting Back: There are two ways to reach the #7 Flushing Line for the ride back. With Shea Stadium as a guide, follow the paths to the LIRR Shea Stadium Station (fewer trains stop here when the stadium is not being used, so check the schedules) and the Willets Point-Shea Stadium IRT station.

For the second route to the Flushing Meadow Park Children's Zoo, carousel, and pony rides, leave Queens Museum by walking directly ahead and left over the pedestrian bridge spanning the

Grand Central Parkway. Just to the left are the Children's Zoo, a small-scale enclosure featuring North American animals which can be hand-fed (free), a miniature barnyard with pony rides, and a traditional whirling carousel. To leave the area, pass relics of the early space age on the left, and walk through the large parking lot to 111th Street. Continue under the LIRR embankment for four blocks through an Archie Bunker neighborhood to the 111th Street elevated station, also a relic of sorts, with original, angled blue and white enamel signs directing passengers for the Upper East Side to transfer to the 2nd Avenue "el." The last train to run on that line did so on June 11, 1940!

While waiting for your train to arrive, note how the trestle sways with the approaching trains. Don't worry; it is actually designed to wobble and shake.

BROOKLYN HEIGHTS
Below and Beyond

New York City Transit Exhibition, northwest corner Boerum Place and Schermerhorn Street. (718) 330-3060. Open daily 9:30 a.m.– 4 p.m. except Thanksgiving, Christmas, and New Year's. Admission adults 90 cents or one token, under seventeen, 45 cents.

Brooklyn Heights and the adjacent neighborhoods of Cobble Hill and Boerum Hill form several of the city's most attractive and liveable neighborhoods, especially for those who work in the Wall Street area or in downtown Brooklyn.

For the visitor, there are quiet streets lined with nineteenth-century residences, the gentle bustle of Montague Street and Atlantic Avenue, the restful Esplanade with its fine views of the harbor and Lower Manhattan, and the historic Fulton Ferry Landing in the shadow of the Brooklyn Bridge.

It is walking territory. Day One is a proposed tour, beginning with a spectacular walk over the Brooklyn Bridge, of the established and emerging Brooklyn Heights districts of brownstones and brick townhouses, grand old hotels and ornate commercial buildings, numerous churches and low-rise apartment houses. Taken together, these present a relatively compact lesson in outstanding urban architecture.

Much less known to people of other boroughs are the delights to be found below the Heights along a relatively short stretch of Atlantic Avenue. On Day Two, you might consider coming here on a Saturday afternoon to explore the two dozen antique and collectible stores that line the avenue side-by-side for several blocks. When your feet tire, try one of the neighborhood's Middle Eastern or French restaurants.

If you get a good start in the morning, stop in at the New York City Transit Exhibition for a view of the subways as they were earlier in this century.

Getting There and Back: Nearly every north-south subway line in Manhattan crosses the East River to converge on the area of Borough Hall where the walking tour begins.

Take either the IND A train to High Street and walk along Cadman Plaza West, in the direction of Borough Hall, to Montague and Court Streets; or the IRT #2 and #3 to Clark Street, beneath the old Hotel St. George, and walk along Henry Street to Montague; or the BMT R (and sometimes the M) to Court Street along Montague; or the IRT #4 and #5 to Borough Hall (and note the colorful mosaics) and follow Court Street to the beginning of Montague; or, finally, the IND F to Jay Street-Borough Hall, the second Brooklyn stop, and walk around Borough Hall to the foot of Montague.

Walking the Brooklyn Bridge

On a fine day, the trek from City Hall in Manhattan over the Brooklyn Bridge is a delightful experience, and one that is a cherished way to work for many of the borough's residents.

To locate the start of the not-so-obvious foot path, cross Centre Street opposite City Hall and to the right of the Municipal Building. A concrete median strip runs between the lanes of bridge traffic, and soon the path rises to a wooden walkway high above the automobiles. For some, the experience is marred by the penetrating hum of rubber tires on the metal roadway grating. It's a sound not unlike an approaching swarm of attacking bumble bees.

The view upward between the spidery cables towards the stone towers is both rhythmic and awesome. Looking to the right are the Brooklyn docks, the Heights, and the old-fashioned skyline of downtown Brooklyn just behind. Below and to the right, the East River empties into the Upper Bay between Governors Island and the Battery.

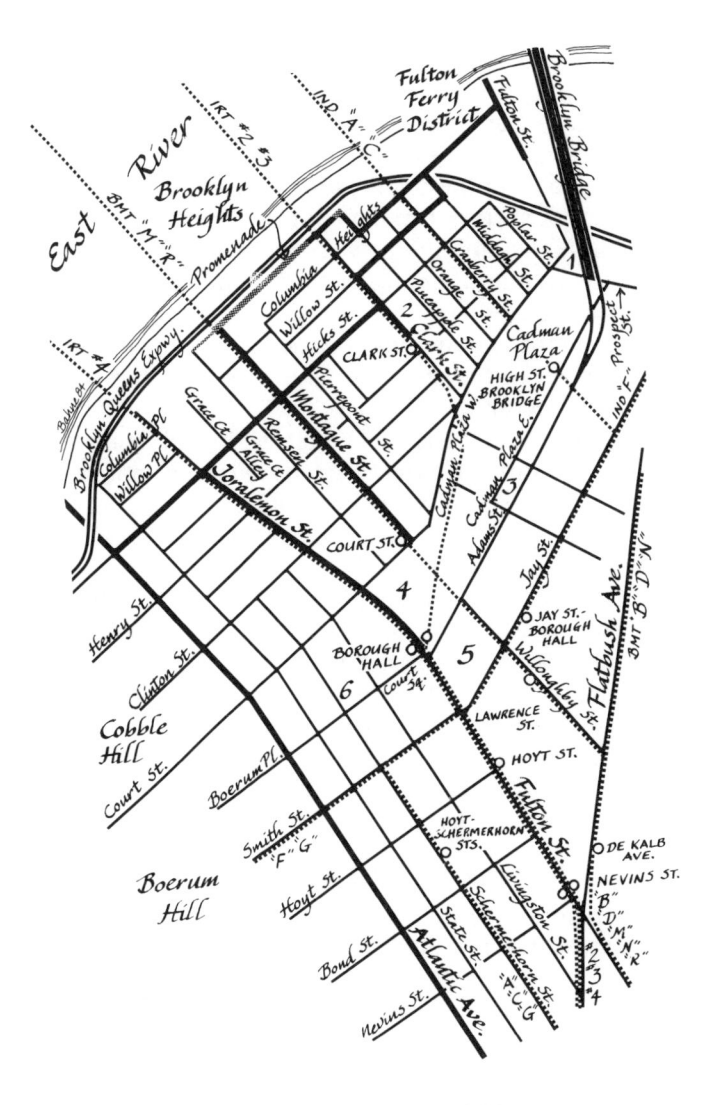

Brooklyn Heights and Vicinity

1. pedestrian entrance to Brooklyn Bridge
2. St. George Hotel
3. Brooklyn General Post Office
4. Borough Hall
5. Transit Authority Headquarters
6. Transit Exhibit

Upriver, the blue Manhattan Bridge partly blocks the view of the containerized banana piers and the former Brooklyn Navy Yard. Between the two bridges on the Brooklyn side, the largely abandoned manufacturing and warehouse district, now known as the Fulton Ferry District, is on the verge of being recycled into modern offices and recreational facilities.

Once past the middle of the bridge, turn around for a wonderful view of the New York skyline, picking out the World Trade Center, the Woolworth Building, and the new towers of Battery Park City. The sweeping vista continues uptown to the Empire State, Chrysler, and Citicorp Buildings.

Before the turn of the century, the Brooklyn Bridge once afforded the highest viewpoint in the city, and its towers were the world's tallest man-made structures.

The wooden promenade turns to concrete again and finally ends in steps down to the street. Go right under the bridge approach to Fulton Street-Cadman Plaza West. From here you can join the walking tour at Borough Hall, or head straight down to the Fulton Ferry Landing.

Two distinctively different areas will be covered on the following two day trips. First, a walking tour of Brooklyn Heights, Columbia Heights, and the Fulton Ferry District, with eating suggestions, and then, for a second day, on to Atlantic Avenue for its Middle Eastern restaurants, bakeries, and antique stores and a hike into Cobble Hill, Boerum Hill, and Carroll Gardens. For those with an interest in the city's transportation history, you might also want to visit the Transit Exhibition, two blocks from Borough Hall.

Day One: Brooklyn Heights

The establishment in 1814 of steam-powered ferry service from Fulton Street Manhattan to Fulton Street Brooklyn quickly transformed the Brooklyn side of the East River into New York's first bedroom suburb. Residential development, aided by additional ferries from Wall Street to Montague Street and from South Ferry to Atlantic Avenue, came fast.

Today more than half of the eleven hundred houses in the Brooklyn Heights Historic District (established in 1965) date from before the Civil War, and only a tiny percentage were built after 1900.

Borough Hall, Brooklyn's oldest government building, dating from 1846 to 1851 and formerly City Hall until the borough was incorporated into New York City in 1898, stands as a beautifully restored Greek Revival-style palace, with a Victorian cupola added in the same year the building changed its name and function. Gamaliel King, a local grocer, builder, and carpenter, was responsible for the original sections. Borough Hall, which stands at a pivotal point between Brooklyn Heights and the definitely less genteel downtown Brooklyn, is open to the public on weekdays, and there are often Brooklyn-related exhibits worth seeing inside.

Montague Street, beginning opposite Cadman Plaza, which was created following the demolition of elevated lines and dilapidated housing, is Brooklyn Heights' main street. In the first block between Court and Clinton Streets, several large office buildings and stately banks form an impressive entrance to the neighborhood. Small stores, cafes, and restaurants line both sides of the street to within a block of the promenade and the river.

One block to the right at the intersection of Clinton and Pierrepont Streets is the Long Island Historical Society, in the process of being renamed the Brooklyn Historical Society. The ornate building, completed between 1878 and 1880 and combining several styles, is best viewed from the opposite corner. Recent photographic exhibits here documented the building of the Brooklyn Bridge, showed the perils caused by the early trolley cars, and recalled some of the borough's oldest private houses. Bus and walking tours are offered in conjunction with some of the special events. (Open Tuesday–Saturday, 12–5 p.m. Admission free.)

Foffe's, 155 Montague Street (718) 625-2558, on the right after the brownstone Holy Trinity Episcopal Church, is a long-established Italian-French restaurant with a 1930s atmosphere of glass partitions and cozy booth seating. The regulars are generally older native Brooklynites rather than the trendy set that dominates the scene outside. Prices are moderate.

At Henry Street, walk one short block to the left to the corner of Remsen Street, where relics from the great French liner *Normandie* now form the west and south doors of Our Lady of Lebanon Maronite Church (1846). The panels show Norman scenes and the liner *Ile de France*. The *Normandie* burned at its West Side Pier while being outfitted as a troopship at the beginning of the United States' involvement in World War II.

The far end of Montague Street runs onto the Esplanade or Brooklyn Heights Promenade, built over two levels of the Brooklyn-Queens

Expressway (B-Q E). However fine an amenity it was considered when finished in 1951, it is a pity that the promenade plan did not call for complete coverage of the noisy highway. The farther away from the railing you stand, the more muffled the traffic. No matter, the view is outstanding, and many local residents come here regularly to stroll, relax, read, chat, and watch the sun set behind the skyline.

The Port Authority of New York and of New Jersey no longer uses the line of cargo piers that abut the promenade, although you may see some ships laid up here. Brooklyn's active waterfront is concentrated down to the left at the Red Hook container terminal.

The panorama from left to right includes Governors Island, the Coast Guard base with its ferries shuttling back and forth, Upper New York Bay with the Statue of Liberty and Ellis Island in the distance, the Staten Island Ferry terminal, Lower Manhattan, South Street Seaport, the Brooklyn Bridge, and the distant towers of mid-Manhattan.

Walk as far as Pineapple Street, not quite to the end of the promenade, turn right, then left on Columbia Heights down past the Watchtower Bible and Tract Society's (Jehovah's Witnesses) headquarters and residences, over the B-Q E, and into the Fulton Ferry District.

Along Fulton Street-Cadman Plaza, on the far side of the busy artery (take care in crossing) stands a group of commercial buildings constructed between 1836 and 1839. They once formed part of the business district leading down to the ferry. Directly behind loom the great stone towers and spidery cables of the Brooklyn Bridge.

To the right at the top end of the block, the handsome Ferrybank Restaurant, 1 Front Street (718) 852-3137, occupies what used to be the Long Island Safe Deposit Company, a cast-iron building completed in 1869. Across the street, the brick Eagle Warehouse and Storage Company building retains its bold raised lettering and fine brick and ironwork in its new role as a condominium.

Cross the street carefully to the red-and-cream former New York City firehouse, constructed in 1926—although it appears to be much older. Until 1924 the ornate terminal for the Fulton Ferry and elevated railway stood here. The attractive little waterfront park allows visitors one of the few places to approach the East River. To the left Bargemusic Ltd., a floating concert hall, offers music programs (718-624-4061). To the right, the highly successful River Cafe,

1 Water Street (718) 522-5200, draws diners from all over the city for its fine food and excellent view. While the menu is expensive, you may choose to have a drink instead, outside in the summer. Across the street, the Harbor View Cafe, 1 Cadman Plaza West (718) 237-2224, offers Neapolitan Italian food at more moderate prices in what was once the important Franklin House, a hotel built in the 1930s. Try the baked ziti with ricotta and mozzarella or the fried calamari and clams *oreganata* style. Ask for a table by the large front windows, which are open to the street in the summer months.

Between the Brooklyn and Manhattan Bridges, Fulton Ferry State Park is the raw beginning of what is planned to be an exciting project that will adapt to new uses the long row of former waterfront warehouses, the Empire Stores built in 1870 and 1885, and several newer and larger manufacturing buildings further inland. Contemplated for Fulton Landing are offices and shops, with the retention of some manufacturing venues and jobs as well.

Return to Brooklyn Heights the way you came, up through Columbia Heights, over the B-Q E, left on Middagh Street, and right on Willow.

Willow Street and adjacent side streets from Middagh to Pierrepont will show you the finest collection of pre-1860 housing in the entire city. The oldest residences, many of them wooden clapboard, date from the 1820s and are mostly located off Willow, such as No. 69 Orange Street. Popular styles were Greek Revival, to be seen at Nos. 101–103 Willow, Queen Anne at Nos. 108–112, and Federal at Nos. 155–159. Note that the last three houses mentioned are not quite parallel to the street, as they were built according to an earlier street grid. Next door, at 151 Willow, the 1880 former carriage house was once the home of playwright Arthur Miller.

Brooklyn once boasted the largest hotel in New York City, the 2,632-room Hotel St. George, occupying the full block bounded by Hicks, Henry, Pineapple, and Clark Streets. Built in five sections between 1885 and 1930, the hotel was originally the center of the borough's social life, yet after World War II it fell on hard times. Today, one part is a condominium, another welfare housing, and the remainder vacant, awaiting renovation into apartments.

At the end of Willow, turn left on Pierrepont, then right on Hicks, crossing Montague and Remsen to Grace Court Alley, a dead-end mews of former stables for residents of Remsen Street. What were common and ordinary buildings back in the nineteenth century are today chic duplex housing worth a small fortune.

It is worth turning right into Joralemon Street for an attractive and less ornate contrast to what you have passed, houses that were once owned by the small business class from the 1840s. On the left opposite a fine row of similar Greek Revival-style houses is No. 58 Joralemon Street. What looks like a typical row house reveals on closer inspection something quite different: the Transit Authority has converted the building to a ventilation shaft for its IRT subway line.

Near the bottom of Joralemon at Columbia Place stands a block of 1890 tenement apartments called Riverside Houses. While these have the air of lower-income housing, you will note the fine brickwork that gives them an unusually solid appearance. Unfortunately, the harbor view was destroyed after the completion of the Brooklyn-Queens Expressway, which here manifests itself as an elevated structure slicing through the neighborhood.

Willow Place, right off Joralemon when returning uphill, is worth a look for a group of Gothic Revival-style duplex houses at Nos. 2–8, a row of brick houses with two-story wooden porches and square columns, the colonnade style once popular in the Heights at Nos. 43–49, and, at Nos. 38–40, 44, and 48, several new townhouses whose style and building materials fit into the neighborhood without intruding.

Follow Joralemon Street back to Court for most of the subway stations that surround Borough Hall.

Day Two: Atlantic Avenue & Environs

In addition to the restaurants listed at the Fulton Ferry Landing and the range of places along Montague Street, there are concentrated pockets of eating establishments at which to have lunch or dinner along Atlantic Avenue and Court Street, south of Atlantic.

On Atlantic between Court and Henry Streets, an intriguing number of Middle Eastern and North African restaurants range from the classy Tripoli, 156 Atlantic (718) 596-5800, to the family-style Son of the Sheik, 165 Atlantic (718) 625-4023.

Son of the Sheik is my favorite place because it attracts a local Middle Eastern clientele, and its unusually spiced food is an exceptional value with entrées in the $6–8 range. It's a one-room storefront restaurant with a warm atmosphere, and the closest subway stop is Borough Hall.

Among the best appetizers are hummus, a delightful mixture of mashed chick peas with garlic and sesame paste, babaganosh, which is largely eggplant and garlic, maza plate, another eggplant dish, and tabouli, a concoction of bulgar (cracked wheat), parsley, mint, cucumber, tomato, and garlic.

Main courses that I have had are baked kibbe, ground lamb with pine nuts and stuffed grape leaves, and shish kebab, seasoned meat roasted on a skewer, with mushrooms, onions, eggplant, tomato, and string beans all sitting happily on a bed of rice. Lamb brain salad, if the name does not put you off, is a novel choice.

Son of the Sheik does not serve alcohol, but you may bring your own, and one liquor store is just down the street on the same side toward the water.

In addition to the restaurants, have a look inside some of the Middle Eastern bakeries in these same blocks—if for no other reason than that they smell wonderful.

About a half-dozen blocks further along, east past the antique section in an unassuming neighborhood, is a far more upscale choice. Lisanne, 488 Atlantic Avenue, corner Nevins Street, (718) 237-2271, is an attractive French continental-style restaurant with white tin walls and ceiling and generously spaced tables in one medium-sized skylighted room. The kitchen, open to view, uses mesquite grilling, and the owner makes the rounds of the tables to explain the frequently changing menu and to take your order. Entrées run from $10 to $18 on weekdays, and on weekends, three-course meals range from $21 to $29 complete, depending on the choice of entrée. The wine list is reasonably priced, and reservations are necessary.

Although not necessarily available on any given day, excellent starters have been the cold pasta with pesto sauce, cured fish, and the goose liver, pork, or scallop patés. For entrées, try mesquite-grilled salmon, swordfish, or monkfish, a North Atlantic variety also known as goosefish, with the consistency of lobster and a wonderful subtle flavor. The sliced breast of duck with cassis and figs makes a good change from the more usual orange or cherry sauces. For dessert, the waiter will roll around the pastry trolley. Or, for something lighter, consider the fruity raspberry or strawberry sorbets.

For antique and collectible addicts, walk both sides of Atlantic Avenue between Smith, Hoyt, and Bond. The stores are mainly, but not always, open from about 11 a.m. to 6 p.m. Monday to Saturday, with a selected few open on Sunday too.

The stores, stacked one after another, display artifacts of the nineteenth and early twentieth centuries, such as huge pieces of oak furniture, art deco tubular furniture, bamboo and wicker pieces, plus the usual hodgepodge of collectibles.

Atlantic Antique Center, 367 Atlantic (718) 624-9044, on the left side of the street, has four rooms of furniture, antiques, and knickknacks. Others have appropriate names such as Circa Antiques Ltd., 374 Atlantic (718) 596-1866, Circa Too across the street, and such folksy titles as in As-Is Thrift Shop, 385 Atlantic (718) 522-3177.

No guide that promotes the use of mass transit could fail to include an exhibit that shows the development of rapid transit on the world's most complex system. The transit exhibit, located just two blocks from Borough Hall and from the many subway lines that converge on downtown Brooklyn, is housed below ground in a former subway station.

At the concourse level are historic maps showing the system's development from the original transit companies, a track layout model indicating subway, surface and elevated lines, historic photographs and color reproductions of the most elaborate mosaic and bas relief station decorations, a film that candidly shows the working of the A train, and a small souvenir shop.

Most people come to see the fine collection of subway cars at track level that reminds us how much style the system once had. A walk through the two lines of cars reveals arched roofs, clerestory windows, ceiling fans, cane seats, and old subway ads that include the Miss Subways promotion. The oldest car is the BMT Q car built in 1903 and the last wooden rail car to operate in North America, lasting until 1969.

THE BROOKLYN MUSEUM & BROOKLYN BOTANIC GARDENS

The Brooklyn Museum, Eastern Parkway, Brooklyn, NY 11238. (212) 638-5000. Open Monday, Wednesday, Thursday, and Friday 10 a.m.–5 p.m., Saturday 11 a.m.–6 p.m., Sunday 1–6 p.m. Closed Tuesday. Suggested contribution $3, but you may pay what you wish; students with valid I.D. $1, seniors and children under 12, if accompanied by an adult, free. Note that some of the galleries are closed part of the day on a rotating basis (except Sunday), so phone first if you have a particular interest.

Brooklyn Botanic Gardens, 1000 Washington Avenue, Brooklyn, NY 11225. (212) 622-4433. Opening hours vary with the season. April 1–September 30, Tuesday–Friday 8 a.m.–6 p.m., Saturday, Sunday, and holidays 10 a.m.–6 p.m.; October 1–March 31, Tuesday–Friday 8 a.m.–4:30 p.m., Saturday, Sunday, and holidays 10 a.m.–4:30 p.m. Admission free, with a small charge for the conservatory and special gardens on weekends.

Often overlooked by residents of other boroughs, The Brooklyn Museum offers special collections not found elsewhere in the city, and the setting is far more relaxed than the frenzied atmosphere of Manhattan's Metropolitan Museum of Art.

Of particular note are the twenty-one rooms furnished in styles ranging from early colonial through the nineteenth century, the Hudson River School paintings, and a sculpture garden containing ornamental pieces saved from buildings now torn down. For fanciers of Egyptology, the museum's collection of statues, jewelry, and large stone objects from the Nile Valley is among the best in the country.

Right next door, the Brooklyn Botanic Garden, in a compact area of fifty acres, boasts many distinctive gardens in miniature. Among the most original are the Japanese Garden, a fragrance garden designed for the blind, and a great collection of bonsai trees.

Both these attractions may be easily visited in one day with a light lunch in the museum's cafeteria or a picnic in nearby Prospect Park. Much of the Garden's park area has been recently restored, and you are likely to find it nearly equal to Central Park in monumental beauty and interest.

Getting There and Back: The subway ride in Brooklyn can be a dingy or pleasant experience, depending on the newness of the cars, but regardless of the train, the Eastern Parkway Station is conveniently located right outside the entrances to both the museum and botanic garden.

From the West Side, take the IRT #2 express marked "Flatbush Avenue," or the IRT #3 express marked "New Lots Avenue" to Eastern Parkway, the third stop after Atlantic Avenue.

From the East Side, take the IRT #4 or #5 (only if the #5 is marked "Atlantic Ave." and not "Bowling Green") to Nevins Street, the stop after Borough Hall in Brooklyn, and make an across-the-platform transfer to the IRT #2 or #3 for the continuation to Eastern Parkway Station.

42 *New York City Boroughs*

From all subway trains, exit from near the front of the train to the street. Once above ground, the 1897–1924-built Brooklyn Museum looms large, and the Botanic Garden entrance is steps from the subway stairs.

On the Museum's first floor, there are displays of wooden statues, mysterious masks and totems from Africa, American Indian objects, and a good collection of prized pre-Columbian jewelry and Peruvian pottery.

The second floor is dedicated to Middle Eastern paintings, ceramics, carpets, and textiles, and South, Southeast, and East Asian sculpture, paintings, bronzes, ceramics, porcelain, and jades.

Perhaps the best collection of all is the Egyptian exhibit on the third floor, which traces the development of the Nile Valley through

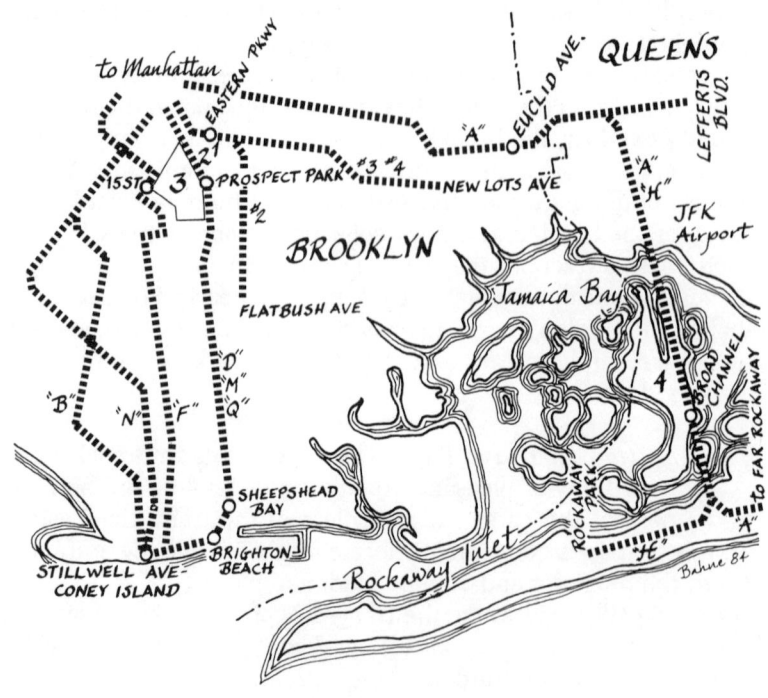

South Brooklyn & Queens

1. Brooklyn Museum
2. Brooklyn Botanic Garden
3. Prospect Park
4. Jamaica Bay Wildlife Refuge Visitor Center

its sarcophagi, gilded and silver statues, and objects made of precious and non-precious stones. Noted pieces include a basalt head of a princess (1800 B.C.), an aquamarine winged scarab, and a sarcophagus for a sacred ibis in gilded wood and silver. The Brooklyn Museum has been engaged for seventy-five years in Egyptian archeology, and its Nile Valley galleries should not be overlooked.

On the fourth floor, there are twenty-one rooms furnished in varying American styles from the colonial through the nineteenth century, with examples of dining rooms, bedrooms, and parlors typical of families spanning the entire economic scale. Since they were originally opened to the public, the period rooms have been recently renovated. Rooms of particular note are found in the reconstructed Jan Martense Schenck House, built in 1675 in the Flatlands and moved here in 1952. A suite of rooms from John D. Rockefeller's mansion, built in 1866 at 4 West 54th Street, Manhattan, is also of note.

The top floor displays Renaissance and Impressionist paintings and sculpture and the development of art in this country. There are good examples from the Hudson River School and a fine collection of watercolors, including major works by John Singer Sargent and Winslow Homer.

Outside at the back of the building you will find a small sculpture garden containing ornamental objects, statues, gargoyles, friezes, and the like from buildings that have been demolished. Several treasures come from old Pennsylvania Station and Coney Island's Steeplechase Amusement Park.

The Gallery Shop, one of the first in the country greatly to expand its inventory and include reproductions of famous works of art, has a good selection of art books, posters, postcards, and craft items. There is also a small, clean cafeteria serving ordinary food on the ground floor to the left of the entrance on the way to the elevators. The floor plan available at the information desk will help you decide how to spend your time here.

On to Brooklyn Botanic Garden, the entrance to which is nearby the subway stairs and to the right of the Museum.

The fifty-acre Brooklyn Botanic Garden was created from a waste dump in 1910, and, while much smaller than its Bronx counterpart, is noted for its spectacular displays of flowers and its variety of distinctive small gardens within the larger botanic garden. There are twelve thousand different kinds of plants from virtually every country in the world, and all species are labeled. Every season of the year has something special to recommend it.

The first section is quite formal, with spring-flowering crab apple and dogwood trees, lilac and wisteria bushes. Paths then lead to some high ground that overlooks the Cranford Rose Garden, best seen from June through September, and the Cherry Orchard to the left, another spring attraction. To the right, you can see native flora as if in the wild, before the coming of human habitation.

The tranquil Japanese Garden, designed in 1914–1915 by Takeo Shiota, is complete with pagoda, shrine, curved drum bridges, stone lanterns, stepping stones, small hills, and a reflecting pool. You can walk alongside the long narrow lake, or enter the grounds free on weekdays and for a nominal sum on weekends. The pavilion built on stilts offers the best view.

A nearby fragrance garden, designed for the blind, uses Braille as well as Roman letters on its labels. Lean over to smell the blossoms.

A formal plaza with pools of summer-flowering water lilies runs in front of the handsome McKim, Meade and White 1917 Administration Building, the plant and gift shop, and the Conservatory, with its dwarfed potted trees, or *bonsai*, of unequalled variety. There may be some disruption to your visit in this section through 1987 during the $16 million reconstruction and building of a new greenhouse and three smaller specialized glass pavilions. Call ahead before you set out for Brooklyn to avoid disappointment.

From the end of the Japanese reflecting pond, a small tree-lined stream runs through the middle of the botanic garden for nearly its entire length to the Children's Garden at the sound end. Here school kids grow vegetables and flowers under the supervision of the education department, the first program of its kind in the world for a botanic garden.

On the far side of the stream, the Rock Garden, created with glacial boulders, is a feast of changing color from early spring to late fall. The spring bulb collection is adjacent.

Be sure to consult the display chart for what plants and trees are in flower each month; except for December and January, there are always some outdoor flora in bloom. No food or drink is allowed within the garden, but there are ample places to sit and enjoy some peace and quiet before returning to the urban scene. The benches at the Overlook give a peaceful long-range view, and the soft grassy slopes around the Japanese Garden Pond allow you to recline while taking in the natural beauty.

It is not recommended, unless you are familiar with the area, to use the Empire Boulevard and Flatbush Avenue subway entrance for the Prospect Park IND D and M subway lines. The station is seedy and poorly maintained. Return the way you came, and enjoy more of the garden.

However, if you would like to visit Prospect Park, the eighteenth-century Lefferts Homestead, the carousel, and the small zoo, the Empire Boulevard/Flatbush Avenue exit from the Garden is recommended. Simply cross Flatbush Avenue and turn right.

Prospect Park, second only to Central Park in its monumental beauty—and much less crowded—was originally laid out according to Frederick Law Olmsted's and Calvert Vaux's design of 1866–1874. It contains 562 acres of woods, plantings, open spaces, playing fields, ponds, a band shell, and a sixty-acre lake with boats for hire.

Right off Flatbush Avenue, follow the path along East Lake Drive for about ten minutes to the Beaux Arts-style boathouse. The path then continues right around Swan Lake, passing Stanford White's croquet shelter at the southern end.

Also just in from Flatbush Avenue are a traditional carousel and the white-shingled Lefferts Homestead. The Dutch Colonial farmhouse dating from 1783 was moved here in 1918. Its stained shingle roof sloping down to form a Dutch eave supported by six columns became a model for many subsequent dwellings. To see its period furnishings, plan to arrive 1–4 p.m. from Wednesday to Sunday. Admission is free. Call (718) 768-2300 for information.

The small Prospect Park Zoo, next door, is a semi-circular sweep of brick buildings decorated with Depression-era WPA artists' murals and bas-reliefs facing a central seal pond. There is a limited selection of familiar animals in traditional caged settings that may please small children. Open every day from 11 a.m. to 5 p.m. Admission is free and fast food is available.

For the return trip by IRT subway, continue walking along the perimeter of Prospect Park paralleling Flatbush Avenue to the Grand Army Plaza subway station. The main Brooklyn Public Library, completed in 1941 in stremlined Beaux Arts style, is across the avenue to the right. Ahead is the Soldiers' and Sailors' Memorial Arch dedicated to Civil War veterans. The arch was completed in 1892 by John Duncan, architect of Grant's Tomb on Riverside Drive in

Manhattan. Tours are available on Sunday. Call (718) 965-6522 for exact dates.

JAMAICA BAY WILDLIFE REFUGE

Jamaica Bay Wildlife Refuge, Floyd Bennett Field, Bldg. 69, Brooklyn, NY 11234. (718) 474-0613. (This is the mailing address, not the location of the Visitor Center.) Refuge open sunrise–sunset every day of the year except Christmas Day and New Year's. The Visitor Center open 8 a.m.–4:30 p.m. Admission free.

Incongruous as it may seem in the midst of a great metropolis, a migratory stopover and nesting ground for thousands of birds using the Atlantic Flyway lies only a subway ride away. Even though Jamaica Bay Wildlife Refuge is within plain sight of the Manhattan skyline and of planes landing at Kennedy Airport, the press of civilization nearby will seem to disappear during a walk through a setting of saltwater marshes and freshwater ponds. From early spring to late fall, Jamaica Bay beckons the professional bird watcher and the amateur nature lover.

While there are resident birds year-round, the spring migration northward occurs mainly in April and May, and the flight south for shorebirds, flycatchers, and warblers begins in August and September, and continues into October and November for other waterfowl, hawks, and finches. June and July are breeding season.

The park rangers at the Visitor Center lead walks during the day and after dark on weekends, show special-interest slides and films, have booklets to sell, and are on hand to answer your questions.

Getting There and Back: Take the A train, marked "Far Rockaway," from any stop in Manhattan or Brooklyn to Broad Channel, located in the middle of Jamaica Bay. (Occasionally, during off-peak hours, you may have to use an A train marked "Lefferts Boulevard," and get off at Euclid Avenue for the Rockaway Shuttle. The subway fare is ninety cents each way, and the ride takes about forty-five minutes from midtown Manhattan. From the Broad Channel station, it is an easy twenty-minute walk to the wildlife Visitor Center.

The A train surfaces in Brooklyn after the Grant Avenue stop, and the neighborhoods of Woodhaven and Ozone Park, mostly single-family detached and row houses, come into view. After the Rockaway Boulevard Station, the line to the Rockaways swings right to follow the former Long Island Rail Road right-of-way, passing Aqueduct Racetrack and Howard Beach Station.

Suddenly, the train begins to climb a causeway and, looking out the windows, you'll have the sensation of putting out to sea. The open waters of Grassy Bay, tidal marshes, and freshwater ponds stretch almost as far as the eye can see. The wildlife refuge's 9,155 acres expanding before you form part of Gateway National Park, a reserve that also includes Breezy Point, Sandy Hook, and Great Kills Park on Staten Island.

While everything outside the train window looks perfectly natural, both the East Pond, lying to the right of the subway tracks, and the West Pond, your destination, are actually ingenious man-made creations.

In 1951, in order to build up the railroad embankment, the Transit Authority needed to dredge sand from Jamaica Bay. Robert Moses, who was then Commissioner of Parks, proposed that the plan include a provision to construct two dikes, thus forming what became only two years later a pair of freshwater ponds. Migrating birds in the thousands were immediately attracted to them to feed, nest, and rest.

Beyond the south end of East Pond, the train begins to slow for the stop at Broad Channel. Leave the station, walk through the little ramshackle community to Cross Bay Boulevard, and turn right. Time permitting, you may wish to explore the tiny backwater settlement of Broad Channel, where many of its pre-war single-family houses are built on pilings over water. Its splendid isolation alone makes it a curiosity for urban dwellers.

Milk Farm, the only game in town and not a very exciting one, is on the boulevard and sells sodas, snacks, and makes sandwiches—in case you decided not to bring your own. Jamaica Bay Wildlife Refuge has several picnic tables outside the Visitor Center in an open setting.

Leave the village by using the left sidewalk of Cross Bay Boulevard and heading north away from the direction of the Rockaways. About twenty minutes from the station, the Visitor Center will appear on the left among the bushes and shrubs.

A National Park Service ranger will issue you a free permit for

Jamaica Bay to use as often as you like. If you return for a second visit within a year, you are put on a mailing list that gives notice of special wildlife walks and slide lectures geared to the changing seasons. Two-hour moon prowls, beginning at 7:30 p.m. and conducted several times a year, explore the refuge in the half-light. There is a spring lecture on horseshoe crab mating and summer photography workshops, just to name a few.

On Saturday and Sunday at 1 p.m. and 3 p.m., there is a narrated slide or film show introducing the refuge's birds, animal wildlife, and flora, followed by a guided walk, usually around West Pond. For first-timers, the park ranger's expertise will greatly add to your own enjoyment and offer a springboard for subsequent visits.

To more fully appreciate what you are going to see, two pamphlets are well worth purchasing. "Birds of the Jamaica Bay Wildlife Refuge" (fifteen cents) is a checklist of all 318 species of birds ever recorded here up to April 1982. The chart included uses symbols to indicate the number of birds of each kind that visit the refuge. Birds that have been sighted only once or twice are charmingly categorized as "accidentals."

The second booklet, "Trail Guide to West Pond" (eighty-nine cents), takes you step-by-step around the one and one-quarter-mile path, and points out geographical and geological features as well as describing the plant, bird, and animal life. At each of the thirteen points of reference, there is a bench where you may sit down to read the useful text out loud to your companions. Urban dwellers usually need all the help they can get to distinguish the difference between a herring or great black-backed gull, or to spot a long-eared owl roosting on its favorite limb of a Japanese black pine tree scanning the ground for Norway rats; this booklet gives it.

If you are making the visit without a guide, follow the gravel path through the thick underbrush bordering the salt marshes. You'll soon break out into wide open spaces with views stretching for miles in all directions. Ahead and to the left are the vast salt marshes and open waters of Jamaica Bay, and to the right the tranquillity of West Pond. The natural setting is ringed in the far distance by the Rockaways, the great span of the Verrazano-Narrows Bridge, and the skyscrapers of Manhattan.

Virtually at your feet, depending on the time of year, are quiet gatherings of shorebirds, ducks, geese, sandpipers, and terns, and, in the trees and brush, wrens, sparrows, and blackbirds. Overhead are osprey, hawks, and gulls ready to dive on unsuspecting fish, horseshoe and fiddler crabs, and rodents. Don't overlook the brilliantly colored butterflies, moths, and grasshoppers, or the wide variety of plant life such as yucca, cattail, and bayberry.

Some regular visitors come at different seasons to experience the widest possible range of bird and flowering plant life. Most nature lovers are quite friendly and enjoy sharing their knowledge, so do not hesitate to ask them what they may have seen on their way around. Bring a pair of binoculars for long-distance vision and to be able to watch the activity close up.

It's easy to spend two hours here, as there is much to see, and it takes time for the novice to learn to spot what is about. In the end, you will discover that you have barely begun to fill out your check list, so plan to come another season, now that you know how easy it is to get here. Then, before you leave, be sure to have your remaining questions answered by the park rangers at the Visitor Center.

BRIGHTON BEACH, SHEEPSHEAD BAY & CONEY ISLAND

Astroland Amusement Park, 1000 Surf Avenue and West 10th Street, Coney Island, Brooklyn, NY 11224. Open 12 p.m.–12 a.m. on weekends only from Palm Sunday to mid-June and in September, and daily from mid-June to Labor Day. Tickets may be bought for individual rides or you may pay $8.65 for unlimited rides.

New York Aquarium, Surf Avenue and West 8th Street, Brooklyn, NY 11224. (718) 266-8711. Open Monday–Friday 10 a.m.–5 p.m., Saturday–Sunday 10 a.m.–6 p.m. Admission adults $2.50, children 2–12 $1.50, seniors 65 and over free after 2 p.m. Monday–Friday.

Three adjacent stretches of Atlantic Ocean beach along the South Brooklyn waterfront offer totally distinctive daytime experiences.

Brighton Beach, a residential seaside community that recently received a large influx of Russian, Ukrainian, and Georgian Jews, has re-established itself as a vibrant New York-style ethnic community. Enjoy a Ukrainian meal in a restaurant under the "el" on

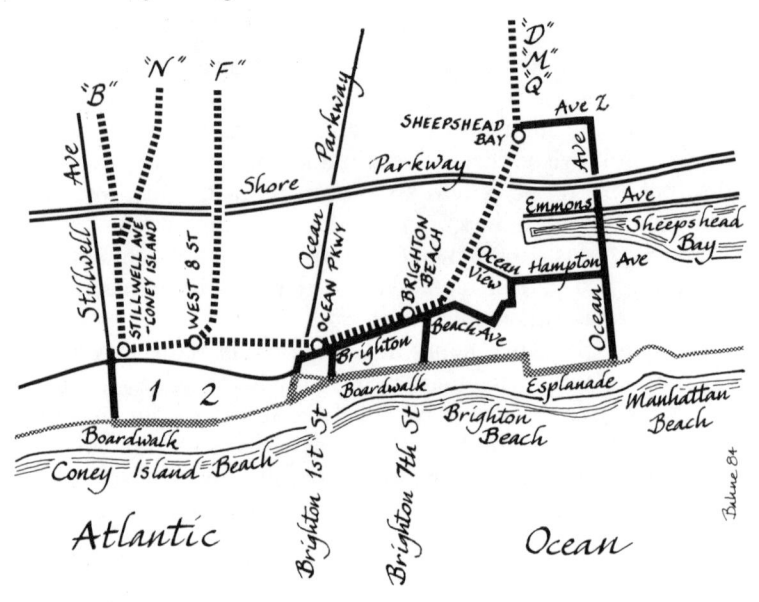

Brighton Beach, Sheepshead Bay & Coney Island

1. Astroland Amusement Park
2. New York Aquarium

Brighton Beach Avenue, shop for cold-weather furs on the street and inside Russian-only-spoken stores, and sample a chilled bowl of beet-red borscht with a large dollop of sour cream during a stroll along the wide boardwalk paralleling the fine sandy beach.

Next door, Sheepshead Bay, best known for its charter and party boat fleet, offering day-long deep sea outings for bluefish, flounder, and fluke, is also a prosperous middle-class community of single-family homes and quiet, tree-lined streets bordering Manhattan Beach.

At Coney Island, spend a leisurely day on the beach, wander through Astroland's midway eating cotton candy and corn-on-the-cob, take a terrifying ride on the Cyclone, one of the world's most jarring experiences, or enjoy the ocean view from a stationary car on the Wonder Wheel.

Bring the kids to the aquarium to watch the whiskered seals and grunting walruses at feeding time, or call in advance to reserve places for a family workshop that explains how to set up an at-home aquarium or for a talk that describes the sleeping behavior of undersea life.

While Brighton Beach and Sheepshead Bay make a natural combination, any one of the three destinations could easily fill an entire day.

Getting There and Back: The route described is to Brighton Beach and from Sheepshead Bay. From the West Side, take the IND D express marked "Brighton Beach" or "Coney Island." Weekdays until 8 p.m. the D operates as an express in Manhattan and Brooklyn, giving a good fast ride all the way out to the end of the line. On weekends the D runs express only in Manhattan. In addition, the IND M local marked "Coney Island" runs from Lower Manhattan, joining the D in Brooklyn.

From the East Side, take the Lexington Avenue IRT #6 local to Bleeker Street and change to the IND D (a transfer is possible *only* in this direction). Or, take the Lexington Avenue IRT #4 or #5 express (but not a #5 marked "Bowling Green") to Atlantic Avenue, Brooklyn and change to the D or M.

The IND Line, shortly after the Prospect Park Station in Brooklyn, comes out from underground and eventually becomes elevated, passing through neighborhoods of small houses and apartment buildings. Get off at the Brighton Beach Station and walk down the stairs to the street, Brighton Beach Avenue.

Brighton Beach

The first-time visitor is immediately struck by the thriving nature of the commercial strip extending the length of Brighton Beach Avenue with the noisy "el" rattling overhead. Instead of detracting from the neighborhood atmosphere, the trains somehow add to the rich flavor of a true old-fashioned ethnic shopping street. Many of the twenty-five thousand residents are Jews, recent arrivals from the Soviet Union, and, by listening carefully between trains, you can hear a lot of Russian spoken. The Russian language also appears on signs and labels in the food shop windows and on some of the clothing goods displayed on the sidewalks. On Brighton Beach Avenue, walk into M&I International Food, the neighborhood Zabar's, for two floors of deli-style meats, pastries, canned items, and sweets. Fish Town, one of the newer food stores, prepares smoked fish without heat, and the results are a milder flavor and a raw moist texture. If this Russian-style of preparation leaves you a bit queasy, they also hot-smoke the fish. Caviar from the Soviet Union, Iran, and our own American shores is in abundant supply, and the prices are generally cheaper than in Manhattan.

The heart of the business district runs only ten blocks, so you can take your time and ease yourself into the slow pace. If you're hungry and want to try some of the simple restaurants, consider Irving's Deli, at the bottom of the stairs at the Brighton Beach Station. Try the $4.95 Combination Plate—roast beef, corned beef, salami, tongue, and turkey with cole slaw or potato salad and pickles, a side dish of kasha (buckwheat groats), and bow ties (noodles) with gravy. Mrs. Stahl's Knishes, another local institution with a similar menu, is at 1001 Brighton Beach Avenue. At Primorski, try their three-course lunch for under $5 that includes a salad, vegetable and beef borscht soup, and grilled chicken in a rich walnut sauce. Lamb is a favorite meat here, as it is at Kavkas just down the street, and it shows up at your table on skewers and in stews with fresh coriander or fresh dill flavoring, accompanied with green pepper, onion, and tomato.

Walking west, Ocean Parkway forms the boundary between Brighton Beach and Coney island. Turn left and head for the boardwalk paralleling the wide beach that stretches for a couple of miles in both directions.

The wide boardwalk, Brighton Beach's fresh air promenade, is rarely crowded except on summer weekends. Joggers of all ages and sedentary older residents, who come for a chat, can be seen enjoying the open space on a sunny day, almost regardless of temperature.

Looking east and south over Rockaway Inlet, the boardwalk is a viewing platform from which to scan the horizon and to look across at the houses on Rockaway Point and to the beaches at Breezy Point. Due south is the Ambrose Channel, linking New York Harbor with the Atlantic Ocean. The boardwalk effectively ties together the amusements of Coney Island, the bustling commercial center at Brighton Beach, and the prosperous single-family homes of Sheepshead Bay.

Sheepshead Bay

To reach Sheepshead Bay via a small section of Manhattan Beach, return to Brighton Beach Avenue by taking one of the numbered streets, Brighton 1st to Brighton 7th Streets. Then, turn right under the "el." After Coney island Avenue, the "el" turns northeast, and Brighton Beach Avenue veers right and becomes less commercial and more residential.

Several of the apartment houses here on the right date from the 1930s, and have rich Art Deco features on their facades and around the entrance courts. Squarish lamps atop stout pedestals flank rounded doorways featuring sunburst motifs and bas-relief metal panels. By going left on Brighton 15th Street, then left again, and right within a very short distance, you cross West End Avenue and begin following Hampton Avenue east. The intricacies of the street grid described here are not as complex as they sound. By continuing along Hampton Avenue, you can get a good feel for the quiet tree-lined community of Manhattan Beach. By turning left on Ocean Avenue, you will reach the pedestrian bridge over the end of Sheepshead Bay.

While crossing the wooden bridge, you will be able to see to the right the large and varied fishing fleet lined up at the docks along Emmons Avenue. On the opposite side of the street, among a row of undistinguished Italian seafood restaurants, the long stucco building with the low Spanish Mission-style facade is the former Lundy Brothers Restaurant, once a notable Sheepshead Bay institution until it went out of business about a decade back.

The public fishing fleet of charter and party boats is the largest on the eastern seaboard, offering skilled fisher folk and novices a chance to try their luck in the open sea. Catches are seasonal, with bluefish and fluke abounding in the summer, blackfish in the fall, cod in winter, and flounder and mackerel in the spring. This list is by no means exhaustive, as the Atlantic fishing grounds are rich in many more varieties.

The serious, hard-core fishers opt for the basic fifty-foot *Jet*, an early boat leaving at 6–7 a.m. and returning at 2–3 p.m. The eighty-five-foot *Betty W II* and *III* are both fairly fast boats and, with snack bar aboard, cater to the middle-of-the-road crowd. For late risers, the *America*, similar to the two *Betty W*s, departs at 9 a.m. and returns about four in the afternoon.

For families with children, some of whom, along with their parents, may not want to fish all day, the high-speed, technologically sophisticated, hundred-foot *Ranger* features a sun deck, heated rails, color TV, and a comfortable coffee shop. On the *Ranger*, even if you don't land a big one, you'll have the day's cruise to remember. Be warned that the boat is elbow-to-elbow on summer weekends during the bluefish season. Also, some people, not used to relatively small boats bobbing on the open sea, may not take kindly to their first trip over water, and there is no going back to *terra firma* until the time is up.

To view the catches, be on the piers in the afternoon from about two o'clock onward. When the fish are running, you can buy what you see coming ashore directly from the boat owners, especially later in the day, when the boats begin to return with their seasonal catches.

There are plans afoot to turn Sheepshead Bay's rather simple waterfront into a major tourist attraction on the scale of San Francisco's Fishermans Wharf. Much controversy is sure to ensue before any definite plans get under way.

To return to the IND subway line, walk away from Sheepshead Bay along Ocean Avenue for two long blocks to Avenue Z, and turn left for the four blocks to Sheepshead Bay elevated station.

Coney Island

Getting There and Back: There are a number of subway lines terminating at Stillwell Avenue, Coney Island. Refer to the *Getting There* entry for Brighton Beach and Sheepshead Bay for the IND D and M trains.

Quite a good line is the IND F train marked "Coney Island," running down 6th Avenue in Manhattan and into Brooklyn. Between Carroll Street and Fourth Avenue, the line climbs high up on a trestle over the Gowanus Canal, and gives good views of the Brooklyn docks and the Upper Bay. The line runs underground to Ditmas Avenue, then on an elevated route all the way to the terminus. Use the West 8th or Stillwell Avenue Stations.

Other routes from midtown Manhattan are the IND B train, which surfaces after the 9th Avenue Station, and the BMT N train, which becomes elevated after 59th Street in Ray Ridge.

All the subway lines end in a huge tangle of tracks and platforms at Stillwell Avenue, with wide ramps built to handle thousands of people headed for the amusement area and beach.

The residential and commercial area is seedy until you pass up the ramps to the boardwalk with its clear view of the beach and the Atlantic Ocean.

The beach at Coney Island ranks among the finest stretches of white sand on the East Coast, attracting large crowds who arrive by subway on summer weekends. On good days at other times of the year, when the crowds are absent, outdoor aficionados come out to stroll the wide boardwalk and to hunt for shells at the water's edge. For most New Yorkers, Coney Island is the easiest and cheapest approach to the Atlantic Ocean.

Astroland Amusement Park still offers some of the world's most famous rides, and the popularity of the wooden-trestle Cyclone, now more than a half-century old, reigns supreme. Roller coaster buffs say that it is the speed bumps, rough riding, and bone-jarring curves, all designed to disorient its passengers, that make the Cyclone special. First-timers find the initial slow climb to the top with a look straight down to be the most memorable experience. The cars can surprise you by taking an alternate route as well as by going in reverse.

Other Astroland attractions include climbing the three-hundred-foot-high Astrotower, riding the rapids on the Water Flume, rocking to the latest songs on the Music Express, and experiencing freefall on the Rainbow.

Apart from the midway's traditional food stands for caramel apples, cotton candy, and egg rolls with onion rings, there's always Nathan's Famous, home of the original hot dog and a feature of the boardwalk since 1911.

Further along the boardwalk, the New York Aquarium, relocated from Castle Garden (now Castle Clinton) at the Battery, is for lovers of all creatures that live in the sea. The curious can have close-up views of fearsome tiger sharks in complete safety, handle the rough spike of a prehistoric horseshoe crab, and watch the underwater habits of sea life in the Bermuda Triangle, including moray eels, giant sea turtles, and lumbering groupers. Penguin feeding, electric eel shows, and dolphin acrobatics are always popular with children.

Special Aquarium tours go aboard the Staten Island Ferry to hear a talk about the currents, tides, and sea life of New York Harbor, and then make a pre-dawn visit to the Fulton Fish Market during its busiest selling hours. Educational programs are designed for adults, children, and whole families, and the Aquarium even has facilities for celebrating birthday parties. Call (718) 266-8540 for details.

NEW YORK STATE

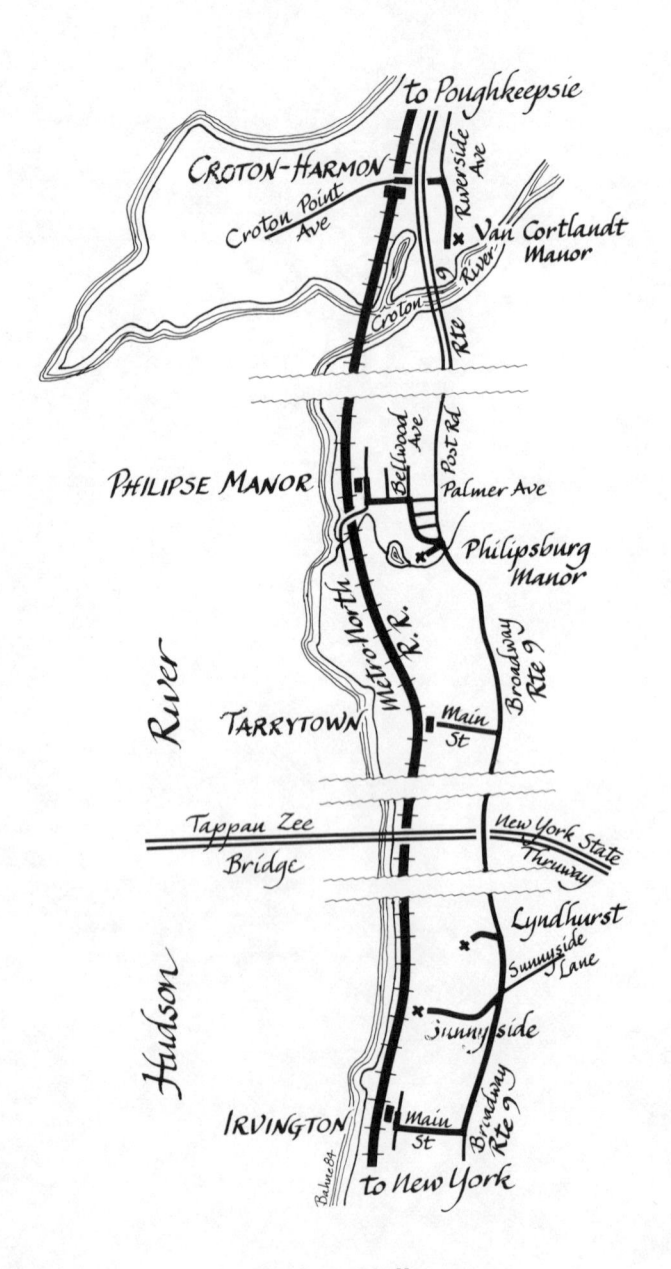

Hudson Valley

STATEN ISLAND
A Ferry Ride to Richmondtown

Richmondtown Restoration, 441 Clarke Avenue, Staten Island, NY 10306. (718) 351-1611 or 351-1617. Open Wednesday–Friday 10 a.m.–5 p.m. (July–August) and Saturday–Sunday 1–5 p.m. (May–December). Admission adults $2, students and seniors $1.50, children 6–18 $1 (under 6 free), family (maximum two adults) $5.

Snug Harbor Cultural Center, 914 Richmond Terrace, Staten Island, NY 10301. (718) 448-2500. Open Wednesday–Sunday noon–dusk, with exhibitions open 1–5 p.m. Admission free.

The Staten Island Zoo, 614 Broadway, Staten Island, NY 10310. (718) 442-3100. Open daily 10 a.m.–4:45 p.m. Admission adults 75 cents, children 6–12 50 cents (under 6 free), seniors free. Wednesdays free.

Richmondtown Restoration, New York City's only historic village, gives the visitor a clear picture of how an American town might have developed from the late seventeenth to the beginning of the twentieth century. Operated by the Staten Island Historical Society, the ninety-six-acre site, located smack in the middle of the city's most rural borough, contains over thirty public buildings and private residences, many of them landmarked, including the nation's oldest surviving one-room schoolhouse.

Several other diversions, easily reachable by bus and train directly from the ferry terminal, can round out a very full day. Except where specifically mentioned, it is always best to return to the ferry's bus station and set out again, rather than trying to travel cross country.

The Snug Harbor Cultural Center, comprising one of the finest collections of Greek Revival buildings in the country, also offers the Newhouse Art Gallery of permanent and changing exhibits usually related to Staten Islanders, a theater group, workshops for children, and outdoor summer concerts. The Staten Island Zoo is well known to New York City children for its unparalleled rattlesnake collection, and Stapleton, an emerging town with a wealth of residential Victorian

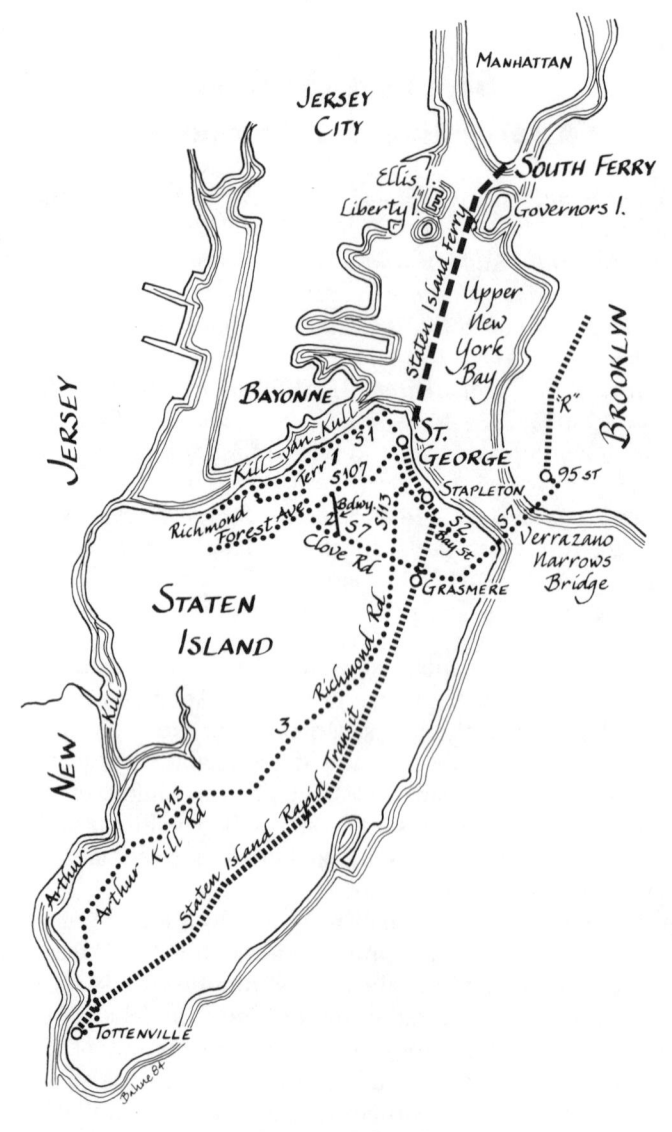

Staten Island

1. Sailors Snug Harbor
2. Staten Island Zoo
3. Richmondtown Restoration

architecture, has a row of antique stores on Bay Street that attract people from all over the city who come for lower-than-average prices.

Rail buffs may like to include a ride on the Staten Island Rapid Transit Line that runs the length of the island from the ferry terminal to Tottenville, and offers above-ground views of New York's most rural borough.

Best of all is the chance to take the Staten Island Ferry, an American institution of world renown. If you have ridden it before, you probably returned to Manhattan without getting off the boat. Here are several reasons to leave the ferry and explore Staten Island's treasures.

Getting There and Back: Relax and enjoy the two and one-half-hour veritable odyssey of train and ferry transport from midtown to Richmondtown. The route is an interesting one, and to vary the heavy diet of road, rail, and water transportation, you can return another way.

To get to the South Ferry at the Staten Island Ferry Terminal, by subway, take the IRT #1 local to South Ferry, or the BMT R to Whitehall Street, across the street from the ferry terminal. The IRT #4 and #5 stop at Bowling Green, a five-minute walk south to the ferry. Or, by bus, the M15, marked "South Ferry," runs at all times south on Second Avenue. The M1, also marked "South Ferry," operates south on Fifth Avenue to the terminal Monday through Friday during the day only. The M6 runs every day from early morning to late at night down Seventh Avenue and Broadway to South Ferry. For specific information, call the Transit Authority at (212) 330-1234.

The Staten Island Ferry, (212) 727-2508, the city's last public ferry operation, is operated by the City of New York's Bureau of Ferries, located in the Battery Maritime Building, One Whitehall Street.

During most of the day, there are departures on the hour and half-hour from both Manhattan and Staten Island. At rush hours, the service increases to every fifteen or twenty minutes, and, at night, the frequency drops to one an hour. The crossing takes twenty-two minutes, more or less depending on tides and harbor traffic.

The bargain round-trip fare is twenty-five cents exact change in quarters payable on the Manhattan side only. Seniors, with Reduced

Fare Cards, pay only a nickel each way, with a special token available at the change booth.

The huge orange and blue Staten Island ferryboats carry over twenty million passengers a year and offer the most commodious form of mass transportation in New York City. About seventy thousand riders use the ferries on an average weekday, and over ninety percent of them are regular commuters. Board the South Ferry from the upper level of the Whitehall Terminal through the door marked "Next Boat."

On a nice day the forward end of the saloon deck is the best vantage point from which to view the harbor during the dash across. While still in the ferry slip, there is a fine view to port of Brooklyn Heights and the decidedly old-fashioned skyline of downtown Brooklyn. A look ahead over the starboard side and to the right of Governors Island will show you the route the boat will be taking down the Upper Bay.

The Statue of Liberty dominates the scene, and the highest land in the far distance, the town of St. George just over five miles away, is your destination. On the New Jersey side and to the right of the Statue is Ellis Island, the former U.S. Immigration Station from 1892 to 1954. It is said that about one American in five has a relative who came through here, and in the peak year of 1907, 1,285,238 were processed on the island.

For many, the passenger cruise liner is the most sought after ship to see, and the paths of these glamorous ships roughly coincide with the ferry's. By phoning the Passenger Ship Terminal at (212) 765-7437, you can learn the arrival and departure times for a full week. If the ship sails as advertised, the liner should pass the Statue of Liberty about forty-five minutes after its departure.

Large container vessels bound for the Port Authority piers in New Jersey or for the Brooklyn docks and giant tankers at anchor are very much in evidence. Approaching Staten Island, the ferry may encounter crossing ship traffic and have to cut its speed.

Once the boat is safely in its slip at the St. George Ferry Terminal, the apron ramps will be lowered, and the majority of passengers will hurry off to their bus or train.

Bus #113 (fare is ninety cents) begins at one of the ramps opposite the terminal, and passes through urban, suburban, and semi-rural Staten Island, in that order, on its forty-five-minute route to Richmondtown, the borough's geographical center.

Richmondtown, founded in the late seventeenth century, was the government seat for Richmond County from 1729 to 1920, when the capital was moved to St. George.

While you can walk freely around the collection at any time, to visit the restored interiors and to watch the excellent craft demonstrations, go to the Visitors Center at the top end of the main street to pay the admission fees. The impressive Greek Revival-style building, which was once the Third County Courthouse (circa 1837), now has a general orientation exhibit showing the development of Richmondtown, including photographic records taken during the relocation of some of the historic buildings.

Directly across the street, the newly opened Historical Museum displays the commercial, industrial, and cultural development of Staten Island from 1800 to the present day. Staten Islanders are proud of their distinctive heritage, and this exhibit is the first to highlight that proud past. The oldest building in the collection, the Voorlezer's House, dates back to circa 1695, and is believed to be the earliest elementary school left standing in the country. Its color contributed to its nickname as "the little red schoolhouse." The *voorlezer*, a lay minister and schoolmaster, lived and taught here, and the building also served as a Dutch Reformed Church—quite a variety of functions for such a small place.

Other places of interest are the Lake-Tysen House, a fine example of an eighteenth-century Dutch Colonial-style farmhouse with fine interior paneling, detail work, and furnishings, and the circa 1837 General Store, containing items that would have been sold about 1910. Adjoining the store is the Stephens House, with 1840–1860 period furniture. Down the street, a carriage house-style building houses historic horse-drawn fire fighting equipment and photographs, and the Restoration's small gift shop.

The ground floor of the Bennett House (circa 1839) has a modest snack bar with sandwiches and soft drinks, and is the only place to eat within walking distance. Upstairs galleries display dolls, games, and toys of early American children. Or, there are two shaded picnic sites on the grounds if you prefer to picnic.

Allow about two hours to cover Richmondtown comfortably and to witness at least some of the craft demonstrations, such as the art of spinning and weaving, candle-making, and old-fashioned hearthside cooking (with samples to taste), performed by skilled, costumed men, women, and teenagers.

Should you wish to return another way, and would like to ride a local transit operation, continue on the #113 bus through a somewhat wild and rural area of the island for another forty-five minutes to sleepy Tottenville, where New York City seems thousands of miles away, and take the Staten Island Rapid Transit Line directly back to the St. George Terminal. As there is only one rail line on Staten Island, you cannot possibly get on the wrong train. The fare is ninety cents, normally payable to the conductor on board, except at Tottenville and St. George Terminal stations where you buy a ticket, not a token. The trains run at twenty-minute intervals throughout the day, thirty minutes in the evenings, and every hour late at night. Call (718) 447-8601 for train information.

The 14.3-mile line had its beginning in the mid-nineteenth century, and from 1899 to 1971 was owned privately by the Baltimore and Ohio Railroad. After the Staten Island Rapid Transit came under Metropolitan Transportation Authority control, the equipment became typical stock of the IND variety, except that it is graffiti-free.

The trip is entirely above ground, and gives passengers a pleasant overview of the island's suburban nature. The jaunt is recommended mostly for rail buffs.

There are several other Staten Island attractions worth considering, and all are easy to get to from the ferry.

From the ferry terminal, take the frequent #1 bus three miles to the stop opposite a yellow brick entrance gate marked "1833," and then carefully cross the busy road.

Before you, amidst eighty acres of lawns and trees, is the largest collection of Greek Revival-style temples in this country, with Victorian and Beaux Arts styles added later. Begun in 1831 as a home for a thousand retired sailors, and once qualifying as the largest and richest charitable institution in the world, the facility closed in 1976, when the seamen were transferred to more modern quarters in North Carolina. Now owned by New York City, Snug Harbor is a growing center for art exhibits, workshops, plays, and musical concerts. The New York Philharmonic has an outdoor concert here every summer, and the audience, many of whom have first enjoyed a pre-concert picnic, sits on the grass. The Staten Island Botanical Garden and the Staten Island Museum are newly established residents.

It is best to phone ahead to receive the calendar of events, as there is something going on all the time. Recent exhibits included the marine art of beloved Staten Islander John Noble (who died in 1984), and a history, in pictures, of the island's transportation links to the outside world.

Or, for a visit to the Staten Island Zoo, take the #107 bus from the ferry terminal for about fifteen minutes, and get off at Forest Avenue and Broadway. Walk five minutes up Broadway to the entrance on the right. The small scale is pleasing, and the zoo is not unlike its charming counterpart in Central Park.

For reptile lovers, there is a singular collection of more than thirty varieties of rattlesnakes. You are greeted by the sign "rattlesnakes are 100% American," because these slitherers are found only in the Western Hemisphere. There are lots of other species of snakes, alligators, lizards, and turtles, and a good range of tropical birds in an uncrowded setting. Many Manhattan children do not feel properly educated until they have ridden the ferry and visited Staten Island's rattlesnakes.

If you wish to go on to Richmondtown, take the #7 bus on Broadway just outside the zoo entrance and transfer (free slip available upon boarding) at Richmond Road to the #113. Once this irregular bus arrives, the ride takes about a half-hour.

For an unusual way back to Manhattan or Queens, hop on the #7 anywhere along its route in Staten Island to return over the Verrazano-Narrows Bridge, with a stupendous view of the harbor from the left-hand side of the bus, to Bay Ridge in Brooklyn, a middle-class community with an Irish, Italian, and Norwegian ethnic base. From 95th Street and 4th Avenue, take the BMT R through Brooklyn to Manhattan and Queens.

Still on the island, to visit a neighborhood specializing in antiques at non-Manhattan prices, make your way to Stapleton, a re-emerging community of Victorian houses offering an intriguing cluster of small shops and one three-story antique center along Bay Street. From the Staten Island Ferry Terminal, ride the Staten Island Rapid Transit two stops to Stapleton Station, or take bus #2 directly to Bay Street. (The thirty-minute walk is quite dull.) Horse of a Different Color at 646 Bay Street specializes in oak furniture and antique clothing. For Art Deco domestic furnishings, try Corner Copia at 680 Bay Street. At 691 Bay Street, the Edgewater Hall Antique Center, in a former bank and Salvation Army building, has three floors of specialized and general dealers. Most of the shops are open from Wednesday to Sunday from about noon to 5 p.m.

PORT JEFFERSON & THE BRIDGEPORT FERRY

Port Jefferson Historical Society, 115 Prospect Street, Port Jefferson, NY 11777. (516) 473-2665. Open Saturday–Sunday May–October, and Saturday, Sunday, and Tuesday July–August, 1–4 p.m. (The Port Jefferson Board of Trade, P.O. Box 15, Port Jefferson, NY 11777 prints a walking tour of the town, with an emphasis on existing businesses.)

For a delightful three-hour ferry cruise across the peaceful waters of Long Island Sound and a view from the upper deck of the *Grand Republic* of the progress of hundreds of sailing yachts, take a train out to the attractive waterfront historic harbor town of Port Jefferson. A summer Saturday or Sunday is the ideal time for this trip, to catch the sun and the maximum number of private craft. As the ferry now runs year-round, a cold-weather crossing can be a briskly different sort of experience for the lovers of the out-of-doors.

Before or following the cruise, spend a few hours enjoying a seafood meal at one of Port Jefferson's waterfront restaurants and browsing through the many specialty shops at the harbor mall. History buffs should call at the Port Jefferson Historical Society headquarters in the Mather House on Prospect Street before taking their walking tour of the nineteenth-century residential section.

Early in the last century, the town developed as one of the North Shore's most important shipbuilding and commercial trading centers, and the Bridgeport ferry has always been a vital element in Port Jefferson's prosperity.

You can also make a circle trip by taking the train to Port Jefferson, sailing one way on the ferry, and returning to New York by train from Bridgeport, Connecticut.

Getting There and Back: From Penn Station, take the Long Island Rail Road to Port Jefferson, usually changing trains at Huntington. The port area is a pleasant twenty-minute walk downhill, and it's worth spending a couple of hours here before or after the one-hour fifteen-minute ferry ride to Bridgeport, Con-

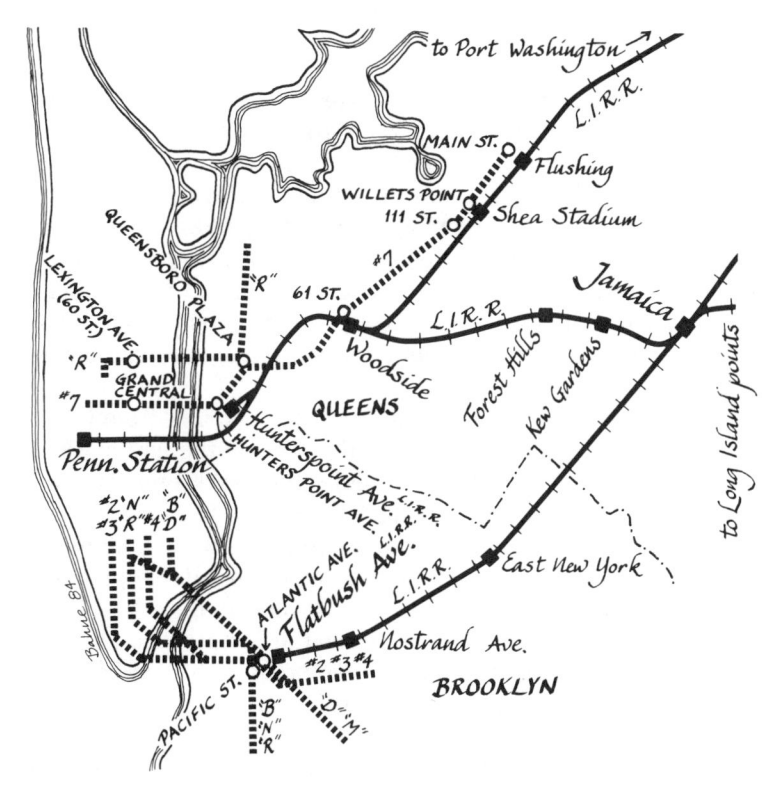

Long Island Gateways

necticut. Or, for a slight variation, stay on the ferry for the return to Port Jefferson and take the Long Island Rail Road back to New York. For yet another routing choice, leave the ferry at Bridgeport and return to New York via Metro-North's New Haven Line to Grand Central. The ferry dock and train station at Bridgeport are a three-minute walk from each other.

You may, of course, take the reverse of the Penn Station-Port Jefferson-Bridgeport route. Take Metro-North's New Haven Line from Grand Central to Bridgeport, and connect with the ferry to Port Jefferson. Stay aboard the ferry and return the same way, or leave the boat at Port Jefferson, do some waterfront sightseeing, walk up the hill to the LIRR station, and take the train back to Penn Station.

Penn Station to Port Jefferson on the Long Island Rail Road (212) 739-4200, one-way off-peak is $5.80, seniors $3.85 (double for round trip).

The Bridgeport and Port Jefferson Steamboat Company, 102 W. Broadway, Port Jefferson, NY 11777, (516) 473-0286 or (516) 473-0631, takes you across the water for the one-way adult fare of $6. If you stay on the boat, the round trip is also $6, while a round trip with stopover is $10. Write or phone for other fares for children, seniors, Ladies Day, bicycles, some of which vary from weekday to weekend. The service runs year-round except during the boat's midwinter overhaul. The ferry line also operates day bus tours to many places in New England using its ferry to Bridgeport. For tour information call (516) 473-0556.

The Metro-North New Haven Line, (212-532-4900), from Grand Central to Bridgeport costs adults going one-way the fare of $8.40 (no off-peak fare on a one-way basis). Off-peak round trips are $12.60. Seniors and the handicapped are $4.20 one way.

The description that follows assumes you're going to Port Jefferson by LIRR, then taking the boat ride to and from Bridgeport, and returning from Bridgeport on the New Haven Line.

On weekends the Long Island trains on the Port Jefferson Branch run every hour and one-half, taking two hours from Penn Station to the end of the line, with a change at Huntington.

Soon after leaving the tunnel from Penn Station, the attractive planned community of Forest Hills appears to the right. Begun in 1904 as a new city district of Tudor-style single-family homes, Forest Hills Gardens quickly grew in popularity with the addition of seven to twelve-story apartment houses in the same style (although the roofs are of Spanish-style red tiles!). The architecturally homogeneous "English village," landscaped by Frederick Law Olmsted, Jr., centers on a main square that leads to the Long Island Rail Road Station. Today, the community of fifty thousand middle-class residents is one of New York's choicest residential neighborhoods.

Just before your train reaches the station platforms, the West Side Tennis Club, home of the United States Open until the tournament moved to Flushing in 1977, appears through the trees to the right.

Down the tracks, Kew Gardens, another planned suburb, has a superficially similar appearance to Forest Hills, although it was and is much less grand.

At busy Jamaica Station, many passengers connect to the Port Jefferson and other trains, which sometimes necessitates even a walk through one train to reach the next one at an adjacent platform. "Change at Jamaica" is practically a household expression. However, you stay put for the fast ride through Nassau County's long string of communities, with the train's whistle sounding its warning at the frequent grade crossings. The wooded countryside of Long Island's North Shore begins at Cold Spring Harbor just before the change of trains at Huntington.

The third-rail electrification is being extended on to Northport, but until the project is completed, you switch to the diesel train here by walking forward along the same platform. The diesel equipment is older, so you may have to look a bit for a clear window, preferably on the left-hand side of the train. Many of the coaches have been recently refurbished inside and out; look for these.

The ride is now through rolling fields, dotted with horse farms, forest patches, and smaller communities. Most of the passengers will have left the train by the time it reaches Port Jefferson, the terminal station.

The twenty- or twenty-five-minute walk to the port and ferry dock is a pleasant one, and very easy to follow. For those who would prefer, a Port Taxi (744-4644) usually meets the train.

Walkers leave the station by the platform back along the train to Main Street, and turn right, passing a small row of ordinary-looking shops. The sidewalk on the left is preferable as you face the oncoming traffic on Route 25-A. For reassurance, little blue and white rectangular signs point to the ferry.

Main Street runs downhill past mostly small Victorian houses into the town's shopping area by the back door. Gramma's Sweet Shop, at the corner of Main and East Main, is an old-fashioned ice cream parlor looking like something out of a 1930s Hollywood film. Step inside to inspect the time-warp interior, and order a large chocolate malt at the soda counter.

The ferry sign points to the right, but you can reach the dock more directly by continuing straight down Main Street to the end. You are in the midst of the tourist district, where large weekend crowds are attracted to the boutiques, antique and collectible stores, and restaurants of all kinds.

For book lovers, visit the Good Times Bookshop on East Main Street, just back from the dock. The store carries a wide selection of new and second-hand books as well as maps and small gift items.

If you are interested in Port Jefferson's past as a major shipbuilding and commercial center, be sure to visit the Historical Society, in the former circa 1840 Mather House on Prospect Street, left off East Main Street. Two generations of the Mather family of shipbuilders lived in this house. To meet the transportation demands of their expanding waterfront business that included the construction of two ferries for the Bridgeport and Port Jefferson Steamboat Company, John Mather built Long Island's first steam marine railways. Nowadays the house serves as an information center and museum, with a seasonal herb garden out back. A recent exhibit displayed a collection of children's toys, games, dolls, doll furniture, and books. The Society prints a useful walking guide for tracing the village's nineteenth-century heritage, much of which appears to be overwhelmed by today's modern and instant old business centers.

Port Jefferson's original business district bordered East Main Street, and many of the contemporary small shops still reveal their clapboard and shingled early nineteenth-century heritage. But for the purest and most original dwellings, many of them belonging to the old sea captains and shipbuilders, zigzag up the hillside's side streets that run between Main Street, your route into town, and High Street, further back. The houses range from the 1812 picturesque Buffet House on East Broadway down by the harbor, to the majestic 1883 Victorian mansion set on the hill on Jones Avenue. As the area of most architectural interest is fairly compact, you can cover most of the historic homes on a walk of about one and one-half hours.

One of the town's most attractive places to eat, and one from where you can watch your boat come in, is Danford's of Bayles Dock, located in a large wooden two-story building with a porch right opposite the ferry dock and plaza. Climb the central wooden steps leading to the open front door, and inside you will find a spacious airy bar with windows giving onto the harbor and square. Danford's is a popular hangout for local and visiting yachtsmen as well as for tourists. The dining room is upstairs, and be sure to ask for a window table that fronts on the docks or on busy East Broadway. The restaurant offers seafood such as broiled scrod, bluefish, and red snapper, with the specials of the day marked on a chalkboard out front.

Upon arriving from Bridgeport, the ferry *Grand Republic* docks bow first, and, once the boat is unloaded, foot passengers may board. Cars park on two decks, and above that the main saloon has a small cafeteria with tables and a gift counter at one end. The room is quite plain, and if the day is nice, you will want to sit outside aft on this deck, protected from the wind, or on the open top deck. There are both fixed benches and deck chairs.

The attractive bar, forward on the saloon deck, has etched glass panels showing several of the historic boats in the company fleet from the *Park City* (nickname for Bridgeport) of 1898 to the *Martha's Vineyard* of 1923, which last ran in the summer of 1984.

The *Grand Republic* is the latest in a long line of ferries that have served this route for more than one hundred years. One of the line's original 1883 stockholders was P. T. Barnum of circus fame. In the beginning, there was a thriving freight trade, with agricultural products being shipped across from Long Island and industrial goods from New England going the other way. Bridgeport passengers used the boat to visit the millionaires' yacht harbor at Port Jefferson, and Long Islanders crossed to Bridgeport for its amusement park and shopping.

The rise in the use of the automobile offset the decline in freight traffic, and today's boat is the biggest yet for the line at 280 feet, with a summertime capacity of a thousand passengers (three hundred in the off-season) and space for eighty-five cars.

Leaving the dock at Port Jefferson, the ferry will make a 180-degree turn to head out of the little harbor, passing the breakwater to reach Long Island Sound. Sand dunes and attractive homes can be seen off to starboard. Ahead is the Sound, which on summer weekends may be filled with sailing yachts and fast motor boats and an occasional coastal tanker bound for New England or the East River.

The crossing takes about one hour and fifteen minutes, and, on the Connecticut side, the ferry passes into the Pequonnock River, an industrial waterway leading to a not very exciting city. If you are taking the non-landing "Mariner's Delight," you stay on board during the half-hour turn-around. Otherwise, foot passengers leave the boat after the first few cars have gotten out of the way. The Shore Line Railroad linking Boston with New York is directly ahead. Pass along the parking lot, under the railroad bridge, and up the flight of stairs to the station's platform for the trains to New York. The ticket office is down to the left, and the bus station down the stairs and across the street.

Bridgeport is a railroad junction for the scenic Housatonic and Naugatuck Valley branch line to Waterbury (see "A Branch Line Train Ride to Waterbury, Connecticut," page 146).

New Haven Line trains run into Grand Central every one or two hours, depending on the time of day and day of the week. Sit on the left-hand side for the one-hour forty-minute ride, with several glimpses of Long Island Sound, river estuaries, marshlands, some fine homes, and the red barn-style New Haven Line stations. See "The Shore Line Rail Route Guide" (page 143) for a complete description of the ride.

BAYARD CUTTING ARBORETUM

Bayard Cutting Arboretum, P.O. Box 466, Oakdale, NY 11769. (516) 581-1002. Open 10 a.m.–5 p.m. Wednesday–Sunday. Closed Monday–Tuesday. Admission on weekends and high-season weekdays $1.50, otherwise free. Children 2–12 free.

Virtually unknown to most New Yorkers, the enchanting 690-acre Bayard Cutting Arboretum on Long Island's South Shore offers a quiet setting to walk among flowering plants, trees, and shrubs. From the Arboretum's winding Connetquot River trail, you can observe a wide variety of migratory and resident shore birds.

Within the sprawling Victorian Cutting mansion, have a look at the former master's private collection of mounted birds and local Indian artifacts. The specimens on display will help with the identification of live species outside on the property.

April through August are the best months to come for the planting bulbs, wildflowers, and flowering trees and shrubs; January to early June for bird watching; and late September to early November for the fall foliage and the southward bird migration. Guided tours are given at 11 a.m. on Sundays.

The only convenient eating facility is a simple cafeteria within the mansion, and be forewarned that picnics are not permitted anywhere on the grounds.

Getting There and Back: The Long Island Rail Road offers regular service, with a change of trains at Jamaica or Babylon, to Great River Station, an easy ten-minute walk from the Arboretum's entrance gate.

The Montauk Branch timetable shows two weekday trains out in the morning and back in the afternoon, and three departures each

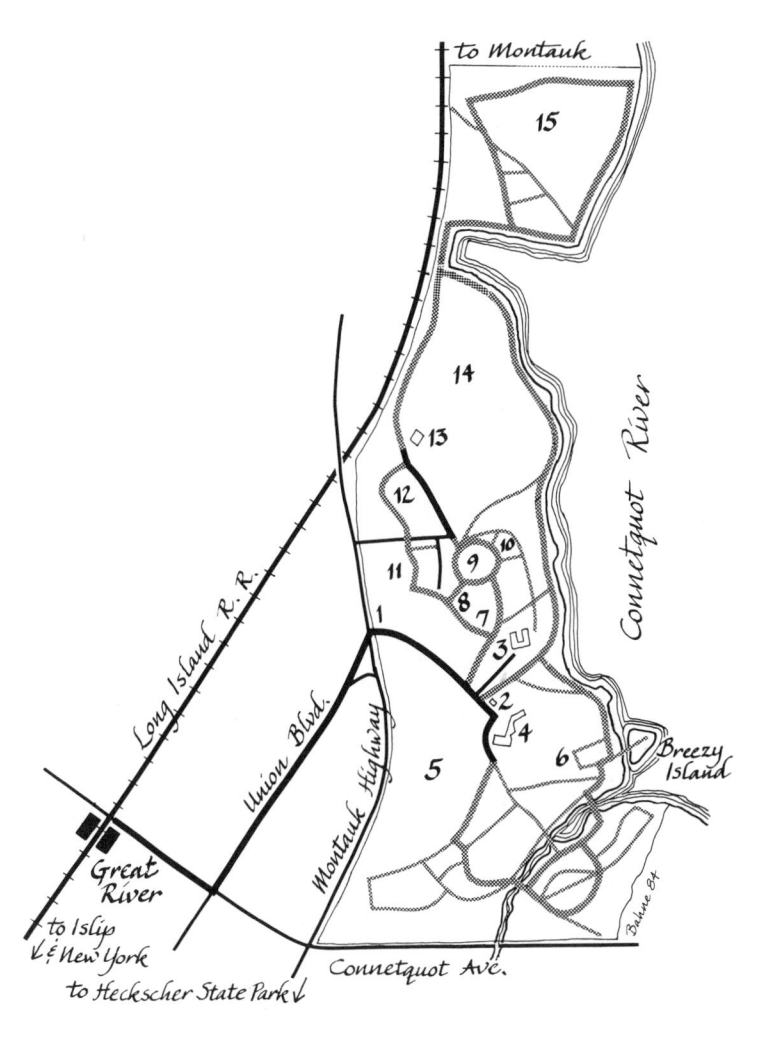

Bayard Cutting Arboretum

1. Park Entrance
2. Shelter
3. Carriage House
4. Cutting Residence
5. Oak Park
6. Native Azalea Garden
7. Pinetum
8. Holly
9. Dwarf Evergreen
10. Gazebo
11. New Pinetum
12. Pinetum Expansion
13. Barn
14. Meadow
15. Native Wood and Bog

way on weekends, with the journey taking one hour fifteen minutes. The off-peak one-way adult fare is $5.20, $10.40 round trip; seniors $3.45 and $6.90, (212) 739-4200. Please disregard literature that says to get off at the Islip Station and take a three-mile taxi transfer.

If setting out from Penn Station, you will have to change from an electric to a diesel train at Jamaica or Babylon. In both instances, it is an immediate guaranteed across-the-platform switch.

After passing under the East River, the train comes out into daylight opposite the parallel Sunnyside rail yards, where Amtrak and New Jersey Transit trains are cleaned, stored, and made ready for their next trips.

The line hurtles past the planned suburbs of Forest Hills and Kew Gardens, then makes the obligatory stop at Jamaica, where, according to the service chosen, you may have to change. If you are traveling aboard an electric train to Babylon, the express run hits eighty miles per hour and easily overtakes the auto traffic on the Sunrise Highway down and to the right. At Freeport, dedicated summer-season buses take riders directly to Jones Beach, and the LIRR offers a complete package, including train fare, connecting bus, changing room, and locker.

Most of the trackside scenery is suburban with a heavy dose of large shopping centers. At Babylon, the end of third-rail electrification, change to a diesel-hauled train. While the equipment is much older, many of the coaches have had their interiors completely refurbished to a high standard. The train now moves at a much more relaxed pace and whistles frequently at grade crossings.

At Bayshore, Tommy's van fleet transfers Fire Island-bound riders to the ferry dock. The Great River stop comes five minutes after Islip.

Leave the station by walking south and right from the grade crossing along Connetquot Avenue, staying behind the white line on the left facing the oncoming traffic. At the first intersection, turn left on Union Boulevard, which has a much more generous shoulder. A large sign across the road reads "Bayard Cutting Arboretum 2000'." Union Boulevard swings gradually left to join Route 27-A, the Montauk Highway. As the two roads become one, cross the street to the Arboretum entrance and the admission kiosk. The total walking time from the station is only ten minutes.

Be sure to ask for a map at the entrance or at the main house, or, to plan your walk, take a look at the detailed map at the shelter, located just past the parking lot, as well as the one in this book. Phone ahead for the schedule of outdoor classical summer concerts, horticultural programs that teach you to create a terrarium, build a bird feeder, or learn the principles of residential landscaping, and lectures about, for instance, floral photography, and other special events.

From the shelter walk to the main house. The late nineteenth-century shingled Cutting residence, partly open to visitors, contains a good collection of mounted birds and Indian artifacts in the ground-floor rooms, all fitted with elaborate fireplaces, heavy woodwork, and stained glass. Unless you fancy archaic Victorian museum displays and period settings (as of course you just might), you will want to spend your time out-of-doors. The simple snack bar has tables on a terrace overlooking the lawn sweeping down to the Connetquot River.

William Bayard Cutting, a successful businessman and investor, started the Arboretum in 1887 according to the plans of Frederick Law Olmsted. After his death in 1912, Cutting's wife and daughter donated the 690-acre estate to Long Island State Park, along with a private endowment for its perpetual upkeep.

The Arboretum contains several sections devoted to specific plantings, and each one can be visited by following one of the five well-signposted trails.

The Pinetum, one of the original areas, contains cedar, cypress, fir, hemlock, pine, spruce, and yew trees, many of them labeled, some with several paragraphs of useful text. New adjacent sections have been recently started with young trees.

The rhododendrons and azaleas, representing the broadleaf evergreen family, are best visited in May, June, and July. Spring and summer wildflowers abound throughout the Arboretum, especially around the ponds and small streams at the south end near the Connetquot River.

The suggested walk leaves the Cutting residence and makes a sweep of the estate's southern portion, and on for a stroll through the broadleaf evergreen and wildflower collections. Follow the Bird Watchers Walk along the shoreline to see swans, geese, ducks, and gulls at almost any time of the year, and many more species of migrating shorebirds from late January through late June. On a fine day, many visitors go down to the riverside benches to read or watch the bird and boating activity. Across the Connetquot, attractive waterfront houses and private docks line the shore.

Continuing northward, the shore path passes an open meadow and crosses a narrow piece of land next to the Montauk rail line leading into a wild area of native woods and bogs, a refreshingly different setting from the Arboretum's planned landscaping. You will also find this the least visited section of the estate. The path loops around and heads back across the meadow, past the barn, and into the evergreen and holly sections, where an elaborate network of paths takes you to every corner of the impressive collection.

Allow two hours to do the Arboretum justice, more if you have lunch in the snack bar or decide to contemplate the river from one of the waterside benches. Picnicking is not allowed, so if you bring your own food, eat it on the train or walk to nearby Heckscher State Park.

The earlier you arrive at the Arboretum, the fewer people you will find, unless there is a special event, as most visitors tend to come in the afternoon.

HUDSON VALLEY RAIL ROUTE GUIDE

For one of the finest short rail rides in the entire country, take an Amtrak or Metro-North train from Grand Central up the Hudson Valley for superb water level views of the towering New Jersey Palisades, the rugged Hudson Highlands, sprawling country estates, the mighty fortress at West Point, and the busy parallel river shipping.

While the scenic feast extends almost 150 miles to Albany, you may enjoy a good portion of these varied sights on a day outing by train en route to the Sleepy Hollow Restorations at Sunnyside, Philipsburg Manor, Van Cortlandt Manor, to the riverside town of Cold Spring and the nearby Boscobel Restoration, and for a weekend at the Mohonk Mountain House. Descriptive chapters on all of these destinations follow. Also see map on p. 58.

The train trip is recommended for any fine day year-round, but the spring and fall offer the most color, and in the winter you can watch large freighters and hardworking tugboats and their tows crashing through the pack ice right outside your window.

Be sure to find a seat on the left-hand side of the coach when heading north.

Hudson River Railroad passenger train service between Chambers Street in Manhattan and Poughkeepsie dates back to 1849. However, it was not until 1871 that a connection was completed at Spuyten Duyvil to bring trains along the Harlem River into Manhattan to the site of the present 1913 Grand Central Terminal. In 1872–1874 the tracks were lowered into a cut with one tunnel section, and by 1913 a new Park Avenue completely covered the tracks from 97th Street south beneath the new terminal. Third-rail electrification reached Croton-Harmon on the Hudson Line in 1913, and since then no further extensions have been completed.

Darkness prevails for about ten minutes upon leaving the Grand Central Terminal area with its thirty-three miles of tracks spread over forty-eight acres. At 97th Street, the line comes out into the daylight from beneath Park Avenue at the southern boundary of Harlem, the most populous black community in the United States. The four-track main line runs over a stone viaduct down the middle of Park Avenue, with the crosstown streets passing through short tunnels beneath. On the left, the large brick post-war apartment houses and the substantial buildings of Mt. Sinai Hospital soon give way to the urban decay of Central Harlem.

Shortly after the pause to receive passengers at 125th Street Station, astride Harlem's main street, the train crosses the Harlem River, spanned to the left and right by a series of ancient swing bridges, into a manufacturing area of the South Bronx. Amidst a tangled network of highways, the Harlem and New Haven Lines split, and the Hudson Line finds a path along the shore of the Harlem River.

Above, the Cross Bronx Expressway leaps the Harlem River to reach the high rocky cliffs on the Upper Manhattan side. After passing the huge brick River Park Towers complex, built on former New York Central land, the Manhattan side reveals a small, scruffy boat basin, a large, abandoned Con Edison power plant, and the sprawling IRT subway yards at 207th Street.

With the train swinging to the left, the line now passes beneath the stone face of Marble Hill and Spuyten Duyvil on the right, with Manhattan now to the south. Although geographically in the Bronx, a recent court ruling officially replaces Marble Hill in Manhattan, where it had belonged before a cut was dug to connect the Harlem and Hudson Rivers via Spuyten Duyvil Creek. Once an important waterway for barges traveling to and from the Erie Canal, the river mainly serves now as a pleasure route for private yachts, Circle Line sightseeing boats, and Columbia University's crew teams.

Columbia's rebuilt Baker Field appears to the left after passing beneath the bi-level bridge that carries Broadway and the IRT #1 line from Manhattan to the Bronx. The top end of wooded Inwood Hill Park stretches from the waterline to rise and meet the Henry Hudson Parkway Bridge before dropping again to the edge of the Hudson River and its open swing bridge.

The partly ruined railroad bridge links the main Hudson Valley line to the West Side freight line, a now unused two-track facility running south along the river past the area west of Pennsylvania Station and ending abruptly at Bank Street in Lower Manhattan. One day Amtrak hopes to operate its New York State passenger trains directly into Penn Station via a tunnel connection from the old freight line. In the meantime, nature is retaking the upper sections of the line.

As the Metro-North train makes the squeaky turn to parallel the Hudson, there's a fine view of the George Washington Bridge and of the Palisades Interstate Park across the river. The rail line is now four tracks, and the train picks up speed, passing with increased rapidity the high-level platforms sandwiched between the rails and the river.

The Country Cane Sugar factory just north of Ludlow station is the route's first major industrial plant that benefits from its riverside location. A freighter bringing raw sugar from South America may be docked on the river's far side.

The city of Yonkers, the fourth-largest urban area in the state, and recently on the verge of bankruptcy, rises with an unremarkable skyline to the right. To the left is the old two-deck Day Line pier, once a regular landing for the sidewheel excursion boats headed upriver to Bear Mountain, West Point, and, about forty years ago, all the way to Albany. These night and day lines once gave the railroads a run for their money, then tried cooperating with them, and, finally, with the added insult of automobile competition, gave up altogether.

North of Yonkers, the shoreline is occupied by both active and abandoned industrial plants, small marinas, and half-submerged wooden hulks. In places, the tracks come within a few feet of the river, which, because it is tidal and salty, is more accurately an estuary or fjord. On weekends, fishermen come down to the river to try their luck.

Just before passing the attractive stone station at Dobbs Ferry, the Chart House Restaurant, to the left, offers steaks and seafood and a river view at New York City prices. The Hudson now widens to form the Tappan Zee, separating New York State's Rockland County on the west from Westchester County on the east. Across the Tappan Zee some lowland that juts out into the water once served as the Erie Railroad's Piermont facility, the end of the line where passengers transferred to ferryboats for the rest of the trip south to New York. Later, when the Erie was permitted access to New Jersey, the company's main line extended down to Jersey City, and Piermont became a branch operation, until it was eventually abandoned altogether.

Just before Tarrytown, the long span of the Tappan Zee Bridge carries the New York State Thruway across the water. General Motors is Tarrytown's main employer, and the rise and fall in the fortunes of the auto industry are often felt at the huge plant here.

Irvington, below Tarrytown, serves as the local stop for Sunnyside and Lyndhurst Castle. Philipse Manor, north of Tarrytown, is the closest station for a visit to Philipsburg Manor.

A long view extends up the Hudson into Haverstraw Bay and the Hudson Highlands, and, at Ossining, the line passes Sing Sing state prison. Slowing down, the train enters the south end of the Croton-Harmon rail yards, the railroad's primary car and locomotive maintenance and overhaul facility. In the days of steam, the New York Central changed engines here for the electric-powered run into Grand Central, but there are few engine changes needed now.

Croton-Harmon is the stop for Van Cortlandt Manor.

Except during commuter rush hours and on the 9:50 a.m. and 5:50 p.m. trains on weekends, all passengers change here to an SPV-2000 diesel rail car or older substitute equipment. Again, secure your seat on the left side.

From Croton-Harmon, the three-track route passes through a wooded area away from the river, then returns to the water at Peekskill, where the line bends to the left and becomes two tracks from here to Poughkeepsie.

Looking south, the often troubled Indian Point Nuclear Power Station occupies a site that the Hudson River Day Line once used as the company's own recreation park and vegetable garden. Across the river, a small pier at Bear Mountain State Park permits boat excursion passengers to land and to frolic amidst bucolic surroundings of lakes, woods, picnic grounds, hiking trails, and open playing fields. The Bear Mountain Inn may be seen through the trees beneath a large American flag.

The river becomes noticeably narrower at the point where the Bear Mountain Bridge spans the gap between the Hudson Highlands. Rocky outcroppings briefly cut off the river view while the train rounds a curve to pass beneath a suspension bridge.

If you blink you might just miss the tiny hamlet of Manitou which, because so few Metro-North trains stop here, gets only a brief mention in the Hudson Line timetable's "Reference Marks" listing. On weekends in the summer months, Appalachian Trail hikers taking the 8:50 a.m. train from New York step off here for trips northeast into New England or southwest across the Bear Mountain Bridge into the Middle Atlantic States.

Unmistakable and rising to the left is a large concentration of gray buildings, forming the United States Military Academy at West Point. At the base of the cliff, a small launch docked near the West Shore Line station brings the cadets and officers over to the Garrison station for trains into New York. The colorful cluster of Victorian buildings surrounding the Garrison depot served as the setting for Dolly's return to Yonkers in the film *Hello Dolly*.

Energetic souls might even consider leaving the train at Garrison for the four-mile hike to Boscobel and Cold Spring. Otherwise, use the more convenient station at Cold Spring for a visit to that town and the shorter walk to Boscobel.

Beautiful cliffs rise across the river with the fine view briefly disappearing in the darkness of the tunnel that passes beneath Breakneck Ridge.

On a small island in the river stands the ruins of Bannerman's, a mock nineteenth-century castle. At Beacon, you can still see the remains of the ferry slip that up to two decades ago connected Beacon to Newburgh on the opposite shore. The ferry service was made redundant with the completion of the first of two spans of the Beacon-Newburgh Bridge that carries Interstate 84.

Between here and the ramshackle town of New Hamburg, there may be a fuel tanker berthed near the tracks. Poughkeepsie is the next and last stop for Metro-North trains and for people joining the hotel car for the Mohonk Mountain House. The tracks, and Amtrak trains, continue north to Albany and Montreal and west to Buffalo, Toronto, and Chicago. Someday you might consider taking an extended train trip across New York state into Canada—or indeed all the way to the Pacific Coast.

SLEEPY HOLLOW RESTORATIONS
Sunnyside, Phillipsburg Manor, Van Cortlandt Manor & Lyndhurst Castle

Sleepy Hollow Restorations, 150 White Plains Road, Tarrytown, NY 10591. (914) 631-8200. The three restorations are open every day 10 a.m.–5 p.m., except Thanksgiving, Christmas, and New Year's Day. Single-visit admission for three Sleepy Hollow Restorations, adults $4, seniors (60 and over) and juniors (6–14) $2.50. Two-property tickets, good for four months, adults $7, seniors and juniors $4.50. Three-property tickets, good for six months, adults $10, seniors and juniors $6.50.

Lyndhurst Castle, 635 South Broadway, Tarrytown, NY 10591. (914) 631-0046. Open April–October, Tuesday–Sunday 10 a.m.– 4:15 p.m. Single-visit admission adults $4, seniors (60 and over) $3, juniors (6–15) $2, children under 6 free.

Four distinctively different periods of Hudson Valley Dutch, English, and American history come alive with visits to Philipsburg Manor (1720–1750), Van Cortlandt Manor (1783–1814), Sunnyside (1835–1859), and Lyndhurst Castle (mostly post-Civil War). The first three are collectively known as the Sleepy Hollow Restorations, and are all best appreciated at a leisurely pace combining an informative guided tour with independent exploring. No more than two houses should be attempted in one day.

Many of the costumed guides are actively engaged in their time-honored trades, and, when there are few other visitors about, asking them lots of questions can be an utterly delightful experience.

The Sleepy Hollow Restorations annual calendar of events lists all sorts of activities throughout the year: you may choose to sample the freshly baked apple pies at Sunnyside; participate in te making of preserves at Van Cortlandt; celebrate the Dutch tradition of St.

Nicholas Day in early December at Philipsburg Manor; or attend the "Summer of Music on the Hudson" series at Lyndhurst.

Both Philipsburg Manor and Van Cortlandt Manor represent Dutch-English-influenced New York at its height, although according to quite different standards of living. The two are easily reached on foot from nearby Hudson Line train stations.

Washington Irving's home at Sunnyside and Jay Gould's Lyndhurst Castle are a good two-mile walk from the train, but the route is a pleasant one. Taxis are also available.

Consider taking along a picnic lunch, as all four houses have special areas set aside for this purpose.

Sunnyside & Lyndhurst Castle

The great American literary figure Washington Irving, beginning in 1835, built a fanciful and exceedingly comfortable home on the east bank of the Hudson. He called it Sunnyside. Nearby, and within walking distance, visit Lyndhurst Castle for its lavish display of wealth and its sixty-seven acres of magnificent trees.

Getting There and Back: On weekdays and weekends, there is hourly local train service from Grand Central at twenty minutes past each hour on Metro-North's Hudson Line. The one-way off-peak fare to Irvington is $3.45 (seniors $2.30). Double for the round trip. See the "Hudson Valley Rail Route Guide" for a description of the scenic train ride.

By taking the 8:20 a.m. train from New York, for instance, you arrive at Irvington at 9:07 a.m. From the station, walk up Main Street, possibly stopping at one of its stores for sandwiches and drinks to make a picnic lunch for after your visit. It's about a half-mile to Broadway, Route 9, where you turn left, walking eight-tenths of a mile to Sunnyside Lane, and turn left again. From here on, there is no sidewalk, and the road twists downhill to the entrance drive. The total distance is about two miles, and Sunnyside should be open by the time you arrive.

Washington Irving bought a little cottage on the property in 1835, and immediately began adding to it to create the gabled, wisteria-cloaked, Gothic- and Romanesque-style fancy we see today. Dinner guests often came to Sunnyside, where they could enjoy beautiful sunsets through the windows looking over the Hudson River. On the house tour, you will be shown the dining room with table set

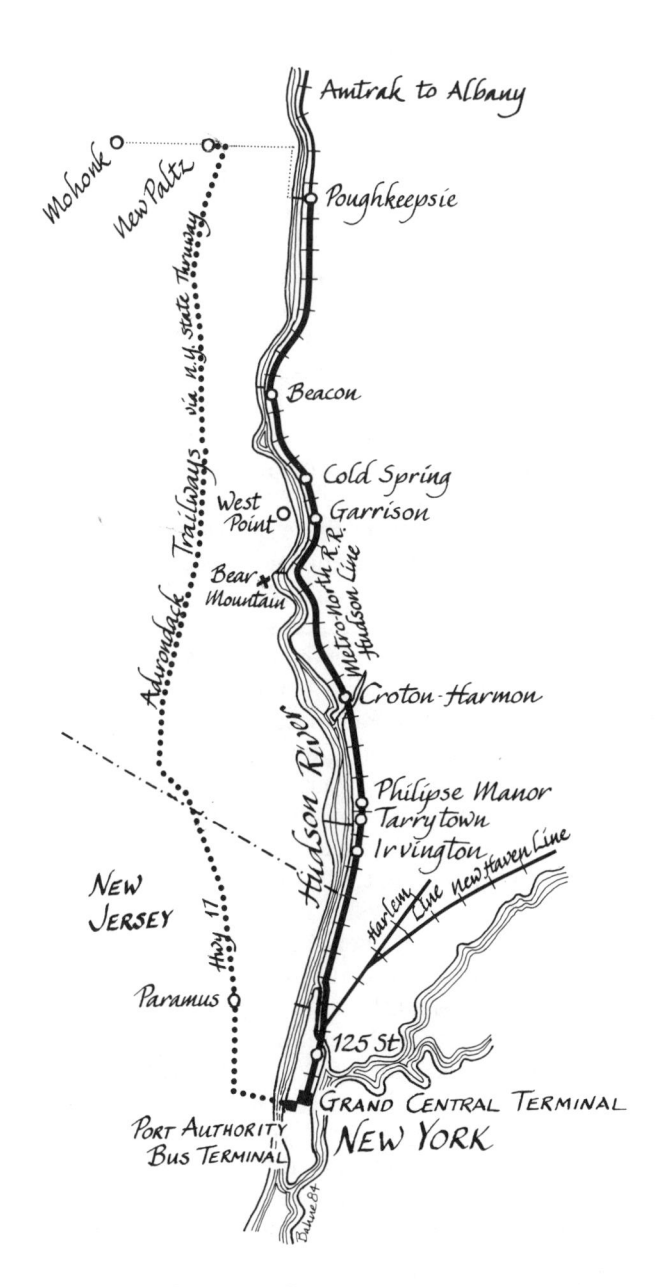

Sleepy Hollow Restorations

as if for the next festive meal. In the kitchen on Thanksgiving weekend, you can watch the elaborate preparations for an authentic mid-nineteenth-century feast.

Washington Irving's study remains as it was in the last years of his life, and it is here amidst his personal collection of books that he wrote the five-volume *Life of George Washington* and parts of other famous works. His publisher, G. P. Putnam's Sons, was responsible for returning his writing desk to this room. In the fall, storytelling at Sunnyside features Washington Irving's familiar stories, including the spooky "Legend of Sleepy Hollow."

Upstairs, each one of the bedrooms, for family, servants, or guests, has its own character. Washington Irving's own bedroom, where he died in 1859, is furnished with a canopied Sheraton bed, and contains some of his clothes and personal effects, such as his favorite walking stick.

Apart from the main house, there are several outbuildings, including a spired and peaked icehouse where the blocks cut from the pond called "Little Mediterranean" were stored for the warmer months. There are twenty-four acres of grounds with woodland paths, and you can stroll about here on your own to enjoy beautiful views of the Hudson at its widest point in the Tappan Zee.

A trip to Sunnyside Restoration can easily be made to include nearby Lyndhurst Castle, a Gothic Revival-style mansion once owned by the infamous financier and railroad baron Jay Gould. To reach Lyndhurst, walk back up Sunnyside Lane to Broadway, Route 9, and turn left. The castle entrance is only three-tenths of a mile on the left. A coupon handed out at Sunnyside reduces the admission here by $1.

Everything here is on an enormous scale: the size of the rooms, the high ceilings, even the furniture. The baronial interior represents the height of nineteenth-century opulence, and is a showcase for Gould's own collection of paintings, his library of rare bound volumes, and an eclectic choice of Victorian furnishings that reflect not only Gould's taste but that of two subsequent owners.

The grounds cover sixty-seven acres, and a map handed out at the gate when you enter will show the location of the magnificent copper beeches, lindens, and the rose gardens, which are best seen in the spring and early summer. Picnics are permitted here and at Sunnyside in attractive shaded settings.

Lyndhurst, separately administered from the three Sleepy Hollow

Restorations, was left to the National Trust for Historic Preservation by Jay Gould's daughter, Anna, Duchess of Tallyrand-Perigord, at her death in 1961. Lyndhurst is Hudson River Gothic at its very best.

To return to Irvington Station, follow Broadway, Route 9, back to Main Street and turn right. Stout walkers might wish to head north along Route 9 through Tarrytown to North Tarrytown where Philipsburg Manor is located, a distance of three and one-half miles from Sunnyside. Alternatively, you could call a taxi, and there is an occasional local bus operating along Broadway into Tarrytown.

Philipsburg Manor

The Philipse family of Dutch ancestry once owned a hefty portion—a ninety thousand-acre tract that extended south to Spuyten Duyvil just north of Manhattan Island—of today's Westchester County. In the early 1700s, Frederick Philipse established his Upper Mills at Philipsburg Manor, a thriving commercial center including a manor house and farm, on the navigable Pocantico River, for the export of flour, corn meal, and sea biscuits.

Getting There and Back: The most convenient stop for Philipsburg Manor is Philipse Manor Station, just two stops north of Irvington (for Sunnyside), and one stop north of Tarrytown. Weekday and weekend Metro-North trains leave Grand Central at twenty minutes past the hour, taking just over fifty minutes. The one-way off-peak fare is $3.85 (seniors $2.55). Double for round trip. The eight-tenths of a mile walk from the station, at the edge of the Hudson River, is a pleasant one through a wooded residential area. Leave the attractive stone depot and walk south up the hill, turning left at Palmer Avenue. Continue for two blocks, and turn right into Bellwood Avenue, which soon swings left along the manor's perimeter and past the still waters of little Pocantico River. Turn right at the traffic light on Broadway, Route 9, and immediately right again through the parking lot to the manor's orientation center.

While waiting for the guided tour, you can browse through the gift shop, with a chart of the grounds, drawings, and photographs for sale. There is also an interpretive center and an introductory film. The actual visit begins with a walk across the two hundred foot oak dam with sluices that control the flow of water leading to the reconstructed grist mill. The mill's waterwheel, today activated by an Englishman with several generations of mill operators in his background, turns the stones used to grind corn into a fine powder. An adjacent dock served overseas sailing ships that made their way from the Atlantic up the Hudson and Pocantico Rivers to reach the manor.

The whitewashed original stone manor is furnished in the quaint style of a simple Dutch farmhouse, with a sparseness that seems uncomfortable by today's standards. In the lower kitchen, you can watch demonstrations of putting up preserves, making bread, and baking biscuits, the latter two done in the open-hearth fireplace and side cavities. To maintain authenticity, the cook will use the original Dutch recipes that produced fine-tasting as well as rather coarse baked goods. Ask to see the recipe for apple fritters, made with ale, sack, nutmeg, and ginger. Outside, the kitchen yard supplies the demonstrators with vegetables and herbs for holiday meal preparations.

The eat-in upstairs kitchen has cabinets and shelves crowded with blue Dutch Delft-style china, Chinese ceramics, earthenware jars, pewter plates, homemade candles, and spice racks. It is here the Philipse family enjoyed informal meals by the fire.

From the bedrooms above, there are views in every direction of the mill, the Pocantico River, and farmland. The working farm has as its centerpiece an original eighteenth-century barn, recently moved here from the Albany area, where sheep and cows are stabled. Sheep shearing and carpentry are two of the regular demonstrations. After the guided tour, it is worth lingering to take in the considerable charm of a fine re-creation of early American life on the farm.

Unfortunately for them, the Philipse family chose the losing side in the Revolutionary War; the vast land holdings were confiscated and then auctioned off to the tenants. After 1785 the Manor ceased to exist as a major trading center.

Van Cortlandt Manor

The prominent Dutch family of Van Cortlandt first came to America in 1638 to establish themselves as large landholders, businessmen, officers in the Continental Army, and government officials, including the first native-born mayor of New York. The family's holdings reached over eighty-six thousand acres, extending from

Croton Point to beyond Peekskill and east to the Connecticut state border. The present restoration at Van Cortlandt Manor represents the period from 1750 to 1815, and includes a large handsome manor house, ferry house, and kitchen, orchards, and gardens.

Getting There and Back: To reach the Manor, take a Hudson Line train from Grand Central to Croton-Harmon. There is hourly (most hours) express service at fifty minutes past the hour, making only four or five stops and taking fifty minutes. Or, there is a slower, by fifteen minutes, hourly local service making seventeen stops. The one-way off-peak fare is $4.25 (seniors $2.80). Double for the round trip.

If you are intending to visit both Dutch restorations, consider the following suggestion: buy an off-peak one-way ticket to Philipse Manor, allowing a morning stopover first at Philipsburg Manor Restoration. Rejoin the train three hours later and buy a one-way off-peak ticket on board for the seven-minute ride to Croton-Harmon, and visit Van Cortlandt Manor in the afternoon. Buy an off-peak one-way fare from here back to Grand Central.

To reach Van Cortlandt Manor from Croton-Harmon station, a fifteen-minute walk, leave the tiny depot and walk north through the parking lot, up the stairs, and east along Croton Point Avenue, passing under Route 9 to Riverside Avenue. Turn right at the shopping center (where if you like you can order sandwiches at the supermarket's deli-counter for a later picnic), and follow the road as it runs straight to the manor. Go directly past the manor house to the visitors lounge for admission.

The tour starts out along the Long Walk, a brick path running between the apple orchards and the flower and vegetable gardens. In the spring, the verges are a mass of colorful tulips.

The manor itself is an imposing three-story stone and wood building set against a hillside, with a double staircase leading up to a covered wooden wrap-around porch. Prior to 1750, the house served as a fur trading post and consisted only of the lower level beneath the stairs, where there is a large eat-in kitchen, parlor, and food storage rooms. There are regular cooking demonstrations using original family recipes, and you might like to inquire into the making of apple butter from apples, apple cider, quince, and orange peel.

The next two floors were added when Van Cortlandt Manor became a permanent home in 1750. The furnishings, much more comfortable than in the spartan Philipsburg Manor, include many fine Queen Anne and Chippendale pieces, and, on the wall, several family portraits. The guide will proudly tell you that members of the Van Cortlandt family lived here until 1941.

At the far end of the Long Walk, in the Ferry House, the manor offered accommodations for travelers using the old Albany Post Road and the ferry that crossed the Croton River. The Ferry House combined a tap room with separate rudimentary sleeping quarters for men and women on two floors. Adjacent, the kitchen that once provided the travelers with meals today shows visitors the art of domestic textile manufacture, as most garments were made in-house.

After the tour, you are invited to climb the hillside for a walk through the woods. During the leafless winter months the walk allows you to view the little Croton River as it empties into the Hudson. For a picnic, there are tables down by the river next to the ice house and entrance gate.

COLD SPRING & BOSCOBEL

Boscobel Restoration, Garrison-on-Hudson, NY 10524. (914) 265-3638. Open Wednesday–Monday 9:30 a.m.–5 p.m. (4 p.m. in March, November, and December). Closed January–February, Thanksgiving, and Christmas. Admission fees include an hour's tour and access to the grounds. Adults $4, children 6–14 $2.

The Village of Cold Spring, a nineteenth-century Hudson River town nestled among the Hudson Highlands fifty-one miles from Grand Central, is a very special destination because of its wide range of exciting sightseeing options. The day or weekend outing, recommended at any time of the year except the dead of winter, is further enhanced by the beautiful train ride up the Hudson Valley.

Some people may not want to go beyond the center of town, which offers lovely walks along the Hudson River, a main street lined with antique and collectible shops, numerous side streets of plain and fancy Victorian residential architecture, and good places for a meal.

For the more ambitious, Boscobel Restoration, a Federal-style mansion with some of the finest early nineteenth-century interior furnishings in the country, overlooks the Hudson from a lofty site within reasonable walking distance from town. Hikers can have a field day exploring the network of trails that fan out to the north with some spectacular views of the Hudson Valley.

For an extended stay, you might consider taking a Saturday morning train up to Cold Spring, spending the night at one of two bed and breakfast houses or at the country inn, all conveniently located near the station, and returning to New York late Sunday afternoon.

Getting There and Back: The one-hour twenty-five-minute train journey from Grand Central along the east bank of the Hudson is one of the most scenic rail rides in the country. For a detailed description see the "Hudson Valley Rail Route Guide."

Metro-North Hudson Line trains depart on weekdays and on weekends at intervals of every hour or every two hours, and most trips require a change of trains at Croton-Harmon, thirty-three miles from Grand Central and the end of the third-rail electrification. The connecting diesel trains may be locomotive-hauled, older commuter coaches, or new SPV-2000 Budd-built diesel rail cars. On Saturdays and Sundays there is a popular through train leaving Grand Central at 9:50 a.m., making only three stops and arriving at Cold Spring at 11:03 a.m. Be sure to sit on the left-hand side.

The off-peak round-trip fare is $11 for adults and $7.30 for seniors.

Upon arriving at Cold Spring and once the train has pulled away, the town's simple layout is easily understood. Main Street, lined with stores and restaurants, begins at the tracks and runs uphill away from the river considerably further than the eye can see. The lower part of town, anchored by a large gazebo at the foot of Main Street's extension, occupies a narrow site between the tracks and the river. Begin your visit on the river side.

Many people pick their way across the two railroad tracks here, and there are no signs that say it is forbidden to do so. To the south, there is a clear view of oncoming trains, but northward the line curves immediately to the right, and New York-bound Amtrak trains pass through town at very high speeds. For the unsure, there is an underpass beneath the tracks.

From the gazebo at the end of Main Street, there are stupendous views of the Hudson River in both directions, from the great, gray pile of West Point downstream to the imposing mass of Storm King

Mountain and Breakneck Ridge upriver. Waterborne commerce using the Hudson consists of oil tankers carrying fuel to the valley's power plants, white banana boats on their regular run from Central America to the Port of Albany a hundred miles to the north, and long strings of barges powered by a variety of hardworking tugs. Numerous private craft and excursion boats, especially in the warmer months, dot the river.

Across the street from the gazebo stands the three-story 1832

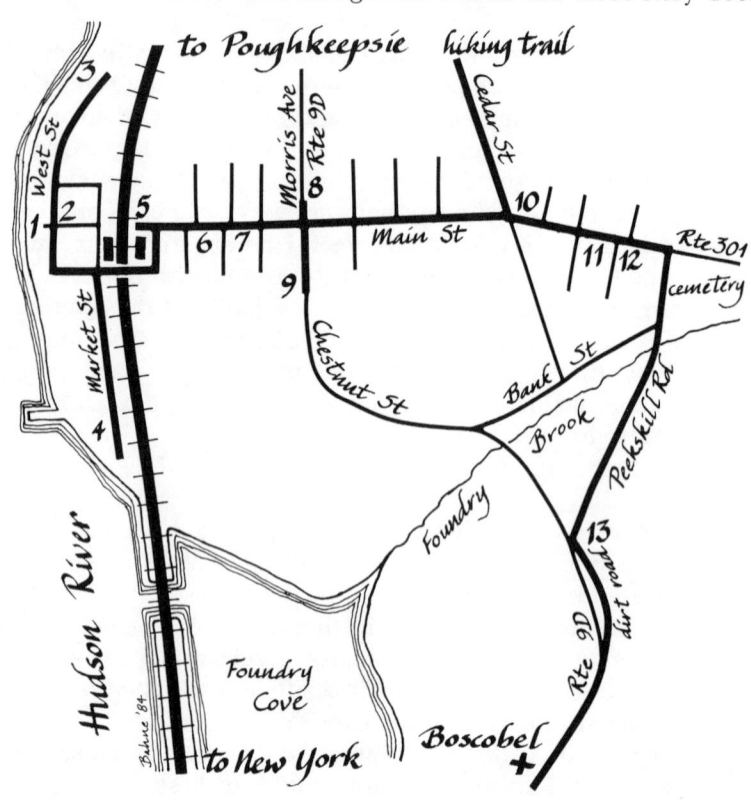

Cold Spring

1. Gazebo
2. Hudson House
3. Dockside Harbor Restaurant
4. Chapel of Our Lady
5. Station One Restaurant (old railroad station)
6. Old Post Inn
7. Antique Mews Guest House
8. Library
9. Foundry School Museum
10. Philipstown Town Hall
11. Hudson Rogue Co.
12. Your Country Store (deli)
13. Plumbush Restaurant

Hudson House, the second-oldest continuously operating inn in New York State, and the only hotel within reasonable walking distance from the railroad station. The fifteen rooms, some with a balcony overlooking the village park and Hudson River, are bright and cheerful. The simple furnishings are mostly nineteenth-century rustic with colonial craft decor. All the bathrooms are new and functional. A double for the night with continental breakfast costs $70.

The inn's Half Moon Bar is a cozy lounge with overstuffed furniture centering around the warming fire. In the summer you may also have a drink in the back garden or on the front porch. For a light meal or snack, the bar serves a cheese board with bread and fruit and a glass of red or white wine for $4.75.

The dining room, serving good plain American fare with entrées that include vegetables ranging from $9.95 to $16.95, looks out onto the river. On Sundays from noon to 2:30 p.m. the Hudson House serves a popular brunch for $12, drawing people from all over the valley. (Hudson House, 2 Main Street, Cold Spring, NY 10516. 914-265-9355.)

In addition to the one conveniently located hotel, there are two good bed and breakfast inns on the right-hand side of Main Street just up the hill from the railroad station. The busier of the two, the Olde Post Inn, is a two-story clapboard house with a wide front porch extending its full width. Upstairs, there are four homey rooms with shared bath decorated in early American style with original antiques and good attention to detail on the walls, tables, and chests of drawers. Rates per night on weekends are $50 for a double with continental breakfast, $5 less during the week. Breakfast is taken in the handsome front parlor to the left of the reception desk. A small craft shop is located in a separate room to the right. On the weekends the tavern is a popular local hangout with live music. Depending on who is playing, you might hear some of the music in the bedrooms. (Olde Post Inn, 43 Main Street, Cold Spring, NY 10516. 914-265-2510.)

Up the street at 73 Main Street, the quieter Antique Mews is a substantial corner brick townhouse offering two double rooms, furnished with a good variety of nineteenth-century antique furniture and knickknacks supplied by the establishment's owners, who are antique dealers as well as innkeepers. The ground floor is basically a store crammed with domestic antique furniture and household items. Double room rates, with private bath and full breakfast, are $65 on weekdays and $75 on weekends. (The Antique Mews, 73 Main Street, Cold Spring, NY, 10516. 914-265-3727.)

Most of the village of Cold Spring lies to the east of the railroad line, and runs for about a mile up the hill into Nelsonville. Just north of where you stepped off the train, the former New York Central Railroad station is now a restaurant called Station One. From the outside the place is unassuming, but once inside the atmosphere improves considerably. The high-ceilinged former waiting room is crammed with colorful railroad signs, black-and-white photographs, prints, and travel impedimenta. Ceiling fans whirl silently above the original wooden benches that form part of the seating arrangement. The food, from a typical small restaurant menu, is reasonably priced and recommended for lunch. To one side there is an old-fashioned soda fountain, and, in another room, a local bar.

Both sides of Main Street present a fairly homogeneous mid-nineteenth-century setting adapted to today's commercial needs as delis, craft shops, and antique and collectible stores. On summer weekends, people flock to Cold Spring to browse through the more than two dozen establishments specializing in old things.

At Marie's Forever Old Shop, 82 Main Street, you can pick through the Victorian and other vintage clothing and even select something to wear at your next wedding. Remember When at 114 Main Street specializes in turn-of-the-century heavy oak furniture, and, at the same address, the Cold Spring Emporium houses sixteen dealers under one roof.

On the side streets, you will find a virtual museum of plain and fancy Victorian houses, and many more going back as far as the late eighteenth century. At the first traffic light, at busy Route 9-D, turn left for Cold Spring's best example of an elaborate Queen Anne-style house with richly decorated porch grafted onto the front of the two-story residence which is finished off with towers.

To the right of the set of lights at 63 Chestnut Street, the Putnam County Historical Society operates the Foundry School Museum. Permanent and rotating exhibits include history and lore of the Mid-Hudson Valley with paintings, photographs, maps, ship models, and other local memorabilia. Phone (914) 265-4010 for the limited opening hours, usually on Wednesday, Sunday afternoon, and by appointment.

While the main shopping district dwindles away east of Route 9-D, continue up Main Street past the white-with-green-trim Philipstown Town Hall on the left and down into Nelsonville. At 255 Main Street on the right-hand side, the Hudson Rogue Company offers an excellent collection of second-hand prints, books, and maps covering Hudson Valley history, including steamboat and railroad transportation. The helpful owner will locate what you would like to inspect, and a half-hour here will greatly aid your understanding of the area's past and scenic beauty.

A bit further along at 289 Main Street, Your Country Deli is the best place for having fresh deli-style sandwiches made, and for ordering up containers of homemade soups and salads.

Boscobel, one of the outstanding examples of New York State Federal domestic architecture, lies along Route 9-D, just twenty-five minutes by foot from the deli or forty-five minutes from the railroad station. By carefully following these directions from Your Country Store, you will avoid most of the busy vehicle traffic.

Continue along Main Street a few blocks to Peekskill Road and turn right. Follow the cemetery on the left to Route 9-D, where the Plumbush Restaurant, set in a mid-nineteenth-century Victorian mansion, appears to the left. Instead of walking the verge of Route 9-D, use the parallel dirt track until it runs out, then cross 9-D. Shortly you will see the entrance to Boscobel on the right.

Boscobel Restoration, an outstanding example of Federal residential architecture, was begun in 1804 by States Morris Dyckman and finished after his death by his wife Elizabeth in 1808. Previously sited fifteen miles south at Montrose, Boscobel, meaning *bosco bello*, or beautiful woods, was endangered by a construction project in the 1950s. It was saved and moved here to its present commanding location overlooking Constitution Island and the Hudson River, and was opened to the public in 1961.

The excellent tour begins at the carriage house and makes straight for the lawn in front of the mansion, where the commentary begins. The graceful front porch, two stories high, is held up by a pair of square outer wooden columns and double sets of two slender round inner columns. Curved strips of wood separate the panes of a single semi-circular window cut into the pediment, and below that hangs three sets of decorative draperies complete with tassels, also executed in wood.

Inside, the main entrance foyer is a grand two-story room from which you can pass directly into the two front rooms, look through the house into the back garden, and reach the second floor via a central staircase that, after the first landing, splits into two narrow stairs to reach the upstairs landing.

Most of the English china and silver seen on the dining room table, sideboard, and in the parlors belonged to the Dyckman family. The library also contains many of their books. The furniture, collected from all over the country, is of the Federal period, with many Duncan Phyfe creations. Phyfe, a New York cabinetmaker in the first half of the nineteenth century, was noted for his artistic use of mahogany in the making of chairs, couches, and tables.

One of the finest rooms in the house is the master bedroom, furnished with a canopied bed dressed with a red-tasseled green fringe around the top and bed frame, with a green drapery flowing down behind the head board. The carpet in green and red nicely compliments the bed covering. Natural light pours into the room from three sides, making the rich colors of the blue-patterned wallpaper and green and white curtains even more vivid.

Lila Acheson Wallace, co-founder of *The Reader's Digest* who died in 1984, gave generous support to the restoration and furnishings.

The tour ends with lemonade and cookies. Visitors are then free to roam the grounds, stroll through the gardens, orangerie, and orchards, and enter the Gate House, Necessary House, Spring House, Carriage House, and gift shop. An annual calendar of events lists summer promenade concerts, year-round nature talks, Christmas candlelight tours, and seasonal flower displays, such as the festival of roses in June.

The outing is well worth the walk from Cold Spring. Allow about three hours to make the leisurely excursion. The entire walk from Boscobel back to the railroad station takes about forty-five minutes.

Serious hikers have several options for short and long walks into the Hudson Highlands with excellent photographic vantage points overlooking the valley. *Hikers Region Map No. 9*, available at shops in Cold Spring, will show the best routes to follow. Study the map carefully before setting out, and be prepared for rough trails. To reach the beginning of the trails, turn left off Main Street adjacent to the town hall, follow Cedar Street one block to Mountain Avenue, and turn right into the woods.

For a relatively short hike of just over three miles, reaching a height of 1420 feet atop Mt. Taurus, climb the Three Notch Trail (B) to where it intersects with the Washburn Trail (W) looping to the left over the mountain and back down to Cold Spring.

A longer, about seven miles, and more challenging walk leaves Cold Spring via the Three Notch Trail (B), passing Washburn Trail (W) to the left and Casino Trail (R) to the right, and after about four miles intersects with Breakneck Ridge Trail (W). Turn left back toward the river, and after one and one-half miles take the By-Pass Trail (R) to the right down to the Wilkinson Trail (Y) that leads directly to the Breakneck Ridge Railroad Station, just north of Breakneck Ridge. An alternate route stays with Breakneck Ridge Trail to its very end where it overlooks the Hudson.

Trains from Breakneck Ridge return to Grand Central on Saturdays and Sundays at 4:33 p.m. and 6:18 p.m. Be sure to consult an up-to-date timetable and carefully read the little reference marks that indicate a stop here, as very few trains do.

MOHONK MOUNTAIN HOUSE
A World Away

Mohonk Mountain House, Lake Mohonk, New Paltz, NY 12561. New York City number is (212) 233-2244; or (914) 255-1000.

Mohonk, a one-of-a-kind nineteenth-century Victorian masterpiece of wood and stone, ringed by balconies and topped with turrets, sits high on a mountain ridge six miles west of New Paltz, New York. Built in sections between 1875 and 1910, the place stretches for an eighth of a mile with four hundred rooms, many with working fireplaces, arranged over six stories.

Built by Quaker twins Albert and Alfred Smiley in 1869, Mohonk has retained its traditional quiet, friendly, and unhurried atmosphere through generations of same-family ownership and the continuity of its most loyal clientele. Mohonk has a few rules that delight regular guests and win over most, if not every, newcomer. For instance, there is no public bar, and, instead, overnight guests may have drinks in their rooms and order cocktails and wine at dinner.

In addition to most of the outdoor activities that people expect from a mountain resort, the property has 140 miles of trails on which to walk, ride horseback, or cross-country ski. Mohonk offers some special attractions every season of the year in a relaxed and curiously anachronistic setting that cannot be found anywhere else.

Getting There and Back: Adirondack Trailways runs frequent buses from the Port Authority Bus Terminal to New Paltz, New York, six miles below and west of Lake Mohonk. The round-trip fare for the one and one-half-hour trip up the New York State Thruway is $29.55. Call the bus line at (212) 947-5300. By prior arrangement, Mohonk's own car will pick you up for $3 per person one way.

You can also take a Metro-North train, about every hour or two from Grand Central to Poughkeepsie, in just under two hours for $14 off-peak round-trip (seniors $9.30). The railroad station is on the east bank of the Hudson some fifteen miles from Mohonk, and the house car costs $20 one way for a maximum of five people. See the "Hudson Valley Rail Route Guide" (p.76) for a description of the scenic train trip, and see page 58 for the map.

The approach to Mohonk is always one of high anticipation. Atop the Shawangunk (pronounced Shongum) Mountains, which run parallel to the Catskills, sits a lonely stone tower guiding the eye to the spot where the mountain house is nestled. Then, once past the gatehouse, the steep winding road climbs ever higher until, there in all its amazing splendor, a fanciful Victorian pile demands your attention.

Mohonk, constructed in a combination of rugged stone blocks and two-tone green clapboard siding, is anchored by huge circular towers housing the best rooms, and is finished off with iron balconies, gables, and dormers. It's an eccentric dream castle that was expanded at the hands of several different architects as business grew, yet all holds together, inside and out.

Within, from the central reception area, long paneled corridors lead off to the left and right to reading and writing rooms, a library, small niches with rocking chairs, and even a grand piano. Looking straight through toward the lake, the lower Lake Lounge provides a quiet spot for enjoying a good book, and is the perfect setting for the daily ritual of afternoon tea. On the floor above, the high-ceilinged main parlor is well-suited for evening lectures, films, and classical concerts. Long porches, lined with old-fashioned rockers, face the Catskill Range; the setting sun in one direction, and Lake Mohonk with its backdrop of rising wooded cliff in the other.

On the lake, you can paddle your own wooden canoe, pedal modern paddleboats, or, around the corner from the mountain house, swim in a secluded area with sandy beach, wooden sun floats, and a lifeguard.

The guest rooms come in an almost infinite variety of shapes and sizes, and some regulars will consider only one that faces the lake, while others want to watch the setting sun or, in October, gaze out over one hundred square miles of luscious fall colors.

The most expensive tower rooms have working fireplaces, private balconies, and appropriately sedate turn-of-the-century period wood furnishings. Standard rooms have fireplaces and balconies and similar, if somewhat simpler, mirrored wooden chests of drawers and chairs in a smaller space. There is a wood delivery sufficient for normal use every day in the winter months, and fire fanatics can purchase extra logs. The cheapest rooms, some also with balconies, have a washbasin only and offer very ordinary plain wooden furniture and hence relatively low rates.

During the fall foliage season, be sure to ask for a room facing the mountains, while at other times of the year many people prefer the lake view. In the summer, the westward-facing rooms are warmer due to the hot afternoon sun, but they also afford splendid long-lasting sunsets. You might also request a room on the two highest floors. Remember that booking the cheapest room is like reserving a miminum-price cabin on an ocean liner: you get what you pay for, although you still have the run of the ship's facilities or, in this case, of the hotel's.

Daily double occupancy rates including three meals run from $208–$224 for the special tower room, $163–$189 for standard rooms, to $132 for those with washbasin only. Single occupancy ranges from $122 down to $69. With a stay of a week or more, as well as any day after late October and before early May, the rates drop about ten percent.

Seven percent tax is extra, and $5.75 per person per day is added to the bill for all gratuities. Guests may leave something additional for the chambermaid and in the dining room if they wish. There is a two-night minimum stay, unless space is available at short notice. Weekends, especially in the fall, and special programs such as Mystery Weekend and Music Week, are booked out well ahead.

There is no air conditioning anywhere in the house, and, except for a few unseasonably hot days a year, the mountain setting provides for cool nights. Television viewing is limited to two small out-of-the-way lounges.

Guests may sign for everything, including wine at meals and all extra-fee activities such as tennis ($5 per court hour), golf ($4–5 per round), horseback riding ($10 per hour), fishing ($3 for a daily permit), carriage rides ($8 per person per hour), and canoes and paddleboats ($3 per hour).

The five hundred-seat restaurant, a vast paneled room with whirling ceiling fans, has wonderful sweeping views of the mountains and sunsets through the western bay windows. Guests are assigned to one table for the duration of their stay.

The food is good hearty American fare with absolutely no pretensions. At the buffet lunch, you can select from four hot dishes and a wide choice of salad fixings. The waiter or waitress serves the beverages and desserts.

At dinner, dresses for women and jackets for men are required. Ties are preferred. The menu includes a wide range of appetizers, relish tray, salad, choice of eight entrées, vegetables, at least a dozen desserts and beverages, including eight types of tea. Typical main dishes are roast strip sirloin of beef, baked stuffed fillet of haddock, roast sirloin of pork, and broiled spring chicken. A special vegetarian dish is always available.

While the house has no public bar, a drawback for some, guests may order beer, wine, and spirits at dinner, alcoholic beverages by the bottle from room service, or bring their own for consumption in the room.

Not all meals need be taken in the dining room; during the warm weather months, schedules for breakfast cookouts and barbecues are posted on the bulletin board.

The Mohonk staff offers short and long hikes, exercise classes, and shuffleboard tournaments in addition to the regular activities and special-theme programs. If healthy outdoor life is not enough exercise for you, there is a new sauna and fitness room in the basement.

There is plenty for children, young adults, the middle-aged and retired to do, and it is not unusual for several generations of the same family to have come to Mohonk year after year.

Many people unwind by reading in a quiet corner, in one of the 114 gazebos scattered around the property, or by taking a map in hand and walking the property, 2,500 wooded acres belonging to the Mountain House and five thousand more owned by the Mohonk Trust. From the base of the skytop tower, 1542 feet above sea level, you can see seven states on a crystal clear day. Now go to a map and figure out which ones they would be.

Mohonk is peacefully active all day long and quietly serene after dinner, especially on a warm evening. Couples stroll through the formal gardens, mount the tower to catch the final rays of the sun, or watch the fading glow of the day from a rocking chair on the porch or from their own balcony.

Even the most harried begin to relax in a few short hours, and once you have sampled the Mohonk experience, it is difficult not to go back year after year.

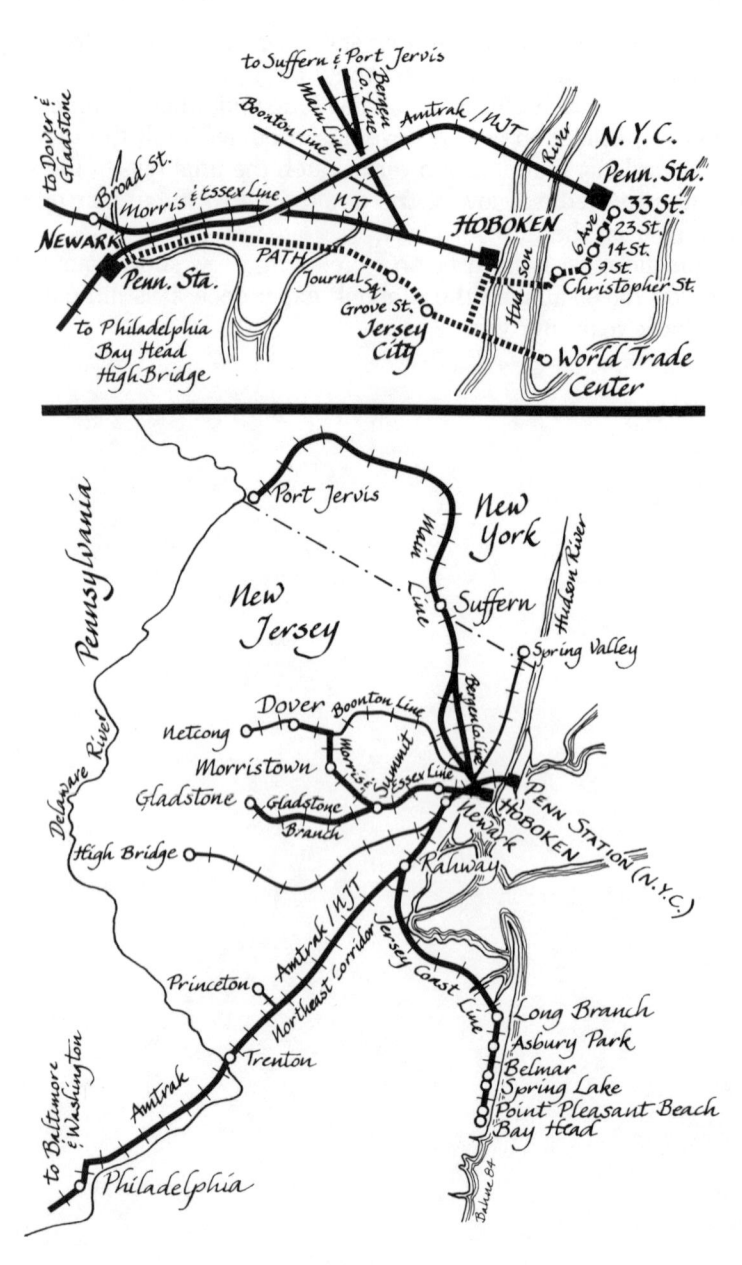

New Jersey

NEW JERSEY AND PENNSYLVANIA

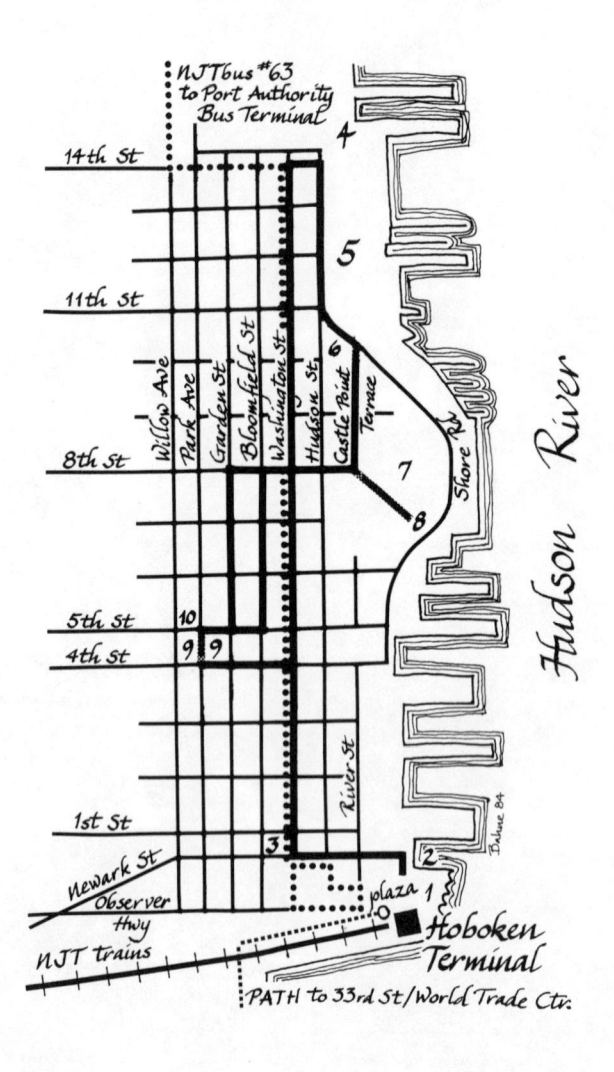

Hoboken

1. old ferry slips
2. S.S. Victoria
3. City Hall
4. Hoboken Shipyards
5. Maxwell House Coffee plant
6. Elysian Park
7. Stevens Institute
8. Castle Point
9. Church Square
10. Library

HOBOKEN
A World of Difference across from Manhattan

Just across the Hudson River from midtown Manhattan lies the distinctly different one square mile town-city of Hoboken, once a great commercial shipping port and waterfront community of the working class. Today, with its convenient location to New York's expanding service industries, Hoboken is rapidly changing into one of the most desirable spots to live for the newly arrived young professional.

A visit here on foot reveals a relatively homogeneous neighborhood of nineteenth-century brownstones along with small pockets of substantial townhouses originally built for the wealthy residents of an important maritime commercial center.

Attached to the underground PATH station where you are most likely to arrive, the landmark Lackawanna Terminal of 1907 stands as the finest surviving example of a combined Beaux Arts waterfront railroad station and ferry house.

Along Hoboken's mile-long Washington Street and adjacent cross streets, a dozen different restaurants mirror the city's past and present, from the huge Clam Broth House, a local tradition since 1899, to the gentrified atmosphere of the recently established Lady Jane's.

Come across the Hudson at any time of year during the day, wearing a good pair of walking shoes, and be prepared to stay until dark to enjoy Manhattan's fairyland of lights from Castle Point and a good meal at reasonable prices.

Getting There and Back: The best route is via the Port Authority Trans-Hudson Corporation (PATH) trains from 33rd Street and 6th Avenue, with four Manhattan stops, direct to the Hoboken Terminal, or from the World Trade Center by direct train, on weekdays, to Hoboken. On weekends, WTC passengers change from the train marked "NWK" at Grove Street, Jersey City (second stop) to one marked "HOB-33." The fare is seventy-five cents exact change. A $1 bill machine will return a quarter.

On weekdays, PATH service runs every six to ten minutes, and on weekends the frequency is generally every fifteen minutes, although at certain early morning and late night hours the wait may be thirty minutes. PATH trains are usually clean and are quite safe. Most trips take less than fifteen minutes. (212) 466-7649.

To go by bus, use New Jersey Transit bus #63 from the Port Authority Bus Terminal on 8th Avenue between 40th and 42nd Street, and get off anywhere along Washington Street in Hoboken. The last stop of this route is the Hoboken Terminal, for the PATH and New Jersey Transit trains. Exact change fare is $1.25 in coins. The service departs every twenty minutes (thirty minutes on Sunday), with less frequency late at night. (212) 564-8484.

Hoboken has been a major destination for one reason or another for well over a hundred years. Before Central Park was laid out, Manhattanites took the ferry over to Hoboken's Elysian Fields for picnics, walks, amusements, and to watch the first game of baseball. Until a serious fire in 1905, Duke's House, next to the historic Lackawanna Terminal, was the favorite watering hole for theater people and the city bigwigs. Several major shipping companies docked their liners at Hoboken piers, one as late as 1962, the date Holland-America's fleet finally moved across to Manhattan.

The Delaware, Lackawanna and Western, later the Erie-Lackawanna, then Conrail, and now New Jersey Transit trains have been arriving and leaving from Hoboken since the middle of the nineteenth century. Until 1967, many travelers crossed the Hudson by ferry, but today the commuting passengers usually switch to the PATH trains.

If you arrive via PATH, begin your walking tour of Hoboken by a visit to the landmarked Beaux Arts railroad terminal. When the Lackawanna Railroad completed the combination train station and ferry landing in February of 1907, it was considered the finest waterfront transportation facility in the world. Crack passenger trains went west through the Poconos to Buffalo and Chicago, and a fleet of ferryboats crossed the Hudson to three separate Manhattan landings.

Today nearly sixty-five thousand people pass through the terminal every weekday to and from New Jersey and lower New York state suburbs. Unlike Grand Central and Penn Station, where the trains are hidden from sight until the track doors are thrown open for boarding, Hoboken's fleet of diesel and electric trains are in full view behind the original iron gates abutting the main concourse.

The central waiting room where tickets are sold is a splendid place, with decorative iron and plaster ornamentation and a Tiffany glass ceiling fifty feet above the colorful *terrazzo* floor.

Off the public square, the rich copper work, turned green with age and oxidation, forms the facade of the old Railroad YMCA, the waiting room, and the arched entrances to the six old ferry slips.

On the far side of the newly reconstructed plaza, the white-hulled ferry, most recently called *Drifters I*, beckons eaters and drinkers to sample its offerings in an authentic setting—complete with rolling wave motion.

The setting, for some, may make up for the routine menus which vary with each management change. Check the place out before spending your money, although you cannot go far wrong to have a drink here.

Built way back in 1930 as the *S.S. Welfare*, New York City's only solely passenger ferry, this "institutional" boat (contrasting with purely public ferries such as Slater Island's) ran for twenty-six years across the East River from East 78th Street Manhattan to serve Welfare (now Roosevelt) Island's several hospitals. Before arriving on the Hoboken waterfront in 1983, the boat had a long stint as a floating restaurant at the edge of downtown Providence.

The pontoon to which the boat is lashed operates as an outdoor bar and cafe in the summer months, and makes for a delightful drinking or dining experience in the early evening. In cool weather imbibers gravitate to the indoor bar amidships. For lunch or dinner, the best tables run along the port side facing the Lackawanna Terminal's richly ornate facade, or are located all the way aft, with glorious views of the Manhattan skyline framed by two finger piers.

The walking tour begins at the terminal, making first for Washington Street, where most of the restaurants are located, then swings around past the entrance to the Hoboken Shipyard and the Maxwell House Coffee plant to Hudson Street and Stevens Institute of Technology, with a few side street options to take in the brownstone and brick row houses along Bloomfield and Garden Streets.

The bow of the ferryboat restaurant points toward the Hoboken Land Building at Newark and River Streets, a handsome brick structure that has inside a beautiful double wooden staircase modeled after those once found on the old Lackawanna ferries.

On the opposite corner, the Clam Broth House, undeniably Hoboken's most famous eatery, has been dishing out reasonably priced seafood of varying quality and generous proportions since 1899.

Suburban Jerseyites pack the several plain rooms on weekends beginning as early as 5 p.m. My favorite choices over the years have been bowls of steamed clams, mussels in white wine, fried shrimp in a basket, and, in season, juicy soft shell crabs. The service is friendly and fairly efficient except when the place is extremely busy.

For local Hoboken atmosphere with no pretention, you can't beat the Clam Broth House.

One block further along is Washington Street, the main commercial artery stretching for one mile to Fourteenth Street. Although the buildings' ground floors have been altered over the years to suit various tenants, the upper floors retain much of their original appearance when constructed during the city's heyday in the last half of the nineteenth and early twentieth centuries.

City Hall, at the beginning of Washington Street and originally built in 1881, was enlarged in 1911, at the same time the city had reached its peak population of over seventy thousand. Today's figure is more like forty-two thousand.

Walking down Washington Street, the numbered cross streets begin with First and rise to Fourteenth, the far boundary for the purposes of the walking tour.

At Second Street, the Brass Rail dramatically mirrors the two faces of Hoboken. On the ground floor, a scruffy neighborhood bar attracts the working class locals, while the second floor is a sophisticated dining-out experience for the newly arrived professional class.

The best selections from the French menu include the braised sweetbreads, escalope of veal, and steak Diane at prices approaching those found across the river. The Brass Rail is a favorite spot for the local gentry to show off the pleasures of Hoboken living and dining to their skeptical urban friends.

Hoboken House, one block further along at Third, has historic value as one of the city's oldest buildings serving food and drink.

On the left between Tenth and Eleventh, Ricco's Ristorante is an excellent and surprisingly inexpensive choice for well-prepared home-style Italian cooking of the baked zitti and linguine with clam sauce variety. The decor is exposed brick walls partially covered with less-than-successful caricatures of famous people. The choice seats are at a table by the window or at one of the old-fashioned wooden booths.

On the corner of Eleventh on the same side of the street, Helmer's holds out as one of the last vestiges of German influence in the city.

Back in the 1870s when the big German Bremen- and Hamburg-based steamship companies moved to the Hoboken waterfront, a great wave of north German merchants and laborers followed. While most of their descendents have since moved to the suburbs, Helmer's remains a magnet for gentlemen of the working class, who come here regularly to treat their wives to a dinner out on a Friday or Saturday night in an unfussy setting. The menu features robust helpings of Wiener schnitzel, bratwurst with sauerkraut, and plain rich cheese cake, with no fancy fillings, fit to be used as ballast.

At the far end of Washington Street, Fourteenth Street, in the shadow of the Hoboken Shipyard, is the setting for a small nest of the city's newer restaurants. Of them all, it's Lady Jane's that has the most inviting menu.

The moderately expensive food is best described as being out of the ordinary, well garnished, and pleasing to the eye. The crisp duckling, for instance, arrives accented with red raspberries ringing the plate, and the sautéed shrimp sits among fresh tropical fruit and ambrosia.

The entrance from Fourteenth Street leads into a vast and usually empty bar, once frequented by shipyard workers. The tiny restaurant in the back has only seven tables in an attractive setting of green velvet and lacy-patterned walls, potted plants and ferns, white linen tablecloths, and carnations.

Regular patrons enter the out-of-the-way and quiet Lady Jane's from Hudson Street via the back door.

Heading back along Hudson Street, parallel to Washington, the world's largest coffee processing plant, Maxwell House, lines the route on the left. Tours are by appointment only. Gradually, the row housing becomes more elegant, until at Elysian Park and the entrance to Stevens Institute, there are large individual houses of varying ornate styles on Hudson Street, and on parallel Castle Point Terrace, which has two blocks of Stevens Institute of Technology's faculty and fraternity houses.

The grounds of Stevens Campus, with some 2,600 day and dormitory students, occupies the most prominent site in the city. For the best view in town, walk through the campus to Castle Point, just to the right of the modern, multi-story Stevens Center, the school's administration building. From here you have a splendid view of the entire Manhattan skyline stretching from the Battery to beyond the George Washington Bridge.

On a Saturday afternoon in the warmer months, many of the port's cruise ships back out into the river across the way and pass below this vantage point. In the evening, the view is even more dazzling, with a panorama of New York's most famous landmarks lighted up. Looking south along the line of vacant piers, a new community of apartments and office buildings is scheduled to rise in the next few years.

For the best neighborhoods of brick and brownstone townhouses, leave Stevens via Eighth Street at the campus end of Castle Point Terrace, and cross Hudson and Washington to Bloomfield and Garden, both residential streets that are benefiting cosmetically from the new wave of professional-class tenants and owners, sometimes at the expense of the older and poorer residents.

Turn left on either street, but especially Bloomfield between Sixth and Eighth, for some of the finest examples of restored houses, row upon row of wonderfully homogenous brownstones. Between Fourth and Fifth, Garden Street forms one side of Church Square Park, given to the city in 1804 by Colonel John Stevens, steam ferry designer and once owner of much of Hoboken. Here is the Public Library (1895), Stevens Academy (1860), still housing what is believed to be the country's first kindergarten, and Our Lady of Grace Catholic Church (1874).

At the corners of Fourth, Garden, and the park, Le Jardin features a varied selection of rich desserts after 7 p.m. The uplifting decor, white walls, wicker tables, white linen, and green carpeting, has been variously described as reminiscent of the inside of a birthday cake, a fairyland, or the setting for a child's tea party. The regular and changing dessert menu is on display at the counter, on the menu board, and you can also see your downfall being prepared in the open-to-view kitchen. Double chocolate fanciers will love the German chocolate cake, chocolate ice cream sodas, and chocolate cheese cake, served with coffee, tea, or milk.

From here, zigzag as the spirit moves back to the terminal or to one of the restaurants that you have passed.

Two hours on foot and another two in a good restaurant make for a fine day in a very different and still changing community only twelve minutes from Manhattan.

NEWARK
Portuguese Seafood in the Ironbound & A Trolley Ride

A short train ride to downtown Newark, a most unlikely destination for the uninitiated, brings you to within a couple of minutes walking distance from an uniquely successful, predominately Portuguese neighborhood known as the Ironbound offering some of the best seafood restaurants, Iberian-style, west of City Island.

The Ironbound's distinctive food shops, moderately priced eating places, and friendly people combine to make a simple outing into a rich experience you'll want to repeat again and again. As a side excursion, take a fast round-trip ride on a classically streamlined trolley into the nearby suburbs, and spend a few minutes admiring the recently restored Art Deco splendor of Newark's Penn Station.

Getting There and Back: There are two different ways of getting auto-free to Newark. The Port Authority Trans-Hudson Corporation runs a usually reliable and nearly always clean twenty-four-hour subway-surface operation called the PATH from two terminals in Manhattan to Newark Penn Station, where you can walk to the Ironbound in a couple of minutes. New Jersey Transit and Amtrak both run non-stop trains from Penn Station in Manhattan to Penn Station in Newark.

The following West Side subway lines serve the World Trade Center (WTC) PATH terminal, one of the two possible departure points: the IRT #1 Broadway local to Cortlandt Street-WTC; IND AA(K) and E trains to the terminus at WTC; the IND A express to Chambers Street, with a pedestrian tunnel connection to the WTC; and the BMT R to Cortlandt Street.

From the East Side, take the IRT #4 or #5 express to Fulton Street, then walk west along Fulton to the end of the street at the World Trade Center. On weekends, enter the complex via Vesey Street, reached by turning right on Trinity Place, then left on Vesey. Once you're inside, the PATH is well-posted.

To reach the WTC PATH terminal, descend two sets of escalators to the PATH concourse. Pick up a useful PATH Map Guide next to the turnstiles to be able to follow your progress through the Meadowlands to Newark.

Look for the lighted signs to Journal Square and Newark since, depending on the time of day and the day of the week, PATH trains use different platforms. There are no token sellers anywhere on the system, so you will need exact change or a $1 bill. Deposit seventy-five cents in coins into the slot until the green "Proceed" sign lights up, or put $1 into the machine, take your twenty-five cents in change from the scoop, and proceed on green. At platform level, make sure the lighted signs at the side of the cars above the doors read "WTC-NWK." Note that each car has two silver plaques near the ceiling dedicating it to a town, village, or borough in New Jersey. A short paragraph gives an historical sketch of each place.

On weekdays during the day and evening, trains leave at least every ten minutes, every fifteen minutes on Saturday, and every thirty minutes on Sunday.

Upon leaving the WTC, the PATH train heads through tubes under the Hudson River, which were the first, along with those on the 33rd Street to Hoboken Line, underwater rail tunnels in the country, opened in 1908 and 1909. Their completion signaled the beginning of the long decline in the numerous cross-Hudson steam ferry services.

In New Jersey, after Grove Street Station, a busy section of Jersey City, the line rises to the surface and remains so all the way to Newark.

The stop at Journal Square, in downtown Jersey City, allows passengers to transfer from the uptown 33rd Street line. The line then passes through an industrial area, dives beneath the Pulaski Skyway, and crosses over the Hackensack River. In what is left of the Meadowlands in this area, the train runs past Conrail's huge rail container yards and relatively new warehouses. The westbound line goes under Amtrak's Northeast Corridor, and then finds itself between the Amtrak line to the left and New Jersey Transit's Morris and Essex Line to the right.

A final stop is made at Harrison, after which the train climbs to the upper level of an elaborate drawbridge spanning the Passaic River and into Newark Penn Station's upper-level terminal. The entire journey from the WTC takes about twenty minutes. Use the escalators or stairs to reach the station's street-level concourse and waiting room.

Newark 111

Before continuing on foot, here are two alternate routes from Manhattan to Newark.

The PATH train from 33rd Street and 6th Avenue is one possibility. Several subway lines directly serve PATH's uptown terminus: the West Side IND D and B lines and the BMT R and N (not all

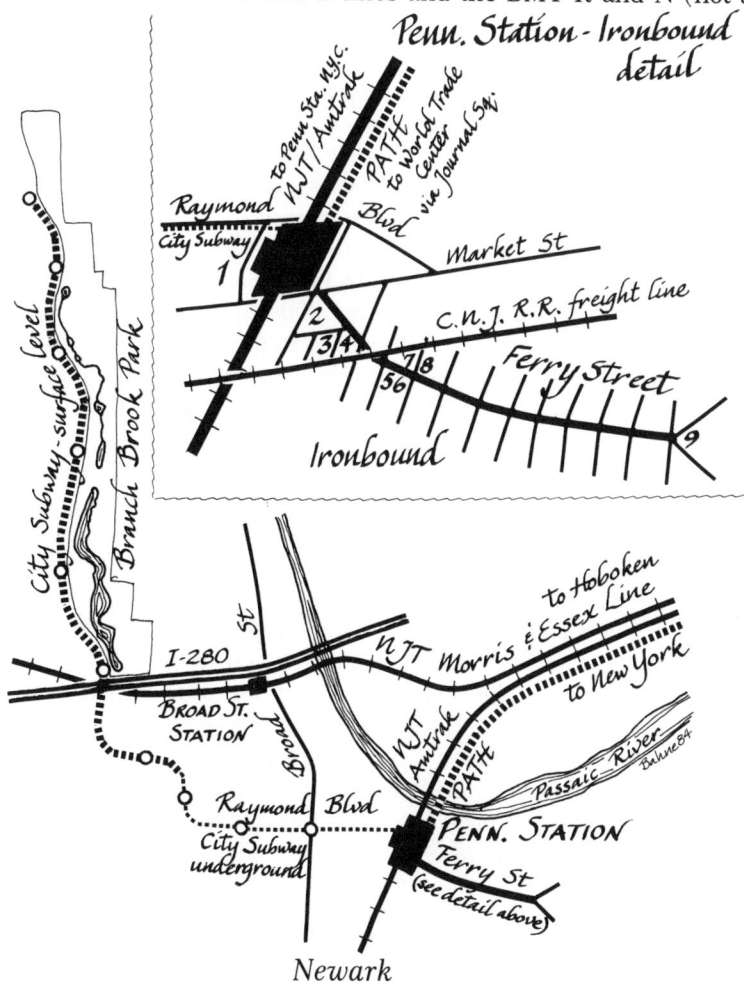

1. Gateway Hilton
2. Peter Francisco Park
3. old church building
4. Forno's Restaurant
5. Peninsula Restaurant
6. Sagres Restaurant
7. Iberia Restaurant
8. Rogue & Robelo's Restaurant
9. St. Stephan's Church

times from Queens and the East Side). North-south bus routes that pass through Herald Square are the M6 and M7 from the West Side and the M4 from the East Side.

To reach Newark, take the PATH train marked "33-JSQ" (for Journal Square) on the weekdays, and *not* the "33-HOB"! On weekends there is only one train marked "33-HOB-JSQ." Both trains require you to change at Journal Square for the "WTC-NWK" train.

The line from 33rd Street, making four Manhattan stops, runs under 6th Avenue, then beneath Greenwich Village, and under the Hudson to Journal Square. On weekends, the line passes through Hoboken, then reverses direction for Grove Street and Journal Square. The entire journey from 33rd to Newark takes about a half-hour, once you are on the train and moving.

Or, a final alternative, leave from Penn Station. Take any New Jersey Transit train with three to four departures an hour on weekdays and two on weekends. Adult fare is $1.50 one way or $2.25 for a seven-day excursion. On Saturday, Sunday, and holidays, the fare is a flat $1. Buy your tickets before you board the train. (201) 762-5100.

On hourly Amtrak trains the fare is $1.50 one way at all times (not good on Metroliners). Buy your tickets before boarding. (212) 736-4545.

Travel time on both non-stop services is about fifteen minutes.

Newark Penn Station, an Art Deco masterpiece completed in 1933 for the Pennsylvania Railroad, has now been restored to its original splendor. Bought by New Jersey Transit from Amtrak in 1984, the transportation facility is NJT's flagship operation for its frequent train service to the North Jersey coast, over the Northeast Corridor to Trenton, and to the Raritan Valley, and for local buses.

Newark is a major stop on Amtrak's Boston-New York-Washington Corridor, and with separate facilities serves as a Greyhound and Trailways depot, and as the terminus for the City Subway.

Penn Station's decorative features are worth a detour. In the high-ceilinged waiting room where Amtrak and New Jersey Transit tickets are sold, note the white wall medallions depicting various forms of transportation. Over the doors to the street are elaborate metalwork designs including the Pennsylvania Railroad keystone embossed with "PRR," a decorative feature repeated in brass letters at the ends of some of the wooden benches. Note the brass and black marble decorative features on the floor. Outside, the Indiana lime-

Newark   113

stone facade features faces of lions and statues of spread-winged eagles.

The 293-foot station and its approaches separate downtown Newark from the Ironbound. A covered walkway links the station's upper level with the Gateway Hilton. Adjacent, a cluster of plain modern office blocks serves as the headquarters for public television station Channel 13 and for New Jersey Transit.

To reach the City Subway, actually a traditional trolley line and a curious relic of the past, follow the signs to the vast underground station decorated with colorful Depression-era murals showing men hard at work. The red, white, and blue trolley cars, whose classic design dates from the beginning of the streamlined era, were completed in the late 1940s. Service is frequent, from every two minutes during the rush hours to every fifteen minutes in the evening. The speedy trip lasts twelve minutes each way, and exact fare, seventy-five cents in off-peak hours, is required.

Once a part of a much larger trolley network, the remaining 3.8-mile line opened in 1935 as a Works Progress Administration project, and in 1984 was heavily rebuilt. A good part of the route operates below ground level in the former Morris Canal bed.

The final section gives a scenic tour alongside Branch Brook Park, ending in a loop at the Franklin Avenue Station in suburban Bloomfield. Many passengers will transfer here to buses to complete their journey home. To return, leave the trolley, walk forward, and rejoin, paying another fare.

Upon returning to Newark Penn Station, pass along the street-level concourse and out the doors beyond the Track 1 escalators. Ferry Street begins at an angle off to the right, across a complicated intersection and around a limestone bank building. You are on the right path when you see a sign that reads "Welcome to Ironbound Memorial Square" and behind that a plain former church building with a cross on top.

Within a block you are in the Ironbound, an ordinary-looking but bustling neighborhood populated mostly by Portuguese from the Iberian Peninsula, the Azores, and Portugal's former African colonies, and by Hispanics. While at first there seems to be nothing special to look at, you will find as you walk along Ferry Street that the community's strong ethnic flavor comes through in the language spoken on the street, in the shop windows, pastry and wine stores, and restaurants.

The Ironbound, surrounded by railroad tracks, began in the middle of the nineteenth century as a German and Irish working-class community with a population laboring in breweries, tanneries, and chemical factories. By the turn of the century, southern and eastern Europeans predominated; today's new immigrants are Portuguese and Hispanic.

While many other Newark neighborhoods have witnessed a drastic decline, the Ironbound's relative isolation has kept it remarkably stable and safe. It is a community that works, and after a couple of hours here, the Ironbound's unique character will become abundantly clear.

If you are feeling energetic, walk the length of Ferry Street as far as the red church with the white steeple at Wilson Avenue, including some forays into residential side streets, then double back. The jaunt will take about forty-five minutes. Built in 1874, St. Stephan's United Church of Christ reflects the area's former German heritage. Ferry Street was originally laid out in 1765 as the main route from Newark to the Hudson River opposite Manhattan, then went through two more phases as a plank toll road and as part of the Lincoln Highway, a cross-country national road. Today Ferry Street binds the neighborhood together, and on weekends small clusters of men gather on street corners for a chat.

Having gotten a feel for the place, it is now easier to select a restaurant.

Five of the most popular, Forno's, the Peninsula, Sagres, Iberia, and Rogue & Rebelo, all featuring Portuguese and Spanish dishes, are within a five- to ten-minute walk from Penn Station. While you may wish to explore for others tucked away on the side streets, it is the convenient Ferry Street cluster that will be highlighted for a first experience.

Most of the Ironbound's popular family-style restaurants share some distinctive characteristics. With a couple of exceptions, they are quite plainly decorated with medium-sized dining rooms. They tend to offer plenty of space between the tables, and have a separate entrance to a bar that caters almost exclusively to the local residents.

The meal portions are enormous, and some seafood selections are plentiful enough for two average eaters to share, although there is usually a slight additional charge to do so. Prices are moderate, and individual entrées run from $8 to about $12, including a small salad. The first item to appear will be a basket of freshly baked Portuguese bread for whetting the appetite and, later, for soaking up the sauces.

Although more will come for the asking, go easy until you are well into your main course.

My favorite Ferry Street restaurant is Sagres, a friendly and simple place on the right-hand side just beyond the railroad overpass. The first patrons start to arrive shortly after 5 p.m., and during the popular hour between 7 p.m. and 8 p.m., all the places will be taken by couples, small groups of friends, and family gatherings, creating a lively local atmosphere. The two lines of generously spaced tables of four run the length of the dining room, and can be easily rearranged to accommodate parties of any size.

The most popular entrées are unquestionably the shellfish dishes, with my very favorite, often to the exclusion of trying anything else, the *mariscadas*, a seafood casserole served in a large black iron pot. The huge portion contains many pieces of lobster, clams, mussels, crab legs, and shrimp, all still in their shells, and small bits of flavorful fish soaking in a tomato, garlic, and wine sauce. As a lot of energy is expended getting at some of the meat with the little two-pronged fork, the exercise may take a whole hour, and you may astound yourself by finishing everything in front of you.

For less greedy eaters, friends who have accompanied me have liked the steamed mussels in hot sauce and the mixed seafood *paella* (the Portuguese pronounce the double letters, unlike the Spanish) with saffron rice.

If you want a change from shellfish, try the breaded veal cutlet with lemon and garlic, or the large and tender sirloin steaks.

To accompany the food, Portuguese *vinho verde* is a popular and reasonably priced light and dry red or white table wine, appearing under many different labels. Some of your neighbors will be ordering pitchers of sangria, white or red wine mixed with chunks and juices of fresh fruit. You may want to ask the waiter to leave out the extra sugar, as the drink is already naturally sweetened.

After dinner, call in at a Ferry Street wine store to see the largest selection of Iberian wines west of Lisbon. Most cannot be had at your local outlet in New York, so you may want to take several bottles home. The most popular brands are priced between $2.50 and $4. Also pop into a pastry shop for a loaf of Portuguese bread or some of the special chocolate desserts.

Ferry Street is perfectly safe to walk at night, and, on weekend evenings, it may be quite crowded with pedestrian and vehicular traffic. Similarly, you need not worry about the PATH and other trains back to the city, and you will find Newark Penn Station well-policed at all hours.

GLADSTONE
A Scenic Train Ride & Lunch, Brunch, or Dinner

The Brass Penny Restaurant, Main Street and Pottersville Road, Glastone, NJ 07934. (201) 234-2080. Open Monday–Saturday lunch 11:30 a.m.–4:30 p.m. and dinner 5–10 p.m.; Sunday brunch 11 a.m.–3 p.m. and dinner 3:30–9 p.m. Reservations accepted only for parties of five or more.

The seventy-five-minute train ride to Gladstone takes you over the newly rebuilt Morris and Essex Line, New Jersey Transit's showpiece commuter railroad offering frequent departures, cheerful modern coaches, and a ribbon-smooth ride. Within minutes of leaving the historic Hoboken Terminal, the inner suburbs seen through the train windows give way to prosperous middle-class communities and then open farmlands and rolling wooded hills.

Where the tracks end, the nineteenth-century-style Brass Penny Restaurant, just a two-minute walk from the depot, serves lunch and dinner every day, but it is the special Sunday brunch that is most recommended. Afterward, take a short walk through the country town before rejoining the train for home. See map, p. 100.

Getting There and Back: For the New Jersey Transit's Gladstone Line, take one of the two PATH services to the Hoboken Terminal. The direct lines run weekdays from 33rd Street and Sixth Avenue and the World Trade Center. On weekends, WTC passengers take the train marked "NWK" to Grove Street, Jersey City (the second stop) and change to one marked "HOB-33" for Hoboken. The flat fare on PATH is seventy-five cents exact change, or insert a $1 bill into a machine and receive a quarter in change. (212) 466-7649.

The New Jersey Transit's Morris and Essex Lines timetable lists the departure times of the PATH connections to Gladstone. If you want additional time to visit Hoboken's historic Lackawanna Terminal and to buy your ticket, take an earlier PATH train. See the Hoboken entry for a description of the waterfront terminal.

Or, to go by bus, a New Jersey Transit #63 bus runs about every twenty minutes (thirty minutes on Sunday) from the Port Authority Bus Terminal at 8th Avenue between 40th and 42nd Streets directly to the Lackawanna Hoboken Terminal. The fare is $1.25 in exact change, coins only. (212) 564-8484.

From Lackawanna Terminal, on weekends, Gladstone Branch electric trains on the Morris and Essex Line run about every one to two hours, making fourteen stops on the way, and more frequently on weekdays. The round-trip excursion fare is $7, good for seven days. (201) 762-5100.

A re-electrification scheme, completed in September 1984, has brought about revolutionary changes to the Morris and Essex's Morristown Line and its Gladstone and Montclair Branches. The old direct-current coaches dating from 1917 to 1930, featuring rattan seats, ceiling fans, and open windows, have been replaced by shiny new alternating-current Arrow III cars, fully air-conditioned, providing faster and more frequent schedules than ever before.

For the trip out to Gladstone, sit on the right (or the left) side going and coming to see everything along the way. Once clear of the Hoboken Terminal yards, the train dives through two tunnels under Bergen Hill to reach the Meadowlands, and makes its first stop at Newark Broad Street (eight miles). Make note of the time on the restored station clock tower and of the city's downtown skyline rising off to the left.

The urban scenery extends to Mountain Station (thirteen miles), a fine-looking building up some stairs to the left. Maplewood (fifteen miles) marks the start of attractive surburban houses, and Short Hills features one of the many fine railroad stations built by the early Lackawanna Railroad.

At Summit Station (twenty miles), where the line passes through a deep cut at the top of the Watchung Mountain Ridge, the train may divide, with one portion going forward to Morristown and Dover and the other down the Gladstone Branch into the heart of Morris County's horse country.

At Murray Hill (twenty-three miles), there are some fine-looking clapboard houses to the right, and, after Berkeley Heights (twenty-six miles), the real country landscape begins. Deep woods and rolling farms, including fields of cows, appear on the right after Bernards ville (thirty-five miles). With so little habitation visible from the train, it is a wonder that this line still operates. The powerful group of weekday commuters sees that it does, however, and now with the enormous expense of re-electrification complete, the Gladstone Branch's future is assured.

An hour and fifteen minutes out of Hoboken, the little train comes to the end of the line at Gladstone. The tracks go no farther, and they never did. Leave the station by the forward end of the train. Directly ahead, three minutes away, is your reward: The Brass Penny, a small white country inn, circa 1840, with a most inviting look.

Formerly a house, then a country hotel, the Brass Penny became a local institution shortly after opening as a restaurant in 1974. Inside there is an attractive bar partly separated from the main dining area, a room with a dozen tables spaced around a central fireplace. In the back is a small second room, and outside a patio used for dining in the summer months. Proper attire is the rule, although jacket and tie are not required, even at dinner.

For Sunday brunch or lunch on any other day, the selection includes a variety of good omelettes with juice, potatoes, muffins or toast, and beverage for $5.95 to $6.75; a generous-sized Reuben sandwich at $4.95; a standard spinach salad for $4.95 and chef's salad for $5.75; and a small lunch steak with fries at $8.95. One of the best meals is the quiche Lorraine with ambrosia, two sausage patties, a warm blueberry muffin, a slice of watermelon, and a pot of tea at $6.50. For a late breakfast, you can have a complete meal from $3.95 to $10.75 (the breakfast steak).

For dinner, the fairly standard menu is extensive and moderately priced. Recommended appetizers include fresh mussels marinara at $3.95 and baked stuffed mushroom caps for $3.25. French onion soup at $2.25, often a favorite choice, is only fair.

Five of the recommended entrées are: Gladstone Sole, a plain choice at $9.95; fresh chicken cutlets sauté in a cream and marsala wine sauce with mushrooms (one of the best selections) at $10.75; stuffed breast of duck, smoked ham, and vegetable with wild rice at $13.50; lightly sautéed and juicy soft shell crabs in season (always good but make sure you have a second choice in case the small supply is exhausted) for $13.75; double-cut loin lamb chops at $15.95; and the seafood assortment with lobster tail, sole, scallops, shrimp, and stuffed crab legs.

To work off your intake of food and to see a bit of the village of Gladstone, leave the front steps of the Brass Penny and either take Overlook Road directly ahead, or follow Main Street to the right to Mendham Road.

Depending on the amount of time you have allowed, you might walk first to the left for about a half-mile to view the prosperous middle-class turn-of-the-century wooden houses, then cross the road and return past the original intersection to the town center, such as it is. (There are few shops.) To the right of where Mendham Road meets Main Street, there is a small pond with a resident collection of swans, geese, and ducks waiting to be fed. The Copper Kettle, an old country store, will be happy to supply you with a box of oyster crackers to disperse fairly among the aquatic birds that are sure to come swimming in your direction.

Since you are an easy ten-minute walk from the station, you can enjoy yourself here until the last moment. Back on the train, make sure you sit on the opposite side for the countryside and attractive little depots that you missed on the way out.

A DAY AT THE BEACH
Five North Jersey Coast Seaside Resorts

Within easy walking distance of New Jersey Transit's North Jersey Coast Line are several of the East Coast's best beach resorts. Five of them—Long Branch, Belmar, Spring Lake, Point Pleasant Beach, and Bay Head—are described here in order of their train stops, each one offering something unique for the day tripper, from an old-fashioned amusement pier midway to Victorian splendor by the sea.

To gain access to any of the beaches, you must pay a small fee that varies from $2 to $5. Lockers, bathhouses, umbrellas, and chairs are available for rent at most of the public beaches.

There can be much more to a visit here than sitting on the sand on a hot summer day. In-season or out-of-season hikes along the boardwalk and through quiet residential neighborhoods are just two of the pleasures that await. Restaurants of all kinds line the seafronts of some communities and the side streets of others. See map, p. 100.

Getting There and Back: New Jersey Transit operates good and relatively frequent train service from Penn Station, sometimes with a change of trains in Newark, to ten seaside towns from Long Branch to Bay Head, a distance of fifteen miles. The ride is a pleasant one, and the beach in all cases is between a five- and fifteen-minute walk from the station. Long Branch is about one hour thirty minutes from Penn Station, with a round-trip ticket good for seven days costing $9.25. The $9.50 round trip to Spring Lake takes about one hour fifty minutes, and to Bay Head Junction at the end of the line it is just over two hours and costs $10 for the round trip.

In the summer, New Jersey Transit runs the Shore Express, making limited stops and cutting over fifteen minutes from the travel time. Check up-to-date schedules for its operations. For a visit to more than one resort, a special excursion ticket allows for unlimited weekend travel on New Jersey Transit trains for one day, and costs $10. Ask also about generous family plan rates. For information, call (800) 772-2222 in New Jersey only and (201) 762-5100 out of state, from 6 a.m. to midnight.

Electric trains run from Penn Station under the Hudson River and across the New Jersey Meadowlands to Newark, where on weekends and most off-peak weekday trips, passengers change to a connecting diesel-hauled train at the same platform.

Upon leaving Newark, with a seat on the left-hand side, the train follows the high-speed Northeast Corridor Line for ten miles to Rahway, then cuts off onto the North Jersey Coast Line. The dome of Rahway State Prison rises to the left, and at Woodbridge the line crosses over twelve lanes of the New Jersey Turnpike. The Outerbridge Crossing span, connecting New Jersey with Staten Island, is seen to the left. After passing through Perth Amboy, the line crosses the mouth of the Raritan River and the Garden State Parkway, Route 9, and Route 35 bridges run parallel to the right.

While skirting Raritan Bay on a clear day, you can see over the marshes to the Verrazano-Narrows Bridge and to the twin towers of the World Trade Center, fourteen and twenty-one miles away respectively.

Just north and west of Matawan at the end of the electrified portion, the line passes over the Garden State Parkway's ten lanes. The countryside now becomes more rural, with lots of wooded sections and even some farmland. Just after crossing the Navesink

River, be sure to look for the gingerbread Victorian Red Bank Station on the left, followed quickly by the attractive stone and peaked-roof Little Silver Station and the Shrewsbury River crossing. The Monmouth Park grandstand rises to the right; New Jersey Transit runs Pony Express trains here on race days.

Long Branch

There is a raw and raucous flavor to Long Branch, where side-by-side boardwalk restaurants and pulsating midway activity, rather than its beach—which is rapidly being eroded by storms—set the tone for this older seaside resort.

To reach the boardwalk, walk one block to the left away from the station, then turn right on Morris Avenue. It's a ten-minute walk through a residential neighborhood from here. At the seafront, the line of informal restaurants begins to the left.

At Max's, a Long Branch tradition and a favorite place to have lunch or an early supper, you'll find customers who have been coming here for years devouring corn-on-the-cob, which is boiled in big iron pots, along with baskets of fried clams and forkfuls of sauerkraut. The eating is done inside at the wraparound counter and outside at picnic tables on a terrace extending out over the breaking surf. There is an appealing, scruffy seaside atmosphere about the place, the service is efficient and friendly, and the prices moderate.

At the popular and crowded amusement pier, there is every kind of midway attraction imaginable—shooting galleries, bumper cars, a tilt-a-whirl, haunted house, children's roller coaster, video games, an outdoor bar, and fishing from the end of the pier, with a twenty-five-cent admission charge for spectators. Across the street are popular water slides and baseball practice machines for beginners, intermediates, and experts. After a day at the beach further south, Long Branch is a good stopover for an injection of fun.

Belmar & Spring Lake

From the train, the first reassurance that the sea is not far away comes briefly to the left between Long Branch and Elberon. Soon after this glimpse of the ocean, large houses appear on both sides of the tracks, and, just before Asbury Park, with its much larger amusement piers and boardwalk, there is another welcome view of the sea at the end of the inlet. Ocean Grove and Bradley Beach come and go, and just after passing over the Shark River, the train stops at Belmar.

It is a fifteen-minute walk down 10th Avenue to the boardwalk, where the atmosphere on a busy summer weekend is honky-tonk. Party boats for blue fishing leave from the Shark River for sails close to shore and further out to sea. Leaving the train at Belmar makes a good approach to Spring Lake from the north, or after a visit to Spring Lake you might walk north into Belmar and take the train back from there. The boardwalk ends briefly at a brick arch dividing the two communities, which are in other ways worlds apart, and so intriguing to experience in one trip.

There is no prettier resort on the Jersey Coast than Spring Lake, a quiet community of splendid Victorian hotel and residential architecture, a long boardwalk, and a fine beach. Spring Lake, which boasts St. Catherine's, a not-so-small replica of St. Peter's in Rome, began as an upper-class Roman Catholic resort community, and soon became known as the Irish Riviera.

The attractive railroad station where you arrive—if you haven't walked from Belmar—is now mostly occupied by the First National State Bank. One decorative wooden door reads "Waiting Room" and the other says "Money." A well-landscaped park with a serpentine lake inhabited by ducks and swans links the station to the seafront, a lovely fifteen-minute walk.

For the main shopping street, walk along the left side of the park to 3rd and Passaic. There are five places to eat on the street, all within three blocks of each other. C. W. Campion's is the most interesting, a spacious Victorian-style bakery and sandwich shop with a high ceiling, table and counter seating. If you are not yet ready to eat, you might take one of their freshly-prepared sandwiches down to the beach.

Between here and the boardwalk on Ocean Avenue, there are several blocks of large Victorian houses of every shape and size. Large turreted houses with circular porches stand next to gingerbread gems with immaculate lawns. Not one looks anything like its neighbor. Spring Lake still attracts short- and long-stay summer visitors to its turn-of-the-century hotels, all located within a block of the beach or facing the boardwalk. Even if you are not considering a stay, have a look inside and lap up the atmosphere of another era, some of it decidedly faded but some still going strong.

By far the most imposing hotel of all is the Essex and Sussex, a huge brick and stucco structure with large columns in front and towers atop. The monumental lobby is furnished with comfortable lounge chairs and couches, oriental carpets, and potted palms. To the left is a huge dining room, to the right, reception rooms, and in back is a courtyard and large swimming pool. Even if a closer look shows that all is not well at the Sussex and Essex, which has the air of barely holding on, one cannot help being drawn inside for a quick look at a once-famous resort hotel.

Nearby, the brown and white triple-turreted Warren Hotel is another Victorian masterpiece that is well-kept both inside and out. The dining room and lounges break off a long, wide passageway, which, with its small clusters of white wicker chairs, acts as another lounge and viewing platform for the outdoor pool activities.

Behind and to the left of the Sussex and Essex on Atlantic Avenue, the Sandpiper Restaurant offers a frequently changed menu and moderate prices. The best choices are the simple and straightforward broiled bluefish and swordfish, or any of the other fresh catches of the day, depending on what the local fishermen bring in. The atmosphere is simple and unpretentious, and the Sandpiper is a good value for an early dinner after a long beach day.

Spring Lake's beach, like most of the other resorts along the North Jersey Coast, is currently being slowly eroded away, even though expensive groins have been built every few hundred yards. However, there is still plenty of sand and elbow room for a few hours or an entire day next to the pounding surf. The long boardwalk stretches for the entire length of the town's seafront, and from this elevation you can choose a favorite spot to lie on the sand or to look inland at the rows of summer and year-round houses and hotels. The promenade has benches for relaxing and two pavilions with changing rooms, a swimming pool, which is popular with children, and a snack bar. You get your beach permits here as well. The northern pavilion is much nicer than its southern counterpart; note the attractive bas-reliefs of fishes and seashells embedded in the walls.

If you wish to visit Belmar after Spring Lake, walk north along the boardwalk and pass through the brick gates that divide the two communities. Walk along Belmar's much busier seafront and then head inland at 10th Avenue to the railroad station, a fifteen-minute walk.

The last two stops on the North Jersey Coast Line, Point Pleasant Beach and Bay Head, are included for no other reason than that they offer two of the finest stretches of sand in the state.

Point Pleasant Beach

The train passes through Sea Girt, Manasquan, and Brielle, crossing the Manasquan River to arrive at Point Pleasant Beach Station. For the beach, walk six blocks down Arnold Avenue to Ocean Avenue and turn right. You can gain access to the water at Bradshaw's Beach, which has a snack bar, umbrellas, and showers for a small fee, or via one of the small hotels that offer daytime admission to their beach facilities and swimming pools.

Bay Head

The rail line ends at a little station shelter with a faded sign that reads "Bay Head Junction," although you cannot change trains for anywhere here other than back to New York. The walk to the dunes along Osborne Avenue is only five minutes. Access to the excellent beaches at Bay Head is more closely guarded than elsewhere, and you will need to buy a non-resident beach badge at the Bay Head Improvement Association office.

Bay Head is largely residential and fairly affluent, with its domestic architecture mostly simple Jersey Coast-style rather than fancy Victorian as at Spring Lake.

A PHILADELPHIA WEEKEND

Philadelphia Museum of Art, Benjamin Franklin Parkway at 26th Street, P.O. Box 7646, Philadelphia, PA 19101. (215) 763-8100. Open Tuesday–Sunday 10 a.m.–5 p.m. Admission Wednesday–Sunday adults $3, seniors, children under 18, and students with I.D. $1.50; Tuesday (when some galleries aren't open) $1.50 and $1.00; Sunday free 10 a.m.–1 p.m.

Rodin Museum, Benjamin Franklin Parkway at 22nd Street, Philadelphia, PA 19101. (215) 763-8100. Open Tuesday–Sunday 10 a.m.–5 p.m. Admission 50 cents.

The Franklin Institute Science Museum, 20th and Benjamin Franklin Parkway, Philadelphia, PA 19103. (215) 448-1200; (215) 564-3375 for taped listing of events. Open Monday–Saturday 10 a.m.–5 p.m., Sunday 12–5 p.m. Admission adults $3.50, students 12–college $3, children 4–11 $2.50, and seniors $2.

Port of History Museum, Delaware Avenue at Walnut Street, Penn's Landing, Philadelphia, PA 19106. (215) 925-3804. Open Wednesday–Sunday 10 a.m.–4 p.m.

For accommodations:
Bed and Breakfast, Center City, 1908 Spruce Street, Philadelphia, PA 19103. (215) 735-0881 or (215) 923-5459.
Bed and Breakfast of Philalelphia, P.O. Box 680-P, Devon, PA 19333. (215) 688-1633.
Amtrak (215) 736-4545; ask for tour desk.

For tourist information:
Philadelphia Convention and Visitors Bureau, Three Penn Center Plaza, Philadelphia, PA 19102. (215) 568-6599.
Philadelphia Tourist Center, 16th Street and JFK Boulevard, Philadelphia, PA 19102. (215) 568-6599. Open daily 9 a.m.–6 p.m.
Philly Fun Phone (215) 568-7255 for two-minute taped message.

Fewer than ninety minutes away from New York, a day or weekend in Philadelphia offers a rich urban experience of fine art museums, important historic sites, spectacular indoor shopping malls, quiet residential neighborhoods, a waterfront of floating attractions, and the largest urban park in the world.

The once dowdy "City of Brotherly Love" has, in the last twenty years, experienced a renaissance, including a burgeoning downtown skyline, extensive townhouse restoration, and the addition of many smart restaurants, ethnic eateries, and new hotels.

On the first day's proposed tour, you can visit the Philadelphia Museum of Art, a monumental repository of American paintings and furniture, period rooms from all over the world, and French Impressionist art. Nearby, the charming little Rodin Museum houses the largest collection of the sculptor's bronze statues outside of France, and the venerable Franklin Institute brings science to life for people of all ages.

Day two starts with an elevator ride to the top of City Hall for a splendid view of Philadelphia's neighborhood parks and rivers, and continues with a shopping tour through the Gallery, a multi-level retail complex, and of the Bourse, which is, by contrast to this swank modern mall, a sedately splendid Victorian restoration. No visit to the city would be complete without a tour of Independence Hall and a close look at the Liberty Bell. As a finale, Penn's Landing on

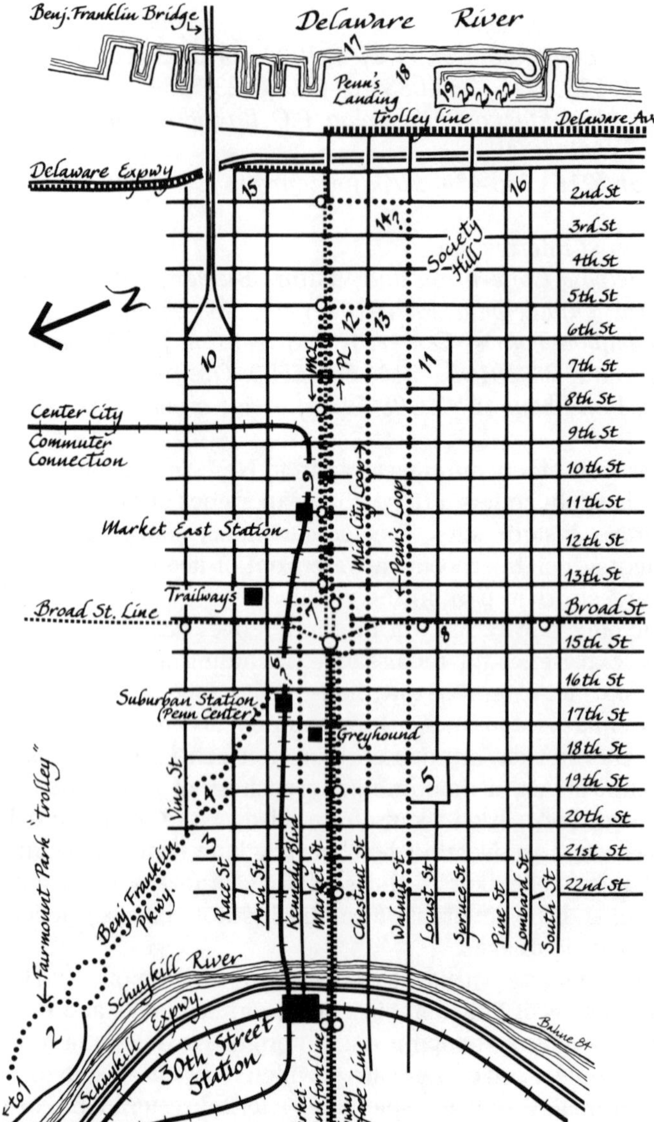

Delaware River
Benj. Franklin Bridge
Penn's Landing
trolley line
Delaware Ave
Delaware Expwy
Society Hill
Center City Commuter Connection
Market East Station
Trailways
Broad St. Line
Suburban Station (Penn Center)
Greyhound
Mid-City Loop
Penn's Loop
MCL
PL
2nd St
3rd St
4th St
5th St
6th St
7th St
8th St
9th St
10th St
11th St
12th St
13th St
Broad St
15th St
16th St
17th St
18th St
19th St
20th St
21st St
22nd St
Vine St
Race St
Arch St
Kennedy Blvd
Market St
Chestnut St
Walnut St
Locust St
Spruce St
Pine St
Lombard St
South St
Benj Franklin Pkwy.
Fairmount Park "trolley"
to 1
Schuylkill River
Schuylkill Expwy.
30th Street Station
Market-Frankford Line
Subway-Surface Line
Bahne 84

Philadelphia

? Visitor Information
1. Philadelphia Zoo
2. Philadelphia Museum of Art
3. Franklin Institute
4. Logan Circle
5. Rittenhouse Square
6. Kennedy Plaza & Tourist Center
7. City Hall
8. Academy of Music
9. The Gallery
10. Franklin Square
11. Washington Square
12. Liberty Bell
13. Independence Hall
14. National Park Visitor Center
15. Elfreth's Alley
16. New Market
17. Moshulu (ship)
18. Port of History Museum
19. Gazela Primeiro (ship)
20. Olympia (ship)
21. Becuna (ship)
22. Barnegat (ship)

the Delaware draws people aboard its fleet of historic ships such as the battle wagon U.S.S. Olympia and the offshore light vessel Barnegat.

Nearly everything worth seeing in the city is walkable, and, when you want to ride, Philadelphia has one of the most comprehensive transit systems in the country, including trolley cars.

Getting There and Back: Amtrak provides the fastest, most frequent, and most comfortable way to travel between the two cities. About three dozen weekday trains, somewhat fewer on weekends, depart from Penn Station, New York, for 30th Street Station, Philadelphia, taking from one hour ten minutes to one hour forty minutes, depending on the number of intermediate stops. All trains except those marked "Clockers" have food service.

The round-trip unreserved excursion fare of $31 is valid for all non-Metroliner Service trains, except for departures from 1 to 7 p.m. on Friday and Sunday, when the fare is $41 round-trip. Metroliner Service fares are higher, and, unless you are hankering for this experience, you will find the trip only slightly faster. Where the Metroliner Service *does* save considerable time is between New York and Baltimore and Washington. Pick up a Northeast Corridor Service timetable, or phone Amtrak for train times at (212) 736-4545 or (800) USA-RAIL, twenty-four hours a day. Be sure to inquire about family-plan fares.

The cheapest way between the two cities is via a New Jersey Transit train from Penn Station to Trenton, with a change to a Southeastern Pennsylvania Transportation Authority (SEPTA) train from Trenton to 30th Street, Suburban Station, or Market East

Station, depending on where in Philadelphia you are staying. New Jersey Transit's phone number is (201) 762-5100; SEPTA's phone number is (215) 574-7800.

The combination of the two commuter runs, which both make lots of stops, takes about two and one-half hours, or about an hour more than most Amtrak runs. However, the savings are considerable, and there are nearly hourly departures. The seven-day round-trip excursion fare on New Jersey Transit between Penn Station, New York, and Trenton is $9.50, and the bargain one-way off-peak fare from Trenton to any station in Philadelphia is $3.25 ($7.50 round-trip). The total comes to $17 round-trip.

Both Greyhound, $27 round-trip, (212) 635-0800, and Trailways, $26 round-trip, (212) 563-9574 for recorded schedules, offer frequent bus service from the Port Authority Bus Terminal to downtown Philadelphia in just over two hours.

While the New York to Philadelphia ride is hardly scenic, there are some interesting sites along the route that are worth mentioning.

At Penn Station, track numbers are posted and announced about ten to fifteen minutes before departure. If the schedule shows that your train is coming from Boston or Springfield, it is well to check the arrival board, in the ticket concourse or at the lower level between the west gates of Tracks 11 to 12 and 13 to 14, for any delays. Trains that originate in New York usually start out on time.

Upon leaving Penn Station, the train passes through the Hudson River tunnels completed in 1910, and then crosses the New Jersey Meadowlands, with a stop at Newark. South of Newark the scenery is mostly urban and industrial. Be sure to catch a glimpse of Rutgers, the state university, to the right, while crossing the Raritan River at New Brunswick. From here to Princeton Junction the train will wind up to one hundred and twenty miles per hour across the flat, partly rural New Jersey countryside. After Trenton, the state capital, be sure to see the famous sign, "Trenton Makes. The World Takes," tacked onto a highway bridge to the right as the train crosses the Delaware River into Pennsylvania. The train gallops past the traffic on parallel Interstate 95, then slows down at the Frankford Junction curve and while passing through North Philadelphia Station.

The best view of all comes a few minutes later while crossing the Schuylkill River. To both sides are the woods, paths, and mansions at Fairmount Park, and, in the distance to the left, the impressive Philadelphia skyline, dominated by City Hall. The rail line skirts the zoo, and when clear of the obstructing rail embankment, you have good views of the Philadelphia Art Museum and of the colorful rowing club houses at the water's edge, before sliding into 30th Street Station.

Completed for the Pennsylvania Railroad in December 1931, 30th Street Station is a shining Art Deco masterpiece. As you ascend the moving stairs from the lower-level platforms, your first sight is of the expansive ninety-seven-foot high ceiling, two rows of dripping crystal chandeliers, and of shafts of diffused natural light streaming in through the repeating series of tall windows. When you reach the main concourse, the station's orderly layout and clear signs will put you at ease about what to do next. Thirtieth Street Station may be one of the most impressive entrances to any major city in this country; its grandeur and its good range of traveler services make every visitor feel important.

Taxis are usually available through the east and west doors. Amtrak ticket holders may have a free SEPTA train transfer to Suburban Station at 16th Street and JFK Boulevard by using the ramp to the upper-level stairways A and B; show your Amtrak stub to the SEPTA conductor.

City Transportation

Southeastern Pennsylvania Transportation Authority operates most of the Philadelphia area's transportation services; call (215) 574-7800, 6 a.m.–midnight. Generally, the services are good, and include subway and "el" rail lines, subway and surface trolleys, trolley buses, buses, and a suburban rail network. The transit fare is eighty-five cents, exact change, with fifteen cents needed for transfers. There are reduced rates ($7) when buying ten tokens. If you are planning to do a fair amount of transit riding, there is an unlimited Weekly TransPass that costs $9. SEPTA maintains a sales office in the concourse at 15th and Market for individual route maps and for the sale of tokens, TransPasses, and an outstanding SEPTA System Map ($1.50).

The Mid-City Bus Loop running along Chestnut and Market between 5th and 17th Streets is a useful service, and is free in off-peak hours.

The Fairmount Park Trolley, (215) 879-4044, is another—and a colorful—way to get around. Rubber-tire replicas of the city's old trolley cars leave the Tourist Center at 16th and JFK Boulevard every twenty minutes from 10 a.m.–4:30 p.m., Wednesday through Sunday, in the spring, summer, and fall, for the ninety-minute, seventeen-mile tour of the 8,100-acre Fairmount Park, noted for its beauty and its multitude of attractions, including the Philadelphia Museum of Art. Adults $1.75, seniors $1, children fifty cents. You have on-and-off all-day privileges. Be sure to get the useful map and guide.

The two full days of sightseeing itineraries described here can all be accomplished on foot, although at the beginning or end of the day you might wish to use the city's public buses, trolleys, or subways to save some time, not to mention your feet.

The first day takes in three of the city's finest museums—the Philadelphia Museum of Art, Rodin Museum, and the Franklin Institute, all located along the Benjamin Franklin Parkway. The second day starts with a trip to the top of City Hall, then passes through Philadelphia's spectacular new indoor shopping centers, tours Independence Mall, and finishes up with a walk down to Penn's Landing on the Delaware.

Day One

To reach the Philadelphia Museum of Art, take a pleasant twenty-five-minute walk from City Hall along the tree-lined Benjamin Franklin Parkway. If you are coming only for the day, arriving at Amtrak's 30th Street Station, leave via the 29th Street exit, and cross the Schuylkill River on the Market Street Bridge. Turn left on 22nd Street, walk eight short blocks to the parkway, and turn left again. The museum rises right in front of you.

The approach to the museum along the parkway is a monumental one. In front of the central stairway, flanked by a series of cascading waterfalls, is a large ornamental fountain featuring bronze figures of deer, moose, and buffalo, with George Washington on horseback as the centerpiece.

The building itself, completed between 1916 and 1928, consists of three interconnected Greek temples of yellow marble. Note the colorful detailed figures in the pediment of the right-hand section.

Inside the East (City) Entrance, the Great Stair Hall, a vast open space of two stories, has Alexander Calder's white mobile, "The Ghost," hanging above your head. Later, you will see the works of Calder's father and grandfather on the route to City Hall. At the second level, a series of sixteen French wall tapestries, designed in the seventeenth century by the Flemish painter Peter Paul Rubens, depict the "History of Constantine the Great."

Begin your visit by entering the first floor special exhibition galleries, where a recent show surveyed "The Golden Age of British Photography (1839–1900)." Included were pictures from the European Grand Tour, taken during the pioneer days of organized travel, English landscapes, and the building of the steamship *Great Eastern*.

In the American collections deeper into this wing, several rooms are devoted to the portraits and seascapes of the Philadelphian Thomas Eakins and to the portraits of Thomas Sully, an Englishman who also made a career in the City of Brotherly Love.

Philadelphia was justly famous for its fine furniture making, and the collection here includes mid- and late-eighteenth-century high chests of drawers, desks, secretary bookcases, tilt top tables, and an assortment of chairs, by Thomas Affleck and many other unknown cabinetmakers.

To the right of the main hall, the long gallery and the parallel side rooms are devoted to a survey of European art from 1200 to 1900. At the far end, one little gallery shows the work of the nineteenth-century English landscape painter John Constable and his son Lionel.

Marcel Duchamp, creator of the term "mobile," has a room devoted to his paintings, sculpture, and a curious mixed media assemblage seen through two peepholes in a wooden door. Beyond, the viewer sees an outstretched nude figure lying on brush and holding a gas lamp, with a painted landscape in the background and a sparkling waterfall. You can come to your own conclusions about the evocative scene.

Climb the great central staircase to reach the second floor, where many of the rooms are fitted as re-creations of elaborate indoor settings and small buildings from around the world. Most of them were commissioned as Works Progress Administration projects from the Depression era.

Entering the medieval European art galleries to the right at the top of the stairs, you pass through a reconstructed cloister from a thirteenth-century French abbey. In the Asian section, one room contains a sixteenth-century pillared temple from South India, richly decorated with granite deities, mythological animals, and human figures. In the next room, you are in the midst of an early seventeenth-century reception hall from the Ming Dynasty that belonged to the Palace of the Duke Chao in Peking. Additional pieces of Chinese furniture, porcelain, and lacquerware are arranged in smaller rooms off to the sides.

In the European Galleries to the left at the top of the stairs, you walk through a sixteenth-century choir screen and around an altarpiece from Dijon, France. Another period room is the panelled and furnished Grand Salon from an eighteenth-century French château.

In one of the American rooms, we stand in the entrance foyer leading into the kitchen belonging to a mid-eighteenth-century Pennsylvania country house, complete with cooking utensils, preparation tables, storage cabinets, and a large fireplace.

In the French Impressionist and related rooms, there are multiple works by Cézanne, Degas, Manet, Monet, Renoir, Pennsylvania-born Impressionist Mary Cassatt, and the post-Impressionist Dutch painter Vincent van Gogh. In the far rooms, there is an extensive collection of the portraits and landscapes of the English painter Thomas Gainsborough.

On the ground floor two flights down, the Museum maintains an excellent shop for art books, posters, cards, and reproductions, a carpeted buffet-style restaurant with a quiet intimate atmosphere, and a basic cafeteria. Here you might experience a Philadelphia Cheese Steak sandwich with onions on a long roll for $3. You may be hungry by now, so consider it; there are no restaurants until you reach the area of Logan Circle.

Leave the Museum via the West (River) Entrance for a splendid view of the Schuylkill and Fairmount Park, the largest urban park in the world. Walk down to the gazebo perched at the edge of the river directly over the wide, fast-flowing spillway. A line strung across the Schuylkill prevents the racing sculls from being swept over the falls. Look upriver at the row of fanciful boat houses, headquarters for the rowing clubs. At night, these are framed with strings of white lights, a fine sight that can be seen from the train on the way back to New York. Above the boat houses stands Lemon Hill, a mansion built in 1800 for the Philadelphia financier and signer of the Declaration of Independence, Robert Morris. To your left, the former, steam-powered city waterworks, dating from 1812, ranges along the embankment in a series of splendid but shuttered Greek-Revival-style buildings.

Walk around to the left of the Museum and follow the Parkway to the intriguing little Rodin Museum at 22nd Street, housing the largest collection of the famous sculptor's work, mostly bronzes, outside his native France.

The entrance to the pretty fountain garden is a replica of the Rodin Memorial at Meudon in France. On the building's front facade an intricate high-relief bronze double door is decorated with many writhing small figures.

The skylighted main hall and side rooms house Auguste Rodin's works both on pedestals and free-standing. The central work of the main hall is "The Burghers of Calais," a famous and dramatic grouping of a half-dozen life-size figures. "The Gates of Hell," a bas-relief, graces the top of one doorway. Rodin's fascination with hands as subject matter can be seen in his "Left Hand," "Clenched Hand," and the "Hand from the Tomb." Busts of famous people are a frequent subject, and there are standing bronze statues of Adam and Eve and the head of "St. John the Baptist on a Platter."

Upon leaving the Museum, continue to Logan Circle by the Free Library of Philadelphia, housing more than six million books and other materials, the Municipal Courts Building of similar design, the Cathedral of St. Peter and St. Paul, the Academy of Natural Sciences, and The Franklin Institute.

The Swann Fountain in the center of the Circle, by Alexander Stirling Calder, father of "mobile" Calder, depicts frogs and turtles with human figures representing the city's three rivers—the Delaware, Schuylkill, and Wissahickon. The Four Seasons Hotel (information following) is also located here.

The Franklin Institute Science Museum recently celebrated fifty years of showing off the outstanding achievements in the field of science to generations of Philadelphians and visitors. Children growing up in the area best remember the giant steam locomotive, a prototype model of a 4-10-2 (wheel configuration) built in 1926 by Philadelphia's Baldwin Locomotive Works. The massive engine has been on display since the Museum opened its doors in the 1930s. You can walk through the arteries of a giant heart and play games at the more recently installed computer center. Philadelphia was once a great shipbuilding center, and another recent exhibit shows the Delaware's maritime heritage in paintings, drawing, photographs, ship models, and a wave tank for testing hull designs. On the top floor, an observatory allows classes of all ages to study the heavens.

The aviation section was still under reconstruction at the time of writing, but it is to be reopened in 1985 with displays recounting the history of flight. Outside, there is a full-size Boeing 707, donated to the Institute by British Airways.

The Fels Planetarium, with an additional admission of $1, has regular seasonal shows every day of the week.

Day Two

This day's events may be considered a relatively more low-brow program of sightseeing, from City Hall through the historic Independence Mall area, down to the Delaware at Penn's Landing. The tour starts where Broad Street meets Market Street in the heart of Center City.

City Hall, the largest municipal building and the finest example of Second Empire architecture in the country, was completed over a thirty-year period between 1871 and 1901. Within are fourteen and one-half acres of office space and public courtyards, and the statue of William Penn atop is the largest piece of sculpture resting on a building anywhere in the world. The sculptural version of Penn is holding a scroll in one hand, and to appreciate the effect it creates, Philadelphians like to show visitors the statue from the Ben Franklin Parkway. You can get the same view on your way from the Museum.

City Hall's construction is a combination of granite and brick faced with marble up to the level of the clocks. The uppermost material looks like stone, but is actually painted cast iron reaching to the top of the 548-foot tower. Alexander Milne Calder, the first of the three artistic Calders, created all the pieces of sculpture on the building, and the effect is richly ornate and worth studying from across the street.

Whether you decide to take the elevator to the top, just beneath the statue, is up to you, but be forewarned that for some it is a claustrophobic and dizzying experience. The reward, however, is a splendid view from forty stories up.

Inside the arch for the Market East entrance, go inside to the end of the hall for an elevator to the seventh floor. From there, follow the double red lines on the floor to the tower elevator, where there may be a wait. The viewing area is a circular caged walkway running around the tower with no solid wall between you and space. Soon, the old Philadelphia zoning law that once allowed no building to rise higher than City Hall will be history, with the completion of a sixty-story office building nearby at 17th and Market. Until then, you have an unobstructed view in all directions—into Fairmount Park, along the Delaware, and out the Parkway to the Art Museum.

John Wanamaker's department store, built in 1902–1911, stands on one corner of City Hall Square at 13th and Market. Have a look inside at the spectacular view of the five-story central court and the huge organ pipes. It's here Philadelphia's children flock to speak to Santa Claus at Christmas time, and the organ concerts are legend.

The first two blocks of Market Street heading east are very tacky. At 12th turn left and enter the new Gallery II underground shopping mall. You first pass beneath the now-closed (as of September 1984) Reading Terminal, which has been supplanted by a new Market East railroad station that carries the city's commuter lines through Center City. The Gallery is an integral part of the entire complex that is designed to bring shoppers downtown by train. Every kind of shop and food under the sun can be found here, and it is worth walking through on any one of the levels, looking over the rail from time to time to see the silver trains passing below. In addition to some 250 individual stores, three of the city's major department stores are located here—J. C. Penny, Gimbels, and Philadelphia's own Strawbridge & Clothier.

You can exit as far east as 8th and Market Streets, where it is only two more blocks to Independence Mall, which stretches for several blocks between 6th and 5th Streets.

The Liberty Bell is now housed in a separate undistinguished pavilion in the mall just to the right of Market Street. There are continuous tours that explain the history of the legendary cracked bell, with time to touch it at the end, from nine to five every day, with extended hours to 8 p.m. in July and August.

One block south across Chestnut Street stands Independence Hall, formerly home to the Liberty Bell. To see the rooms where the Declaration of Independence was adopted and where the U.S. Constitution was written, you must join a tour leaving every twenty minutes from a waiting room just to the left of the main building. The hours are the same as for the Liberty Bell, and, in the summer, you can expect a wait if you arrive in the middle of the day. In the summer, there are also sound and light shows every evening. After the tour, be sure to enjoy the quiet beauty of the small park behind the Hall before going on. Some of William Penn's original urban planning, the city squares and handsome brick buildings, can be appreciated here.

Just east of the Mall, the red sandstone building that once served as the Philadelphia Bourse Building has recently been recycled into one of the city's finest shopping centers with office space on the upper floors. Built in 1893–1895 for Philadelphia's Maritime and Stock Exchanges, the structure underwent some major alterations to re-adapt it to today's needs. The original two-story stained glass ceiling was removed to create a ten-story central atrium with a clear glass roof. On either side, above the original ceiling, the brick walls have been replaced with glass to allow the offices to share the natural light from above.

The ornate plaster work, colored tiles, and iron balconies remain, with a mezzanine floor added to increase the retail selling space. The main floor has pushcarts, an information center, and rows of shops to the side. Escalators and stairs take you to the mezzanine and to the third floor, where eighteen international food outlets sell fast food from around the world. Some visitors may find the space more intriguing than the stores and choice of snack bar restaurants.

From the 4th Street exit to the Bourse, it is a fifteen-minute walk, preferably along Chestnut Street, to the river at Penn's Landing. Some of the city's oldest commercial buildings and institutions can be found on these three blocks.

To reach Penn's Landing, where Philadelphia's waterborne trade once centered, cross the depressed highway (I-95) via a park platform overpass. You can also look down on Delaware Avenue where, in the warmer months, a local group of trolley enthusiasts run vintage streetcars along a wobbly one-mile line. For $1 you can sample what it was like to travel the streets on rails in cars that are much older than those currently running in regular service on some of the city streets. Phone (215) 627-0807 for details of days of operation.

At the river's edge, the black-hulled sailing vessel *Mosholu* was originally built in 1904 for the lucrative nitrate trade from Chile to Europe. The ship is now permanently moored here as a restaurant and museum. The setting below decks is a good one for lunch or a drink. Large windows have been cut into the hull to allow views of the Delaware River and the skyline of Camden in New Jersey across the way. The menu is reasonably priced, with a selection of overstuffed deli-style sandwiches, the usual salads, and fresh fish and shellfish.

After a meal, climb up to the ship's museum, where for a small admission charge you can get the feel of the cramped eating and sleeping quarters that the sailors of old had to endure during the long weeks and months at sea. A good black-and-white photo display shows how the vessel was restored, as well as portraying some of its career as a cargo vessel under sail. The sloping open decks show off the rigging and equipment needed to run the ship while at sea. Walk all the way foreward and aft to appreciate the *Mosholu's* great length, marked sheer, and fine lines.

Just south of the *Mosholu*, the modern Port of History Museum has changing art exhibits—but what will interest most people is an excellent and wholly honest slide and film show of Philadelphia's past and present. Much of the current story is told by local citizens, who make quite candid comments about their own experiences, ranging from happy to humorous to not so happy. One does come away with a good understanding of what draws together and divides this great city.

Again to the south of the *Mosholu*, ship enthusiasts will find a superb collection of historic vessels moored in an artificial basin. In the summer months, there may also be some unexpected visitors from other ports.

The permanently moored fleet is headed unquestionably by the American battleship *U.S.S. Olympia*, which served as Admiral Dewey's 1895 flagship that, during the Spanish-American War, won the sea battle at Manila Bay. From these decks came the famous slogan, "Fire when ready, Gridley."

The *U.S.S. Becuna* is a World War II submarine, and, if you want to experience the confined quarters of this warship, board her by all means. The red-hulled lightship *Barnegat*, built in 1904, once helped mark the shipping lanes leading to the mouth of the Delaware River. The lightship as an aid to navigation is almost an extinct species in this country, as the lightships required large, expensive crews living on board to maintain the vessel and operate the equipment.

A foreigner is the *Gazela Primeiro*, an 1883-built Portuguese barkentine, the last example of a once-common type of fishing vessel. Today, she still goes out under sail on excursions as the oldest operating wooden sailing ship in the world.

All the above-named vessels have small admission charges that vary from $1 to $2.50, and usually allow visits to more than one ship.

There are seats to rest on all along Penn's Landing, so you may pace your walk with intermissions to enjoy the slow-motion rhythm of Philadelphia's waterfront and river.

The best way to return to Center City or 30th Street Station is to walk to the subway station at 2nd and Market, where there is a direct line (69th Street direction).

Hotels

The three hotels listed here have been selected for their good value at their respective price levels and for convenient locations, which make it possible to visit many of the city's attractions on foot.

The Four Seasons Hotel, facing Logan Circle and the Benjamin Franklin Parkway, is considered by many discerning travelers and Philadelphians to be the city's best hotel. Completed in 1983 with a light-colored granite facade, the Four Seasons is only eight stories tall (no building fronting on Logan Circle may exceed eighty feet). In order to make the venture an economical proposition, in view of the city's height regulations, a thirty-story office building called One Logan Square rises across a courtyard at the rear of the property.

Upon entering the hotel, one is immediately struck by the bright airy feeling created by large windows bringing in natural light, and by the pink marble floors partly covered with thick, simple-patterned carpets, the use of light woods on the walls, and the lack of obstruction as one moves from the lobby to the public rooms and restaurants.

In the summer months, drinks are served in the Courtyard Cafe which adjoins the entrance lobby and opens onto the center court between the hotel and office building. At other times of the year, the Swann Lounge offers drinks with a view of the Calder-designed "Swann Fountain" in the center of Logan Circle. The spacious room has a separate bar to one side, and during the week offers a limited lunch menu that includes a hot entrée in a chafing dish, quiche, sandwiches, and salads. Afternoon tea with finger sandwiches is served daily for $7.95, and at night there is musical entertainment.

Opening off to the left, the Swann Cafe, a small wood-paneled room, serves lunch, and an all-day menu is available until the wee hours. Recent recommended items include chilled cream of leek soup with chervil for $3, cold salmon and cucumber with mayonnaise sauce for $8, and breast of chicken in a cream sauce with mushrooms for $7.

For the hotel's most elegant dining in a handsome, dark-paneled room with some tables by the windows facing the circle, the Fountain Restaurant gets rave reviews. Two recommended choices from the menu are sautéed scallops with scallions and lime sauce at $12.50, and grilled medallions of veal with turnip sauce for $15.50. The Fountain Restaurant also serves breakfast, lunch, and brunch.

The same bright atmosphere is found in the large bedrooms and suites, some with an adjoining sitting area and some with separate sitting room. There is twenty-four-hour room service, twice-daily maid service, and your shoes may be shined while you sleep. Ask for a room on one of the higher floors facing Logan Circle.

Rates for the Guest Rooms are $125–$175 single occupancy and $150–$175 double occupancy, plus a nine percent hotel tax. Rates for Four Seasons Rooms (small suites) and suites are higher. On weekends the hotel offers several packages. For instance, One Enchanted Evening, $160 plus tax for two, includes a Four Seasons Room, champagne, flowers, Home Box Office, use of the Spa, breakfast in the room, and gratuities. (Four Seasons Hotel, One Logan Square, Philadelphia, PA 19103. 215-963-1500 or, in New York, 800-462-1150.)

The eight-hundred-room Franklin Plaza Hotel is seven blocks from City Hall at the edge of the Center City business district. The modern twenty-six-story hotel has recently undergone extensive renovations. Upon entering, your eye is carried upward to the huge lobby atrium, extending from which are many of the Franklin Plaza's eating places. For intimate and elegant dining, try Between Friends for dinner, which offers a continental menu. To view all the bustle in what is a very busy place, have lunch at the terrace restaurant in the main lobby. For one of the best Philadelphia views while dining, Rooftop Horizons on the twenty-sixth floor has a very popular buffet lunch and dinner with dance music.

The hotel's athletic facilities are extensive, with indoor pool, health club, tennis, racquetball, and squash courts, and a running track.

The most favorable rates are on Friday, Saturday, and Sunday, when the room rates are $59 plus tax whether single or double occupancy. You will find the rooms to be medium-sized, well-equipped standard accommodations. Ask for the highest floor available facing Center City. (Franklin Plaza Hotel, 17th and Race Streets, Philadelphia, PA 19103. 215-448-2000.)

For visitors who would like to be among Philadelphia's most famous historical attractions, the Holiday Inn at Independence Mall offers a convenient if predictable experience. Benjamin and Deborah Franklin's 1790 gravesite is less than a block away, and the waterfront at Penn's Landing a fifteen-minute walk.

There is a restaurant, coffee shop, and a bar lounge located on the main floor. The 364 rooms are standard Holiday Inn-style, and usually a good value for the money. Singles are $77 and doubles $85 plus tax. King-size beds are $4 extra. Weekend rates—you must specifically ask for these—are $65 single or double for Friday or Saturday nights. The hotel has an indoor swimming pool. (Holiday Inn-Independence Mall, 4th and Arch Streets, Philadelphia, PA 19106. 215-923-8660; central toll-free number is 800-HOLIDAY.)

CONNECTICUT AND RHODE ISLAND

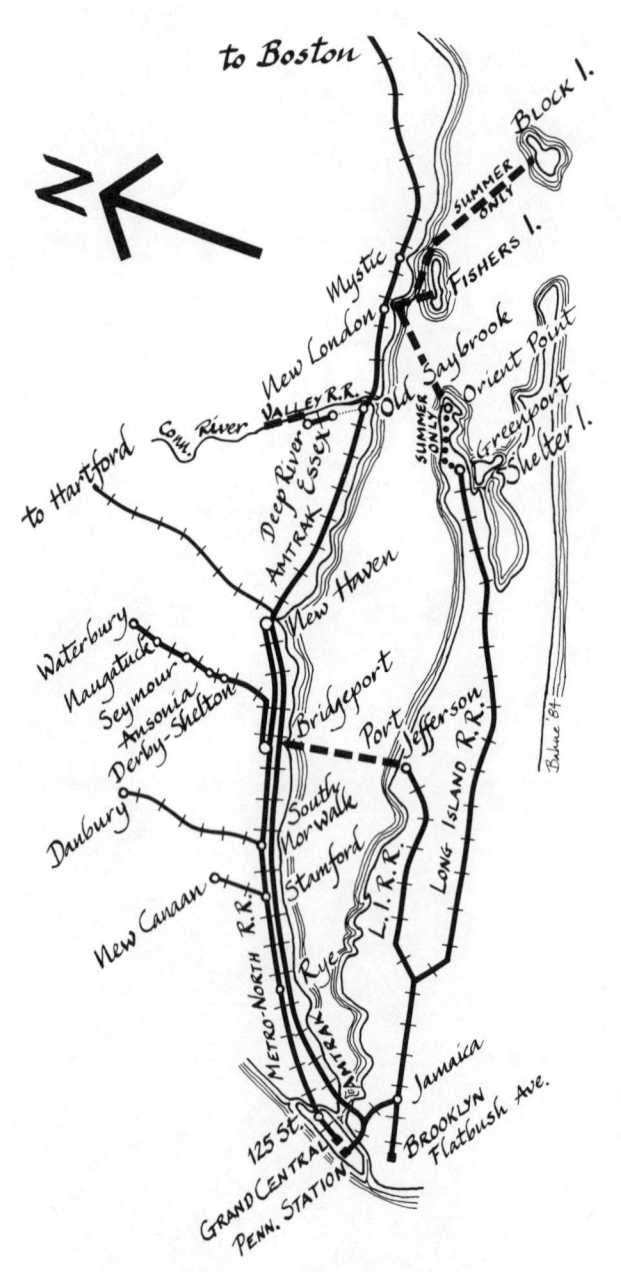

Connecticut Shore Line

SHORE LINE RAIL ROUTE GUIDE

This descriptive route guide may be used in connection with outings on the Waterbury Branch Line, ferry trips to and from Port Jefferson, the Essex weekend, the walking tour of New London, ferry rides to Fishers Island, Block Island, and Orient Point, and the weekend outing to Mystic. (All of these destinations are described in following chapters.)

The Northeast Corridor Line from New York into New England provides the rail traveler with one of the richest feasts of seascape viewing found anywhere in the country. Once known as the New York, New Haven, and Hartford Shore Line to Boston, today's Amtrak trains follow the same scenic coastal route along the northern edge of Long Island Sound.

For trips that use Metro-North's New Haven Line, trains originate at Grand Central Terminal, and for those outings beyond New Haven, Amtrak's Penn Station is the starting point. The two rail lines leave New York via different routes and meet at New Rochelle about ten miles before passing into Connecticut. Make sure to take a seat on the right-hand side for all outbound trips.

If you've taken the Metro-North from Grand Central, you'll spend the first ten minutes of the ride in total darkness under Park Avenue. At 97th Street, though, the train bursts into daylight and follows a high-level stone viaduct down the middle of Park Avenue through Central Harlem. The Mt. Sinai Hospital complex rises prominently to the left behind some relatively modern housing projects, then the neighborhood rapidly deteriorates into older tenements and the ugly scars of abandoned buildings.

Most trains pause at 125th Street Station astride the main street of Harlem before crossing the Harlem River and passing into a manufacturing area of the South Bronx. The Hudson Line to Poughkeepsie and Albany splits off to the left, followed by the Harlem Line to White Plains, Brewster, and Dover Plains. The scenery remains mostly seedily urban until the MTA Line joins Amtrak's Hell Gate Route at Shell Tower.

Or, if you left from Amtrak's Penn Station, you'll follow a different route to Shell Tower. From the gloomy platforms at Penn Station, the train travels eastward under the East River, coming out from underground in the Sunnyside section of Queens on Long Island. The extensive rail yards for Amtrak and New Jersey Transit run parallel down to the left, and at the Harold Tower interlocking, the elevated Hell Gate Route separates from the Long Island Rail Road Line and begins a wide swing through Astoria, then back over the Hell Gate passage of the East River.

On a clear day the view of the Manhattan skyline is magical, and it is worth getting up from your seat to take in the glorious spectacle unfolding on the left. Just after crossing the East River, the train curves right, passing over Wards and Randalls Islands. Below are parks, playing fields, tennis courts, and Manhattan State Hospital. The small vessels tied up at the river's edge are New York City's sludge boats or, more popularly, "honey barges," which haul treated waste out to sea for dumping. Adjacent are the grounds and buildings belonging to the New York City Fire Department Training Academy. A red city fireboat is usually moored here. If you happen to see a red brick tenement in flames, it is only a planned exercise to simulate an actual fire. If you're lucky, you might see department trainees in rain slickers wielding fire axes, climbing fire escapes, spreading rescue nets, and directing powerful water jets.

Leaving the Hell Gate Bridge, the rail line drops into a cut through the South Bronx, then crosses the Hutchinson River. To the left rises the huge Coop City apartment complex. Just short of New Rochelle Station, the Amtrak line joins the Metro-North route from Grand Central. From here on to New Haven, the two routes are one and the same, sharing four electrified tracks.

The train's speed increases, and the pace may be too rapid for you to read the frequent commuter station signs. The parallel New England Thruway turns into the Connecticut Turnpike at the state border toll booths. The rail line will dive over and under the highway many times on its way up the coast.

The first suburban tree-lined streets appear in Connecticut, and glimpses of Long Island Sound begin after Greenwich and at Cos Cob. The latter place is well known to commuters as the site of a wheezing old power plant that is occasionally reluctant to provide sufficient electricity for the overhead wires.

At Stamford, a city with one of the lowest unemployment rates in the country, a cluster of corporate headquarters rise around the new transportation center under construction. Many trains stop here, and passengers change for the eight-mile New Canaan Branch, except on through trains during the rush hour. After departing Stamford, coach storage yards appear below and to the right.

Metro-North trains stop at South Norwalk to make connections with the twenty-four-mile Danbury Branch.

The scenery improves substantially, and at Westport the first of th route's attractive wooden barn-style stations appear, a legacy from the New Haven Railroad days. Many of the houses within sight of the tracks are worth hundreds of thousands of dollars. The first tidal marshlands open up on the right between Westport and Green's Farms. Southport, another very well-to-do bedroom community, lies near the limit of intensive daily commuting, forty-nine miles from Grand Central.

The simple dock for the ferry across Long Island Sound to Port Jefferson appears just before Bridgeport's station platforms. To the left is a fanciful Moorish building housing P. T. Barnum's circus memorabilia collection, as well as this industrial city's main business district. Passengers for the thirty-two-mile Waterbury Branch change here to a diesel rail car, with four trips a day up the Housatonic and Naugatuck Rivers. (See the following chapter for more detail.)

Leaving Bridgeport, the train first crosses the Pequonnock, then the Housatonic Rivers, and twenty-five minutes later enters New Haven, seventy-two miles from Grand Central and the last stop for Metro-North trains. The electrified section ends here, and Amtrak passengers experience lights-out for about seven minutes while a diesel locomotive is added. Those people destined for Hartford and Springfield normally have to change trains.

Historical New Haven station, closed for several years, is being rebuilt into an intermodal transportation center for trains and buses.

Once clear of New Haven's urban influence, the landscape becomes genuinely rural for the first time. Rocky hillocks rise from the tidal marshlands through which flow meandering streams. Isolated houses stand on tiny islands just off shore, and the sweep of Long Island Sound is visible for long stretches. There are many attractive coastal towns between here and Old Saybrook, where travelers for Essex leave. Note the handsome nineteenth-century wooden station on the right. As the train rumbles across the bridge spanning the beautiful Connecticut River, be sure to look both ways for splendid views.

Between Old Saybrook and New London (twenty-nine miles), the

Shore Line parallels the sandy beach at Rocky Neck State Park and again along Niantic Bay, running less than a hundred feet from the water's edge.

All trains stop at New London, once an important whaling town and today the home of the United States Coast Guard. Ferries for Fishers Island, Orient Point, and Block Island (seasonal) depart from the several piers to the right. Note the fine brick railroad station to the left. (See "Island Destinations from New London" for details.)

Leaving New London, the line swings right across the Thames River, where a look upstream may reveal the Coast Guard sail training ship, *Eagle*, and, either way, a nuclear submarine or two on the Groton side. General Dynamics maintains its important Electric Boat shipyard here.

Just before the Mystic River Bridge, water laps at the line on both sides. The new bridge and track realignment are important parts of the Northeast Corridor Improvement Project designed to give better Amtrak service. Look up and down the Mystic River for acres of moored yachts.

The two-tone wooden Mystic Depot sits handsomely on the left, the final station on this route guide. From here, the Shore Line follows the coast into Rhode Island with short stretches along Narragansett Bay, and on to Providence and finally Boston, 231 miles from New York. The relaxing all-rail route into New England offers a leisurely alternative to the hectic pace of plane travel and the heavy traffic encountered on the turnpike.

WATERBURY
A Branch Line Train Ride

The few remaining branch lines that offer rail passenger service in this country, other than distinctly commuter operations, are cherished relics from the past that provide smaller communities with local service as well as make connections to main line trains.

The thirty-two-mile run from Bridgeport to Waterbury, Connecticut, leaving New England's scenic Shore Line at Devon, will give today's traveler an insight into the heyday of the industrial revolution that made Waterbury and adjacent towns the center of the brass industry in America.

The one-hour branch line ride, each way, passes large occupied and vacant red brick factories that face the railroad and the Housatonic and Naugatuck Rivers. Waterbury's McKim, Mead and White-designed railroad station was, when completed in 1908, the New Haven Railroad's most prestigious building.

The stopover at Waterbury between trains allows for a walking tour to the city's impressive main square, a grand town center of public buildings on a human scale, and to the nineteenth-century residential district to view the homes of the brass industry tycoons. A visit to the industrial arts collection at the Mattatuck Museum will give a glimpse into Waterbury's inventive past. Here are displays of clocks, watches, buttons of every description, and ordinary household items once made of brass instead of today's omnipresent plastic.

Getting There and Back: On weekends, you have the choice of two New Haven Line departures from Grand Central at 8:05 a.m. and 12:05 p.m., with a change of trains at Bridgeport, same platform, arriving at Waterbury at 10:20 a.m. and 2:20 p. m. respectively. Trains return from Waterbury at 11:18 a.m., 3:18 p.m., and 7:18 p.m., arriving back at Grand Central two hours and twenty minutes later, allowing for a stopover of one, five or nine hours. Weekday schedules are very similar. A five-hour stay is recommended, and the trip may be made at any time of the year. The round-trip off-peak fare is $14.35, seniors $9.50.

See "Shore Line Rail Route Guide" (p. 143) for a complete description of the scenic trip from Grand Central to Bridgeport. For the ferry connection from Bridgeport over to Long Island, see "Port Jefferson & the Bridgeport Ferry" (p. 66).

A single Budd Company SPV-2000, the latest type of diesel rail car, usually protects the Waterbury Branch Line. Operating from the eastbound platform at Bridgeport, the little train pulls up to board its passengers after the New Haven-bound train that originated at Grand Central leaves the station. Aboard the rail car, a partial center divider separates the smoking and non-smoking sections. Amfleet-type reclining seats with pull-down trays offer a comfortable though slightly cramped ride. The scenery is equally interesting on both sides, so choose a seat on the right, facing the direction of travel, both going and coming back.

Five miles down the track, after crossing both the Pequonnock and Housatonic Rivers over an elaborate pair of old drawbridges, the rail car wobbles left, leaving the main line to begin the leisurely twenty-seven-mile run up the valley.

The maximum allowable speed of fifty miles an hour feels just right for the track conditions and for viewing. At Derby-Shelton the line leaves the Housatonic River and begins to parallel the Naugatuck, with the river first on the left, then on the right, side of the train. A mile and one-half further along, Ansonia is approached through an open set of flood gates that were installed to protect the town from the disastrous overflows that once plagued the entire Naugatuck Valley.

The American Brass Company, one of the valley's three original major concerns, still maintains a small operation here and at Waterbury, although the company today is a mere shadow of the once large-scale manufacturing industry that by the time of the Civil War made the Naugatuck Valley the nation's center for brass-making. Immigrants from northern, central, and southern Europe arrived in great waves from the early 1800s onward to fill the labor requirements. After World War II, the industry went into an irreversible decline, largely due to the popularity of cheaper plastic goods. Today the valley is a depressed area of relatively high unemployment, although, with companies relocating to the Waterbury area, the economy is improving and the number of new jobs increasing.

After passing through Ansonia's north-end flood gates, the train closely follows the river that only a couple of years ago washed out the line but spared the town. There was an unsettling period of several months afterward when it was rumored that the railroad would not be rebuilt.

At Naugatuck, the town's handsome railroad station houses the local newspaper. Then, just under an hour after leaving Bridgeport, the train comes to a final stop at the northern end of Waterbury's under-used freight yards.

Stepping off the train, the immediate scene is a depressing one of broken platforms, missing canopies, and the dull facade of what looks like a closed railroad station. However, walk around the building to the city side and cross the street to the large gazebo. From Library Park, McKim, Meade and White's glorious 1908 station building can be fully appreciated and photographed. When completed, Waterbury's station was the most elaborate of all the structures belonging to the New York, New Haven, and Hartford Railroad.

The long arched brick structure with its slender tower, a copy of the *Campanile* in Siena, Italy, and four working clocks has since 1958 served as the offices for the *Waterbury Republican-American*. The only evidence that the building is a railroad station, apart from the clearly obvious fact that it looks like one, are the posted timetables on one window and a small crew office at the back.

Waterbury received its first trains in 1849, and before World War II travelers could head in four directions: to Danbury, Winsted, Hartford, and, of course, south to Bridgeport and New York. The present service of four trains a day beginning and terminating at Waterbury has operated virtually unchanged for more than twenty years.

To reach the Green, the city's central square, take Grand Street beginning in front of the railroad station. Just after the modern Waterbury Superior Court, turn left into Church Street and walk two short blocks. The late nineteenth-century commercial, public, private, and church buildings surrounding the Green reflect the city's impressive heritage as the brass capital of the nation. The view from the open square is an unobstructed one, and on a nice day local residents will be seated on benches around the Victorian clock, chatting away.

The Mattatuck (the original Indian name for Waterbury) Museum on the Green at 119 West Main Street is located in an old house with more recent extensions in the back, and serves as a fine introduction to Waterbury's industrial past. The original rooms are modeled after a country store, a settler's cabin, and a Victorian parlor; three centuries of changing lifestyles and tastes are thus spanned in this inventive exhibit.

Every manner of brass items are on display, from impressive clocks and ammunition casings to fine watches, water kettles, and more mundane products such as hinges, fasteners, screws, pins, and coins. Topping all of these is a wonderful collection of hundreds of plain and fancy brass buttons in more shapes and sizes than one thought possible. The portrait paintings, landscape scenes, and modern art works are all by Connecticut artists.

Admission is free, and the museum is open Tuesday through Saturday 12–5 p.m. and Sunday 2–5 p.m. (except July and August). Closed Monday throughout the year. Plan your visit around the limited opening hours and allow an hour. (Mattatuck Museum, 119 West Main Street, Waterbury, CT 06702. 203-753-0381.)

Another useful address is the Waterbury Convention & Visitors Bureau, City Hall, Grand Street, Waterbury, CT 06702, for a map of the city and highlights of places to see.

If you decide to take the second train back to New York, you have five hours fully to explore the town and to have a meal. The Mattatuck Museum puts out a pamphlet, giving a route diagram and short history of each house and its owners, that will take you on a good walking tour lasting about two hours from Main Street. The tour passes most of the city's finest houses built for the rich Waterburian industrialists between the middle of the nineteenth century and the first decades of the twentieth. With advance notice, the Mattatuck Museum will conduct the walk.

During the heyday of the brass, clock, and button business, owners not only chose Gothic but Italian Villa, Queen Anne, Georgian, and Greek Revival styles, all of which are visible in the compact neighborhood on the tour. Money was no object to these industrialists, and good taste often took second place. Some residences have been relocated, such as the 1845 Leavenworth House, which was moved from a lot facing the Green to another part of the family land on Park Place. The Benedict-Miller House, completed in 1879 at 32 Hillside Avenue, is an extravagant and eclectic combination of Stick-style wooden siding, bricks, fish scale shingles, and fanciful spindles.

For lunch consisting of something more than a coffee shop meal, there are a half-dozen restaurants on or near the Green. A recommended restaurant is Dreschers, on Leavenworth Street near the back door to the Mattatuck Museum.

ESSEX
A Weekend at the Griswold Inn

The Griswold Inn, Essex, CT 06426. (203) 767-0991.

For a serene weekend in one of the oldest inns in America, centrally located in a nearly perfect river town, you can do no better than the Griswold Inn in Essex, Connecticut. A veritable museum of maritime art and memorabilia, the Griswold offers good American seafood, comfortable rooms, and nightly musical entertainment.

During your escape you may wish to do little more than venture down to the little park and maritime museum where the town meets the Connecticut River, stroll along the eighteenth- and nineteenth-century residential streets, and browse through the numerous antique stores.

Those in search of more activity may walk to the edge of town for a delightful half-day excursion combining a ride on a steam-hauled railroad with a cruise up the Connecticut as far as East Haddam.

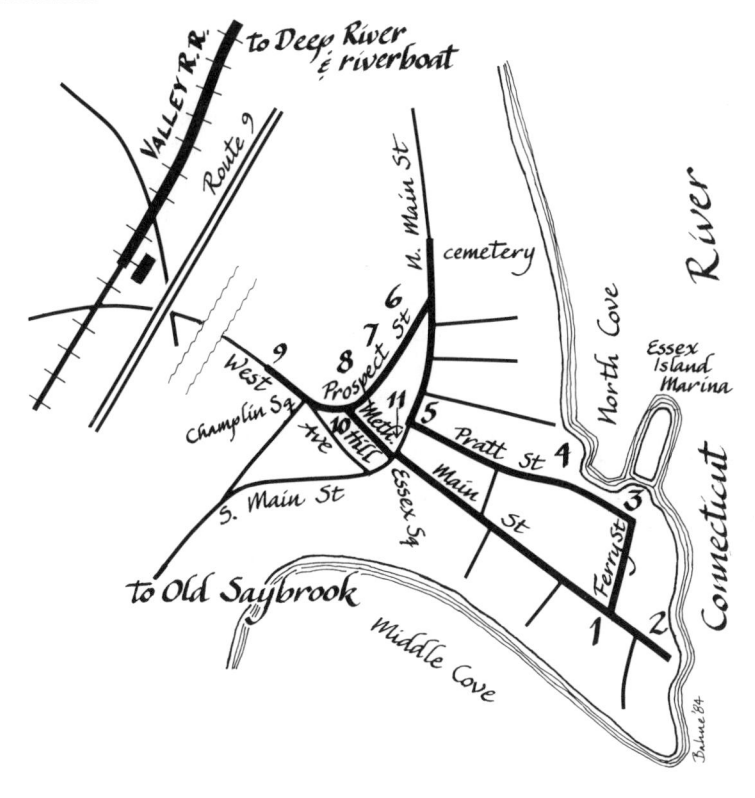

Essex

1. Griswold Inn
2. River Museum & Steamboat Dock
3. Dauntless Yard
4. The Gull Restaurant
5. Bookstore
6. Baptist Church
7. Catholic Church
8. Historical Society
9. Pratt House & Smithy
10. Congregational Church
11. Drugstore

Off-season is perhaps preferable to the summer months, when hordes of people descend on Essex to sample its many pleasures.

Getting There and Back: From New York's Penn Station, four Amtrak trains a day serve the nearby station of Old Saybrook, four miles from Essex. The Griswold Inn will make arrangements for a taxi transfer. The round-trip excursion train fare is $29.50, and the taxi costs $6.50 each way.

For a detailed description of the scenic two-hour fifteen-minute train ride up the Connecticut coast, see "Shore Line Rail Route Guide."

Upon stepping off the train at the Old Saybrook Depot, there is an immediate feeling of being transported back into the last century. The wooden country station, built in 1873, sits peacefully alongside a straight stretch of track and faces a little spur line that runs north to the tourist-oriented Valley Railroad. Inside the high-ceilinged waiting room with its comfortable wooden benches, only present-day Amtrak posters intrude on the nineteenth-century atmosphere.

In about ten minutes after leaving Old Saybrook, the taxi begins the winding approach to Essex, a neatly arranged town of eighteenth-century Colonial and Federal houses and nineteenth-century Victorians nestled in an abundance of trees on a gentle slope leading down to the river.

The Griswold Inn, a three-story white frame building with a covered front porch, sits on Main Street to the south of the commercial heart of Essex, only a five-minute walk from the Connecticut River.

The oldest portion of the twenty-room inn dates from 1776—and yet in more than two hundred years of receiving guests the Griswold has had only five owners. Today's innkeeper, in charge since 1972, is William Winterer, who also owns restaurants in Middletown and Saybrook Point.

In the main house, the annex, and the newly redecorated Hayden House across the narrow side lane, the variety of accommodation spread over two floors ranges from comfortable double- and twin-bedded rooms to more elaborate two-room suites, furnished with an eclectic variety of period American furniture and some good antiques. Some rooms, including the suites, have working fireplaces, and the lounge makes for a cozy retreat after a day of sightseeing. All the rooms are air-conditioned, and, by Mr. Winterer's choice, none have televisions or phones.

As the walls are thin, you may hear your nearest neighbors; and be sure to ask for a room that is *not* located above the Tap Room, where the late-night entertainment can keep you awake. For the quietest rooms, ask for one of the three newly completed one-room suites in the early nineteenth-century Hayden House. The Hayden House has two lounges on its ground floor which are also open to the guests staying in the main building and annex.

Rooms, with continental breakfast, are $52 for a double, with suites from $56 to $75. Reservations for summer weekends are hard to come by, as Essex then is particularly crowded with day as well as overnight tourists. The fall, winter, and spring seasons are heartily recommended for those in search of peace and quiet.

On the ground floor behind the reception desk, the Tap Room, a handsome bar, features live musical entertainment every night, ranging from jazz and Dixieland piano to sea chanties, concerts, and opera, drawing both local residents and visitors. In one corner an antique popcorn machine dispenses the hot buttered version.

The four dining rooms all have a particular historic theme, making each a veritable museum of Americana. The Steamboat Room is modeled after the dining room of one of the New York to Hartford night sidewheelers that once regularly called at Essex. Decorative artifacts include ships' bells, binnacles, and clocks, lights from the masthead and pilot house, steamboat advertisements, and the name boards of well-known yachts. The Library, once the original parlor for the inn, is a book-lined dining room with a fireplace and walls covered with a remarkable collection of sixteen paintings by Antonio Jacobsen, one of this country's most important turn-of-the-century marine artists. In the Gun Room, nearly sixty firearms show the development of the rifle and hand gun beginning with the fifteenth century. The Covered Bridge, built from the remains of just such a structure, has its walls and sloping ceiling covered with more than a hundred paintings, prints, and photographs of mostly American sidewheel steamboats and transatlantic liners. Many of the Hudson River and Long Island Sound steamers are original Currier & Ives prints. You need not be bashful about inspecting these at close hand, even when there are diners present, as the regulars are used to the curious leaning over their tables. The entire collection is the envy of many maritime museums.

Breakfast at the Griswold Inn is normally a continental buffet affair, served in the Library—along with *The New York Times*, if you want to remain connected with the outside world. On Sundays, however, the Griswold's chef outdoes himself with an elaborate hunt breakfast served from 11:30 a.m. to 2:30 p.m. The buffet may include any of the following foods: scrambled eggs and grits, ham, bacon and sausage, chicken livers, lamb kidneys, smelts or sea perch, creamed chipped beef, home fried potatoes, and hot cornbread. To enjoy this weekly event to the utmost, get up early and eat something light, or sleep late and let the hunt breakfast be your first meal.

Lunch can be a sandwich, fresh fish, or the Griswold's own sausages, made from a two hundred-year-old recipe. For a change of pace, some guests will want to eat lunch out.

The food at dinner is unfussy and thoroughly American, featuring such recommended entrées as barbecued ribs ($12.95), fried or sautéed soft shell crabs in season ($13.95), broiled salmon ($13.25), sixteen-ounce New York strip steak ($14.95), and a nest of Canadian quail ($13.95). All entrées come with salad and vegetables. Wines are reasonably priced, beginning at $4 to $5 for a half bottle and $9 for a full one. For beer drinkers, John Courage Ale is an excellent choice. The soups change daily, and for one of the richest and best-tasting desserts try the Original Mudslide Pie, a hefty concoction of coffee and chocolate ice cream, with chocolate pieces, almonds, marshmallow, and fudge topping.

After a full dinner you might consider taking a walk along a now-peaceful Main Street before retiring to bed.

For the active sightseer, a complete day of touring might begin with a short walk to the Steamboat Dock at the foot of Main Street, where the town fronts on the broad expanse of the Connecticut River. As early as 1656 there was a wharf established here, beginning a long era that saw Essex become a major trading port and shipbuilding center.

The handsome three-story dock building dates from the 1860s, and once served as the landing for night steamers between New York and Connecticut River towns as far north as Hartford.

Inside the former terminal, the Connecticut River Steamboat Dock Foundation has established its River Museum, with a growing collection of paintings, models, and artifacts relating to Connecticut River maritime history. One of the featured exhibits is this country's first submarine, the *American Turtle*, built in 1774, and used, without much success, against the British during the Revolutionary War. On the top floor, a cargo hoist raised freight from the ground-floor unloading area to the second and third floors. Barrels and sacks are stacked about to suggest the produce shipped out from the Connecticut Valley. It is appropriate that one of the detailed ship models should be the sidewheeler *City of Hartford*, in 1931 the last steamer to call at this very building. Some of the maritime artworks belong to William Winterer, owner of the Griswold Inn. Foundation volunteers can give you more information about the changing special exhibits.

Hours for the Connecticut River Fondation, P.O. Box 261, Essex, CT 06426, (203) 767-8269, are Tuesday through Sunday 10 a.m.–5 p.m. from April 1 to December 31. Admission is adults $1.50, seniors over 65 $1, children under 16 50 cents.

The walking tour continues back up Main Street, then turns right on Ferry Street and leads down to the Essex Boat Works, where yachts are built, repaired, and stored. For a closer look at the large fleet of private sailing and motor yachts that reside or call here during the summer season, take the free motor launch over to the Essex Island Marina. A simple restaurant opposite North Cove and the island marina is the Gull, serving typical American and seafood fare but with particularly good views of the boatyard activity through the large front windows.

Walk up Pratt Street past attractive homes to North Main, which leads into the village's compact commercial center. The Clipper Ship Bookshop just right on North Main offers an excellent selection of nautical books, area guidebooks, local pamphlets, and a large second floor of used books. Most of the antique stores are located around Essex Square and along Main Street leading back to the Griswold Inn. Unless you have a lot of money or are a serious collector, you will find most of the wares very expensive. However, just looking is always free.

Continue past the bookstore for three short blocks to the junction with Prospect Street. On the right is Riverview Cemetery, where many early Essex families, such as the Pratts and Haydens, and sea captains are buried. Walking up Prospect Street takes you past the 1845 Egyptian Revival Baptist Church, the Roman Catholic Church, formerly a dormitory for the Hill Academy, a boarding school, and now the 1832 Essex Historical Society Building. You may find that the walk past these buildings is sufficient, and there is no need to go inside.

If you wish to return to the Griswold Inn, walk down Methodist Hill to Essex Square and Main Street.

For a full day away that includes the Valley Railroad and a boat ride, follow Prospect Street as it bears right to meet West Avenue. A couple of Essex's very oldest sections are located on the right side of the street. The Pratt Smithy, with basement and forge dating from 1678, once forged the village's household, shipbuilding, and horseshoe ironwork. More recently, the village smithy custom-made replacements for buildings under restoration and yachting hardware. The Pratt House, with the middle section dating from about 1701 and the front portion from 1732–34, belonged to the Pratt family, who ran the nearby forge. The house, now a museum with eighteenth-century furnishings and artifacts, is open in the summer, and is owned by the Society for the Preservation of New England Antiquities.

West Avenue leads away from town to elevated Route 9. Turn right under the highway, using the green and white bike route signs as a guide. The Valley Railroad Depot is just up the grade on the left. The total distance from the Griswold Inn by the most direct route is one and one-third miles, a good half-hour walk along pleasant streets.

The Valley Railroad, built to parallel the Connecticut River from Old Saybrook to Hartford, egan operating in 1871, and by 1933 the line had closed down its passenger services. Freight traffic ceased in the 1960s, and the railroad was abandoned. Then, in 1971, the Valley Railroad re-opened as a short line tourist hauler running in conjunction with a scenic river trip.

The ticket office also serves as a gift shop of railroad memorabilia, and nearby in a stationary grill car you can have a light lunch of hot dogs, hamburgers, or sandwiches while waiting for the next train. (The best plan probably would be to eat in Essex before coming out here, however.)

Departures vary from as many as six a day on summer weekends, five on weekdays, to more reduced schedules in the late spring and early fall and weekends only in December. School groups and other large parties sometimes take over the early departures. It is a good idea to call before you make the trip out.

The round-trip train ride takes only fifty-five minutes, but most people opt for the combination train and boat package lasting two hours ten minutes. Train and cruise fare is, for adults $7.95, children 3–11 $5, parlor car extra fare $1.50. (The Valley Railroad, Essex, CT 06426. 203-767-0103.)

The historic equipment owned by the Valley Railroad comes from many different railroads, and includes several steam locomotives, open-window coaches with cane seats, and the parlor car "Wallingford," with plush red lounge chairs and stained glass partitions. On most of the regular trips, the parlor attendant will serve soft drinks, wine, and beer.

The line heads north through deep woods, with the train whistle sounding the alarm at grade crossings, and in spots passes close to the Connecticut River. About five miles from Essex, the train backs down to the Deep River landing, where passengers make a direct connection for a delightful water trip up the unspoiled Connecticut River. The sites mentioned below are those that can be seen from the excursion; they cannot be reached without a car.

Within fifteen minutes the boat crosses the path of the Chester-Hadlyme Ferry, a cross-river operation that dates to 1769, and since 1947 has been operated by the State of Connecticut. Today, the ferryboat *Selden III* takes cars for seventy-five cents and passengers for twenty-five cents. Up the hill beyond the ferry landing stands Gillette Castle, an eccentric fortress home built in 1913 by William Gillette, an American stage actor who made the role of Sherlock Holmes so famous.

Further up the river at East Haddam, the Goodspeed Opera House dominates the right bank. It is fully restored to its 1876 condition and functions in the summer as a music theater.

At this point the boat heads back to the landing and the train to Essex. Walk to the Griswold Inn the way you came, following West Avenue into Essex Square and then down Main Street.

If you are staying at the Griswold Inn for the weekend, you may wish to tour the town of Essex one day and save the Valley Railroad for the next.

ISLAND DESTINATIONS FROM NEW LONDON
Block Island, Fishers Island & Orient Point

If you love islands and the ferries that take you there, consider riding up the scenic Connecticut shoreline on an Amtrak train and boarding a boat for a weekend on Block Island, or for a short round-trip voyage across Long Island Sound to Fishers Island or Orient Point. When there is time to kill between the train and the ferry, New London offers an interesting walking tour beginning right outside the historic railroad station.

Block Island is a very special place of natural beauty, with winding paths along high cliffs, bird watching sanctuaries, fine sandy beaches, and a variety of comfortable accommodations in Victorian-era hotels and inns. Bike riders will find the eleven-square-mile island ideal for touring.

If you simply like to be out on the water, the half-day ferry trip to nearby Fishers Island or further afield to Orient Point on the tip of Long Island's North Fork will satisfy your maritime yearnings. These latter two suggestions might appeal to those who are making an extended stay in Mystic, a mere fifteen minutes by train from the ferry docks in New London.

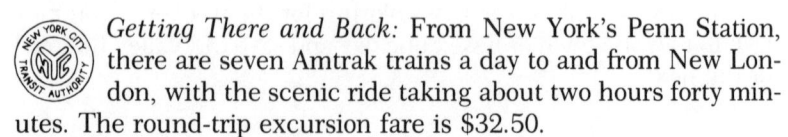

Getting There and Back: From New York's Penn Station, there are seven Amtrak trains a day to and from New London, with the scenic ride taking about two hours forty minutes. The round-trip excursion fare is $32.50.

Between Mystic and New London, there are three trains a day taking only fifteen minutes, and the round-trip excursion fare is $6.50.

For a description of the coastal trip, see "Shore Line Rail Route Guide."

New London

The riverside city located on the Thames (rhymes with James) grew up with the whaling industry and other maritime pursuits to become one of the most important ports on the New England coast.

Today, the Coast Guard, Navy, and shipyards keep the area, which includes Groton, humming to a somewhat different tune. Downtown, the city is attempting, with some success, to retain its architectural heritage and commercial core.

The historic district is anchored by the elegant, three-story red brick 1887-built H.H. Richardson railroad station, where you will arrive. Located on a curve along the riverfront, New London's station is an unusual intermodal transportation hub for Amtrak's Northeast Corridor trains, Greyhound buses, local transit operations, and ferryboat services to Fishers Island, Orient Point, and Block Island. No other city in this country can boast so many different means of transportation radiating from the same place.

The landmark building itself, incredible as it may seem, was once threatened with demolition in the 1960s. Instead, a well-organized community effort saved the structure, restored the exterior and interior, and modernized the station platforms and canopy. The successful project set a precedent for other cities, and, as a result, nearly every station of historic value on the Boston-Washington rail line has also undergone or is slated for restoration.

Whether seen from the city side across the small park or from the river as you approach by ferry, the railroad station presents an equally handsome facade of symmetrically balanced windows of varying shapes and sizes and two pairs of eyelid dormers protruding from a gracefully angled roof.

The arrival of the Shore Line train is an important event that occurs every hour of the day. The distant whistle announces the train's approach, then the crossing gates are lowered, bells clatter, and red lights flash. The town comes to a standstill for a few moments as the train, blocking the main street, lets off and takes on its passengers. There is a flurry of activity as people head off to cars, buses, and boats. The conductor gives the high sign for the all aboard, the engineer signals back with a hoot of the horn, and the silver train glides out of town. New London's traffic then again moves freely back and forth across the tracks.

In the station's basement are recruiting offices for the Army, Marines, Navy, and the Air Force, and a newsstand and snack bar. Walking tour maps and service guides may be obtained either at the station or at the kiosk on the City Pier.

If you have about an hour, the following route will take you past many of New London's most historic buildings. To visit some of the

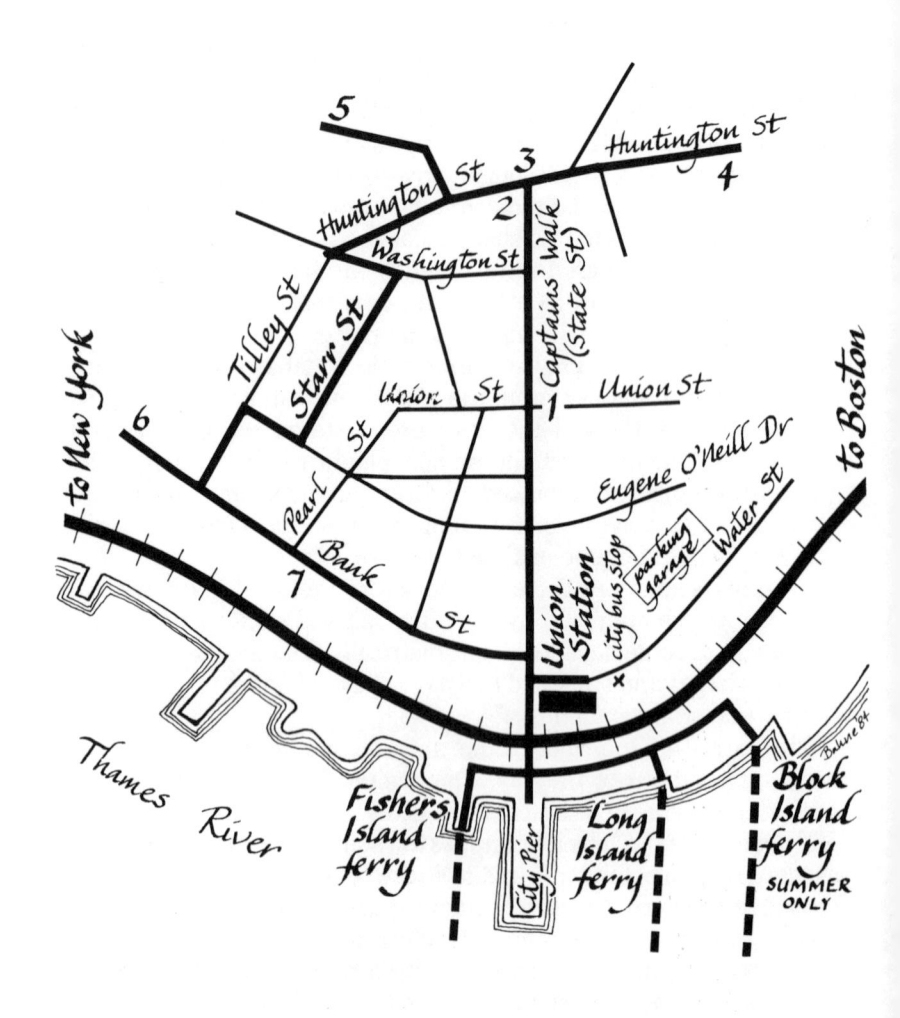

New London

1. Nathan Hale School
2. Public Library
3. State Court House
4. Whale Oil Row
5. Hempsted House
6. Shaw Mansion
7. Custom House

interiors, allow another hour, at least. Leave the railroad station via Captain's Walk, which begins at the City Pier, crosses the tracks, and heads uphill into the business district. Within a block the street becomes a pedestrian mall, one of the first attempts thus to turn around a declining downtown shopping area. A few empty storefronts mar what is otherwise an appealing idea. The 1774 Nathan Hale School on the right and the Public Library on the left, where the Captain's Walk meets Huntington Street, are the most noteworthy buildings. The 1784 State Court House is directly ahead.

Turn right on Huntington Street and walk one and one-half blocks to Whale Oil Row, the site for a series of nineteenth-century Greek Revival-style houses. Number 3 is the Tale of a Whale Museum, a former whaling captain's house, with a whaling memorabilia collection, and Number 1 is the Southeastern Connecticut Chamber of Commerce, for tourist information. Telephone here is (203) 739-0208.

Double back on Huntington past the Court House to Jay Street (also U.S. Route 1A) and turn right for the 1678 Joshua Hempsted House, one of the few surviving seventeenth-century dwellings in Connecticut, and the oldest house still standing in New London. The land on which the wooden frame house stands is part of a six-acre land grant that the Hempsted family, one of the founders of New London, received in 1645. The 1678 portion was added to in 1728 and lived in by family descendents until 1937. A detailed diary, dating from 1711, aided the restoration, and a copy of this may be inspected inside, along with many of the Hempsted's original furnishings.

On the same property stands the Nathaniel Hempsted (Huguenot) House built in 1759. The construction is unusual for this area because the building material is granite cut into two-foot thick blocks, crafted by exiled French Protestants or Huguenots from Nova Scotia. There are now only two granite houses left in the state, this one and the nearby Shaw Mansion seen later in the tour.

Inside there are seven rooms furnished with eighteenth-century wooden cooking and eating utensils, pewter ware, ceramics, wrought iron household items, and furniture. Both houses, on the National Register of Historic Places, may be visited, with a small admission charge, from May 15 to October 15, 1–5 p.m. For further information, write the Antiquarian and Landmark Society, Inc., 394 Main Street, Hartford, CT 06103. (203) 274-8996.

Return to Huntington Street, turn right, then first left on Washington Street, and first right on Starr Street for two splendid rows of fully restored and utterly charming early and late nineteenth-century wooden houses. These come in two sizes, with the larger and more elaborate group at the top end of the street. The biggest houses have three stories, are slightly raised above the sidewalk with three front steps, and a few have small front first- and second-story porches. Further down the street toward the river, the smaller and plainer houses are virtual carbon copies of each other, with semi-circular attic windows, and are framed with engaged pilasters and have ornately carved little roofs over the front doors. All the Starr Street houses are privately owned and occupied, so you will have to enjoy them from the outside.

At the end of Starr Street, turn right then first left on Tilley Street, then first right on Bank Street for the granite Shaw Mansion, similar in construction to the Huguenot House. Head back along Bank Street toward the center of town, passing the impressive New London Custom House facing out to the river. Bank Street leads back to Captain's Walk.

Two Ferry Rides: to Fishers Island & Orient Point

These two ferry trips are breezy outings for those who love being out on the water, and are probably less important for their destinations, which for most people would have limited appeal. Pick a sunny day to enjoy the passing scene and to meet your fellow passengers at the railing.

The shortest ferry ride from New London is the forty-minute trip each way to Fishers Island, a tightly controlled vacation colony of the very rich with a year-round population of 250 climbing to two thousand in mid-summer. Small ferries leave year-round with two to ten sailings a day, depending on the season. The fare is $3.50 each way payable on board. Children under twelve are half fare. (Fishers Island Ferry District, Box H, Fishers Island, NY 06390. Main office 516-788-7463. New London Terminal 203-442-0165.)

The *Munnatawket* is the best ferry, with a large cabin, open forward deck, and narrow promenade running completely around the boat. The smaller *Olinda* is less comfortable for the foot passenger; its sailings are indicated in red on the schedules. Nearly all the supplies that the island requires move from the mainland on the ferry, so the loading can be quite interesting, with the freight often consisting of building materials, food, and cars towing boats on trailers.

The route follows the Thames out into Long Island Sound past the monumental New London Lighthouse, an historic square structure built on a rock.

At Fishers Island, the older buildings to the right of the landing once belonged to the Coast Guard, and they are slated for restoration. The layover between trips may be less than a half-hour, depending on the traffic.

The island is nine by one and one-half miles, and the center of town, such as it is, with a few stores and a small hotel, is about a twenty-minute walk from the ferry. But unless you fancy huge houses seen only through the trees, it is best simply to go for the boat ride.

Year-round service is provided for passengers and vehicles from New London to Orient Point, on the very tip of the North Fork of Long Island. There are from three to twelve sailings a day, depending on the season, with the crossing taking about one and one-half hours, one way.

The ferries are much larger than the Fishers Island boats, and vary from spartan open-deck types to the much more comfortable *Cape Henelopen*. For the round-trip ferry ride, the fare is $9 for adults and $4.50 for children under twelve. The non-landing ride takes just over three hours. The route leaves New London via the Thames and crosses Long Island Sound, passing Fishers Island to port and Plum Island to starboard before rounding Orient Point to land. (Cross Sound Ferry Service, Inc., Box 33, New London, CT 06320. Main office 203-443-7394.)

Block Island

Once a day at 10 a.m. (with an extra trip at 7:15 p.m. on Fridays) from about June 9 to September 9, a passenger ferry, with limited space for cars, leaves from near the railroad station in New London for Block Island. For the morning sailing, check the very latest Amtrak schedules to make sure that the first train from New York connects with the boat.

Upon leaving New London on a three-hour crossing, the ferry sets a course along the Connecticut coast, then passes between

Fishers Island and Watch Hill, a famous old Rhode Island resort, and rounds Block Island's now-abandoned granite North Point lighthouse (1867), docking in Old Harbor.

The return trip leaves daily at 4 p.m. with an extra Saturday sailing at 6 a.m., and there are good train connections into New York. For those making the same-day round trip, allowing about three hours ashore, the fare is $10 for adults and $7 for children. If you are staying over, then the round-trip fare is $18 for adults and $12 for children. (Interstate Navigation Company, Box 482, New London, CT 06320. Main office 203-442-7891.)

A special note: if the first train from New York does not connect with the morning sailing from New London, you may take the train to Kingston, Rhode Island. From there it is a ten-mile, $12 taxi ride to the State Pier, Point Judith (Galilee), Rhode Island. The same company runs up to eight trips a day to Block Island with a sailing time of one hour fifteen minutes. Unlike the New London route, this ferry runs year-round, being the island's principal link with the mainland.

The rambling three-story Spring House, built in 1852, is the largest and oldest hotel on the island, drawing a fiercely loyal clientele that comes back year after year. Its Victorian atmosphere and special setting, strategically positioned atop a hill overlooking the Atlantic Ocean and a freshwater pond, provides for a soothing weekend visit.

From a wooden rocking chair on the veranda, you can watch the sailboats darting around Old Harbor and the slow-motion sight of bicyclers moving along the island's country lanes. In the evening, many of the guests take their drinks from the hotel bar out to the lawn chairs to catch the setting sun.

Inside, most visitors will find the accommodations a spartan example of mid-nineteenth-century design, with all-wood furniture and comfortable beds. Light sleepers may be bothered by noise coming through the thin walls from the adjoining rooms.

Most of the rooms come without private facilities, although there is a washbasin in one corner. Choose a quiet southward-facing room for a rolling view of hillsides dotted with white clapboard houses and swept at night by the powerful beam of the island's lighthouse, visible for thirty-five miles at sea.

The dining room is most cheerful in the morning, but the large space and bright lighting does not offer much intimacy at dinner. Breakfasts are always good, and the food at dinner ranges from well-prepared meats and routine desserts to surprisingly poor seafood. It is best to order before 7:30 to insure that your dinner choice is still available. Lunch is not served at the Spring House.

While you can tour the island by rented bicycle or moped during the boat's layover, consider spending a night or two here to get the true feel of the place. After the last boat has left for the day, you will find that Block Island has a quiet charm and simplicity that make it a favorite place to explore for those looking to shun the frenzied and trendy atmosphere of Martha's Vineyard and Nantucket at the height of the season. First settled in 1661, the island and town of New Shoreham have a year-round population of only five hundred.

All the boats from New London, Point Judith, and Providence now arrive at Old Harbor, a settlement of largely Victorian architecture on the National Register of Historic Places. Some of the most notable structures are the National and Surf Hotels and the even older, rambling Spring House impressively set atop a hill overlooking the town.

By far the best way to spend your time is to rent a bicycle at one of the five Old Harbor locations and head out of town on a two-and-one-half-mile ride clockwise around the island. The noisy mopeds are the bone of contention on Block Island, and you will have to check on their availability.

The first landmark approached is the massive brick Southeast Lighthouse built in 1874 and set on a bluff 150 feet above the sea, boasting the highest beam in New England. Going to the edge of the clay cliffs here is not unlike being on the bridge of a ship. Cargo vessels and tankers making passages along the coast file by only about two miles distant. Many people liken the scenery and surf to those of the northern California coast. Just to the south, the Mohegan Bluffs rise to a height of two hundred feet above the rocky shoreline.

The southern half of the island consists of rolling moors of bayberry and rugosa roses and continuous Atlantic Ocean views. The winding road passes the shingled Vail House, freshwater ponds, and the sunken woods at Rodman's Hollow, a protected cleft in the island's surface that forms part of the Block Island Conservancy. In the fall, the Audubon Society offers walking tours in this wild area to watch the migrating birds flocking here to rest and feed on their way south.

Most of the roads that lead down to the west shoreline at places like Dorry's and Grace's Cove are not paved, but for those who like frequent sea views they can still be negotiated by bicycle.

A favorite viewing point for watching the sailboats come and go is the former Coast Guard station alongside the cut made for the entrance into New Harbor.

Beach addicts will find the State Beach, about a mile's walk from the Old Harbor and most of the hotels, to be a good and generally uncrowded one. There is a pavilion for changing and a snack bar for lunch.

You will find that Block Island has very little night life, and most people who come to stay for a few days do so for the peaceful nature of the place.

MYSTIC

Mystic Seaport Museum, Mystic, CT 06355 (203) 572-0711. Open every day except Christmas. May–October 9 a.m.–5 p.m., November–April 9 a.m.–4 p.m. Admission adults $8.50; children 5–15 $4.25.

Mystic, Connecticut, is best known for its nineteenth-century Seaport Museum, an elaborate restoration dedicated to the town's proud shipbuilding past. Within the compound are more than three hundred ships and small craft ranging from the former whaler *Charles W. Morgan* to tiny catboats and canoes. You can watch demonstrations of ship model repair, barrel making, and lifesaving at sea. In the summer there are outdoor sea chanty programs and musical concerts. During a cruise on the 1908 steamboat *Sabino*, watch the coal stoker feed the boilers and the tall stack belch black smoke into the sky on the boat's way downriver.

Take a walk through the town's historic district to see the way Mystic's sea captains used to live. Visit Mystic Aquarium for the hourly dolphin shows, and shop for clothes and gifts in charming Olde Mistick Village, an effective recreation of an eighteenth-century small-town setting.

For the more adventurous, run away to sea on a windjammer cruise for an overnight or even longer sail into Long Island sound.

The 135-mile ride up the Shore Line by Amtrak train, with superb views of the Sound and coastal resorts, is both relaxing and scenic. Then for a couple of nights choose one of the three places conveniently located close to the railroad station and to most of Mystic's popular attractions.

Getting There and Back: Three Amtrak trains spread evenly throughout the day serve Mystic from Penn Station, New York in just under three hours. For one night away, consider taking the morning train up on a Saturday and returning Sunday evening. Be sure to sit on the right-hand side on the way up, and on the left-hand side on the way back to catch what you missed the first time. Round-trip excursion fare is $33. For a detailed description of the trip, see "Shore Line Rail Route Guide."

Stepping off the train from New York, Mystic Depot offers a warm welcome. The historic station, dating from 1905, served as the model for Lionel's Lionelville Station. Amtrak and local community organizations have combined their efforts to restore the two-tone wooden structure set on a brick foundation and to improve the platforms and provide attractive plantings. During the day, when the station is open, you can get Amtrak train schedules here (but not tickets). Ask about tourist information, and patronize the gift shop and art gallery, all run by friendly people.

The three recommended places to stay in Mystic will provide a free transfer on request. Visitors with a minimum amount of hand luggage, though, can walk to any of the hotels.

The Whaler's Inn (20 East Main Street, Mystic, CT 06355, 203-536-1506 or toll free 800-243-2588) is located three-tenths of a mile from the station. To walk, head toward the white Congregational Church, then turn left at the monument on East Main Street for two more blocks. The Inn is on your left just before the Mystic River Bridge.

The Whaler's Inn, occupying a site used for a hotel since 1861, offers the best rates in town and a convenient central location for reaching most of Mystic's attractions on foot.

For the lowest, bargain-rate rooms, book into the main three-story hotel building, a non-descript sort of place with small, very plain air-conditioned units spread over the second and third floors. The rooms at the back are much quieter than those overlooking the busy

168   *Connecticut and Rhode Island*

street. If you are looking for more than a cheap rate, the two-story motel section, completed in 1978–1979 and surrounding the parking lot at the rear of the hotel, offers larger and more cheerfully decorated air-conditioned sleeping accommodations.

There are three levels of rates depending on the season, plus two-night room-only packages that include tickets to the Mystic Seaport Museum and the Mystic Marinelife Aquarium; bed and breakfast

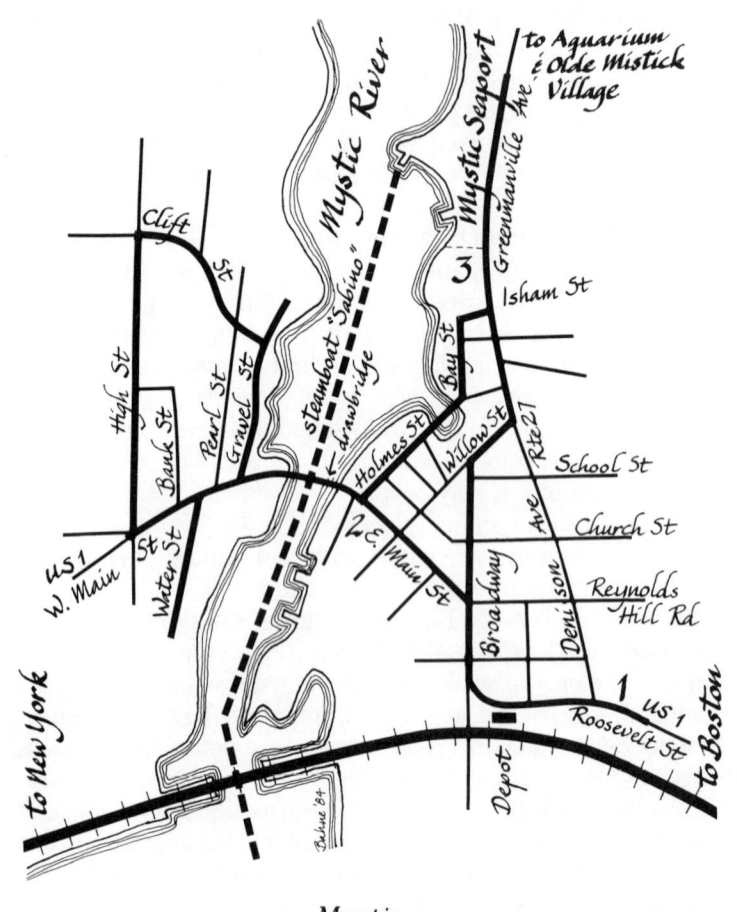

Mystic

1. Inn at Mystic
2. Whaler's Inn
3. 1833 House

rates with admissions to the town's two main attractions; and a rate including tickets to the very special Christmas Lantern Light Tour in December. One-night rates, depending on location and season, range from $38 to $85 double occupancy. Also, phone Amtrak for their Whaler's Inn packages.

The Whaler's Inn's simple family restaurant, the Binnacle, is best for breakfast, and the Flying Bridge, an outdoor patio dining area is a cheap choice for lunch. Here you can watch the hourly opening and closing, punctuated by a steam whistle, of the 1924-built bascule (counterbalance) drawbridge and the fleet of boats passing through. Seafood of the most ordinary type is offered here—fish and chips, shrimp in a basket, codfish cakes, and crab casserole, all for under $6.

The hotel's registration desk, located in the back of the gift shop, has helpful printed information and a staff that is genuinely happy to answer your questions and even give you a lift somewhere if necessary.

The compact commercial center of Mystic lies just across the drawbridge from the Whaler's Inn. For dinner and a good view, try the Steamboat Cafe. Turn left once across the drawbridge and follow the river walk for a couple hundred feet to the entrance. The second-floor bar and dining room overlooks the Mystic River and features good fresh fish, broiled lobster, and soft shell crabs (in season) at moderate prices. As the restaurant is very popular a good part of the year, it is best to make reservations. (203) 536-1975.

If you would prefer to stay in a bed and breakfast establishment at low cost and offering no frills, the 1833 House (33 Greenmanville Avenue, Mystic, CT 06355, 203-572-0633) offers four basic rooms with private or shared bath. The location is a mixed blessing as, while it is conveniently near the Mystic Seaport Museum, the house fronts on Greenmanville Street, the heavily used artery linking downtown Mystic with many of its attractions and the Connecticut Turnpike. From the railroad station, it's a three-quarter-mile walk first in the direction of the white-steepled Congregational Church, then past it along Broadway to the end, right on Willow Street and left on Denison Avenue, which turns into Greenmanville Avenue. The 1833 House appears on the left. With advance notice or a phone call from the station when you arrive, the owner will pick you up.

Singles with shared bath are $22; doubles with shared bath $40; doubles with private bath $44. A family unit of two rooms with bath is $60 for four persons.

Not to be missed is a late afternoon stroll through the town's private residential neighborhood, where many of the most impressive early- to mid-nineteenth-century houses belonged to Mystic's native sea captains.

The one-hour walking tour begins by crossing the drawbridge and turning right along Gravel Street running parallel to the Mystic River. Greek and Gothic Revival styles predominate in these handsome residences that once faced a row of shipyards on the opposite shore. All historic buildings have wooden plaques for identification, and the Chamber of Commerce booklet is a very helpful guide.

On Gravel Lane, make special note of No. 15, an 1835-built Greek Revival house which had some Italian Villa-style features added later. The first owner was a cabinetmaker who made coffins in his basement, and he then sold it in 1847 to a clipper ship captain. Just beyond Clift Street, No. 27, with leaded glass sidelights on either side of the handsome front door, was built in 1834, and a small building at the rear once served as a station on the underground railroad for runaway slaves from the South. No. 29, built in grand Greek Revival style in 1837, was once owned by Captain Edward L. Beach, author of the books *Run Silent, Run Deep* and *Submarine!*.

Heading away from the river up Clift Street, several of the houses you'll see were once owned by the prominent Clift family. No. 100, built in 1854 by Captain Isaac Gates, is a large Greek Revival house noted for its "five over four and a door" style, meaning five windows on the second floor and pairs of two windows on either side of the central front door.

At the top of Clift Street, turn left on High Street. At the corner of High Street and Academy Lane stands an 1842 Victorian house owned by the Clift family. Inside, a landing on the stairs between the first and second floors is large enough once to have held a chamber orchestra (the then-owner, Caroline Townsend Clift, was a lover of music).

Among the fancier houses are simpler and earlier ones built in Cape Cod style, some of them dating back to the second decade of the nineteenth century. High Street leads into West Main Street, Route 1, where you might note the imposing 1861-built Union Baptist Church.

Mystic Seaport, the chief attraction, is an easy and pleasant half-mile walk from the Whaler's Inn. Follow Holmes Street, beginning just opposite the hotel's patio restaurant, along the river's edge to

Bay Street, and turn left, continuing two blocks to the end, where you turn right on Isham Street. At this point, you are within inches of the museum, which is on the opposite side of the fence. Go one block more, then turn left on Greenmanville Avenue where you'll see the museum entrance and store just on the left.

The Seaport Store, just outside the ticket kiosk, has an excellent bookstore, with a good range of nautical and New England titles, and an art gallery on the second floor, as well as a good gift shop on the ground floor. Buy the $1 guide here for a full description of each vessel and exhibit.

Mystic Seaport's activities are many and varied, and you may want to write ahead for a calendar of events to help plan your trip. In the winter there are regular introductory and advanced evening classes to learn the basics of blacksmithing and woodcarving. In June, a full weekend is set aside for a sea music festival that takes place on the decks of the training ship *Joseph Conrad* and at the Village Green, where the audience gathers around on the grass. The July antique and classic boat rendezvous draws dozens of pre-1940 sailing yawls, sloops, schooners, and wooden cabin cruisers. In the fall, the annual schooner race begins at Mystic with the entrants on view at the seaport museum.

There is enough to see and do within the grounds to spend the better part of a day. For a fast food lunch, be prepared to line up for very ordinary food at the Galley. Or, for a more substantial and better meal, try the outdoor or inside dining facilities at the Seaman's Inne. Stick to the basic entrées.

Using the map provided at the entrance, begin the tour by going left to the Preservation Shipyard, an active facility that does regular overhauls of the museum's ship collection as well as work on outsiders' boats. Retracing your steps, you next pass the dock for the little excursion boat *Sabino*, built in 1908 and the sole remaining coal-fired steamboat in this country. Take a half-hour trip on the Mystic River for $2 (children $1.25), or, better still, wait until the end of the day for the one and one-half-hour trip for $4.50 (children $3), or for the evening music cruises at higher rates depending on the program. No museum admission is charged for the evening trips, and the *Sabino*'s season extends from the end of May to mid-October.

The longer evening trips head downriver through the raised highway and railroad drawbridges and past yacht marinas and riverside restaurants to Long Island Sound and back. Open to view is the throbbing engine room, where you can watch the stoker shovel coal into the boiler, a rare treat in these days of oil-fired diesel engines.

The museum's featured vessels where boarding and inspection are permitted include the *Joseph Conrad*, a permanently moored training ship built in 1882. Visiting school groups may use her as a dorm during the educational sessions. The best known of the museum's vessels is the *Charles W. Morgan*, the last survivor of a once-great fleet of wooden whaling ships that had an extended career from 1841 to 1921 roaming the seas in search of the giant mammals. Be sure to see the captain's gimballed bed designed to alleviate the effects of a pitching ship. Some three hundred ships and small boats make up the impressive waterborne fleet, including catboats, duckboats, dories, sailing yachts, lifesaving boats, fishing boats, whaleboats, and several types of canoes.

Lining the river and pathways are a varied collection of original nineteenth-century buildings brought here from all over New England to recreate maritime history in a typical village setting. Inside most of them are trained staff demonstrating particular skills of the period, such as woodcarving, rolling pills, ship model building, barrel making, spinning, and weaving. In addition, there are indoor exhibits dedicated to oystering and lobstering, nautical instruments, ship figureheads, catboats, lifesaving, paintings, furnishings, and more.

The Stillman Building houses an exhibit on New England's maritime history, an excellent scrimshaw collection, and a ship model exhibit. In the model restoration shop you can see how its craftsmen maintain the collection with regular repainting and rerigging just as if for full-sized vessels.

In the Mallory Buildings, the life and contributions of the shipbuilding, ship- and yacht-owning Mallory family are on display in the form of oil paintings, ship models, shipyard tools, and family furniture.

The oystering exhibit chronicles the rise and fall of New England's oystering industry, once the most important fishery of all in this country. The centerpieces are an 1824-built dugout canoe, the oldest boat in the museum's collection, and an 1890s New Haven sharpie (an oyster dredger). Around the shed are photographs, tools, various containers, and graphs, all of which help to make up a very complete story.

As the grounds stay open past the exhibits' closing hour, there is no rush to leave, and the *Sabino* excursion can be left for the end of the day.

Longer windjammer cruises lasting a full day and overnight or more have their headquarters here, and first-time sailors might want to test their sea legs by taking a day sail on one of them out into Long Island Sound. On a fine day a cruise under sail is a great way to take the sun and to meet fellow travelers while stabilizing yourself on a sloping deck. Generally, the auxiliary engine is used only for getting into and out of the harbor. If the weather turns poor, you can expect to share very cramped quarters below deck.

Overnight and longer cruises are the only way to get any kind of feeling for what it was like in the hardworking days of sail-powered vessels. While you will eat better and live in more comfortable quarters than the early sailors, and experience the glorious sensation of being on the open sea, you will also undergo the rocking and rolling motion, sharing tight quarters, and having close social contact. While you might take a chance at a last-minute booking for the day sails, if you are intent on an oveernight windjammer cruise, you should make early reservations.

The Seaport's Education Department operates the sixty-seven-foot *Rachel B. Jackson* and the sixty-two-foot *Brilliant*. Call (203) 572-0711 for information.

Out O'Mystic Schooner Cruises (7 Holmes Street, (203) 536-4218), just down the street from the Whaler's Inn, owns the well-known hundred-foot *Mystic Whaler* and the recently acquired hundred-foot *Mystic Clipper*. Day cruises with continental breakfast and lunch are $49–$59, depending on the date. An intriguing option invites passengers to stay overnight *before* the cruise for $75–$109, depending on the cabin and date.

Voyager Cruises (77 Steamboat Wharf, just across the drawbridge, (203) 536-0416), has the largest fleet headed by the eighty-five-foot 1888-built *Charlotte Ann* and the sixty-five-foot *Voyager*. Day sails with lunch and refreshments lasting from 9:30 a.m.–4:30 p.m. cost $40 weekdays, $45 on weekends. Children are half fare. Optional overnight stays before or after the daytime cruise are $15–$25 single and $35 double.

Two additional attractions, located about one-and-a-half miles from the Whaler's Inn, are Old Mistick Village, a shopping center set in an eighteenth-century colonial compound (open Monday–Thursday and Saturday 10:30 a.m.–5:30 p.m., Friday to 9 p.m., 203-536-4941) and the Mystic Marinelife Aquarium (open daily 9 a.m.–6 p.m.) in the summer, 9 a.m.–4:45 p.m. in the winter, 203-536-3323).

The aquarium has hourly sea lion, dolphin, and belukha whale demonstrations inside a large 1,400-seat air-conditioned theater. Sea Island is an outdoor two-acre re-creation of their natural habitat for resident seals and sea lions. Inside there are thirty separate exhibits featuring more than two thousand underwater creatures from all over the world.

APPENDIX
New York Area Transportation Operators

New York City Transit Authority
INFORMATION: (212) 330-1234, twenty-four hours a day.
OFFICES: 370 Jay Street, Brooklyn, NY 11211
PLEASE NOTE: at certain times, you may have to wait to reach a clerk, but when you do, he or she will probably be very helpful and well-informed. For bus and subway maps, write Customer Services, Room 832, at the above address, and be sure to enclose a Number 10, stamped, self-addressed envelope for each item requested.

The Transit Authority buses and subways are owned and operated by a subsidiary of New York State's Metropolitan Transportation Authority, which also runs Metro-North and the Long Island Rail Road.

THE SUBWAY The city's underground and elevated rail lines receive much bad press, but New York's subways make up the world's most elaborate urban rapid transit system, serving nearly every city neighborhood and point of interest. Other cities may have shiny new metros, but they are not nearly so useful and comprehensive. While traveling during rush hours is never fun, off-peak and weekend riders will usually find that the subway will take them where they want to go quickly, efficiently, and cheaply.

Every recommended subway routing that appears in this book is described in sufficient detail for you to decide whether you want to take it, and alternate routes that cannot be recommended are left out altogether.

All subway lines have twenty-four-hour service, although the frequency may be reduced and some through train service eliminated late at night and on weekends.

Maps The entire subway system, operating in all boroughs except Staten Island, is spread out on one map, with important service information for each line listed in the upper right-hand corner. On the reverse side, every line is individually sketched to show all stations, express and local, as well as connecting subway and bus routes. Subway transfers noted can be made without paying an additional fare, but in nearly every instance switching from a subway to a bus requires an additional token.

The subway system is enormously complex, so for routes with which you are not familiar, study the map carefully. There may be more than one way to go and to return, and be aware as well that express trains do not stop at all stations.

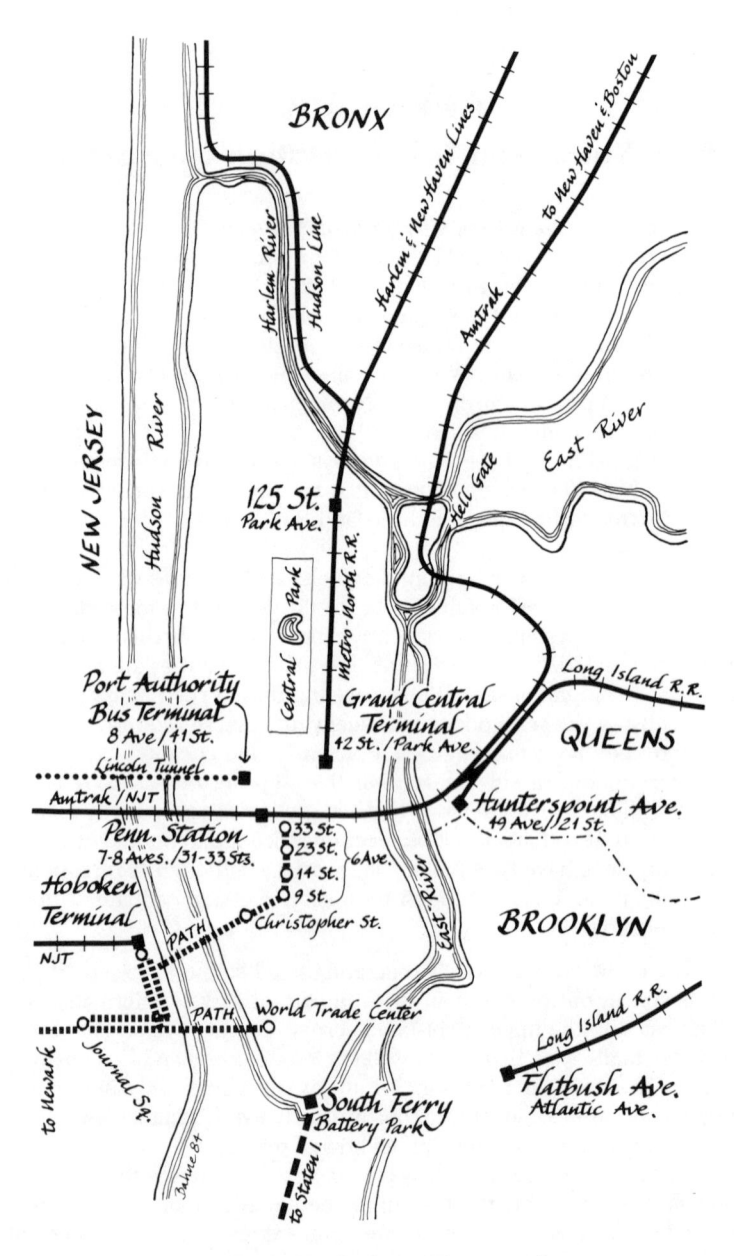

New York City Terminals

While many people still refer to the three subway divisions, the BMT (Brooklyn Manhattan Transit), the IRT (Interborough Rapid Transit) and the IND (Independent Subway) Lines, the Transit Authority is encouraging its three and one-half million daily riders to think instead in terms of route numbers and letters.

Locally, for instance, the Lexington Avenue Line may be referred to as the "Lex," the East Side IRT, or, more specifically, the local or express, the Number 4, 5, or 6, or by its destination, as the Pelham Bay Train or the train to Dyre Avenue. So, if you ask several different people which train to take somewhere, you are apt to get a variety of responses, and they may all be right.

For most travelers, the train number and final destination are most important. If you know these, you will know both the route and whether the train is going at least as far as you want it to go. The Transit Authority is in the process of relettering many of its trains, so during the long transition period you may see differing designations for the same train. AA or K; CC or C; GG or G; LL or L; QB or Q; and RR or R.

Maps are meant to be available at all subway stations, but this is too often not the case. Keep trying every time you're near a station. The information booths at Grand Central Terminal and the Long Island level of Penn Station are usually the best bets. Incredible as it may seem, many subway stations do not have maps posted. All subway cars do, if they haven't been torn out by vandals.

Fares On the subway, you may only use tokens in the turnstiles, unless you are a pass rider. Tokens, good for one ride of any distance, including transfers, cost ninety cents for ages six years and up. People, 65 and over, whether a resident of the city or not, may apply for a Reduced Fare Program for the Elderly card. Write to: Department for the Aging, Reduced Fare Program, 280 Broadway, Room 212, New York, NY 10007. Many senior citizen centers will issue the card with proof of age.

Token booth attendants will make change for bills up to $20. Some token booths sell "Ten Paks" with ten tokens sealed in a plastic bag for $9, no savings, but convenient. Even if you are an infrequent subway user, buy more than one token at a time to avoid long lines. When there isn't a line, add to your supply. Tokens are also good on the city buses. At some subway entrances, during off-peak hours, the token booth may be closed, and there is usually a sign at street level indicating this.

Equipment The condition and age of the trains varies enormously from line to line. Most IND trains have better equipment than the IRT trains, but with the new Japanese-built cars coming onto the IRT, the situation is changing on some lines. Graffiti is rampant throughout the system, with important exceptions where the battle appears to be shifting. Some trains are air-conditioned. Others should be and are not, and the remainder haven't yet had the air-conditioning units installed.

Safety Using normal precautions and some common sense, the subways are as safe as most of the city's residential and commercial neighborhoods.

Many stations have off-hour waiting areas located near the token booths that are marked by overhead yellow bands. When there are not many people on the train, it's advisable to ride in the middle of the train near the conductor. The motorman's car at the head of the train is a good place, too, although late at night there may be few passengers riding this far forward. On many trains, the last car is the smoking car, although the practice is illegal.

Transit police ride many trains and patrol platforms, and even if you don't see one, he or she may be close by. Some Transit Authority police are in plain clothes.

There are, of course, no toilet facilities on any train, and very few stations have unlocked facilities for public use. Try a nearby restaurant. Bicycles are not allowed on trains under any circumstances.

CITY BUSES   You can certainly see more from a bus than from a subway (elevated lines excepted), which makes them often a more pleasant way to travel, yet buses can be a slow and tedious way to travel for long distances. Buses, particularly in midtown Manhattan, are subject to almost constant daytime traffic congestion. As many of the outings in this book are designed for a leisurely day, though, certain long bus rides are recommended for their interesing itineraries.

Many routes do not operate twenty-four hours a day, so be sure to check before you plan a trip that calls for a very early departure or late return, especially on weekends.

Maps Bus maps are much more difficult to come by than subway maps; they are never available on the bus. The best sources are the information booths at Grand Central and the Long Island Rail Road concourse at Penn Station. Failing these suggestions, write the Transit Authority at the address above.

Each of the five boroughs has its own map. The maps show the routes, and have information about frequency and hours of operation. Many bus stops have service charts called "Guide-A-Ride," which indicate the number of the bus or buses that stop there, the route, frequency, and hours of operation. Bus schedules are often erratic; the intervals between buses on the chart may bear no relation to how long you have to wait for the next one to come along. Where the timetable shows six buses an hour, though, it's more likely that you will be able to climb aboard sooner than when only two per hour are scheduled.

Some stops have shelters, too, often with intriguing advertising panels, and the number of these amenities is increasing.

Make sure that the bus is going at least as far as you are, as many operate abbreviated routes or have routes that divide along the way. The bus should have a number and destination sign (newer buses with digital signs may in addition show some of the route) on the front. If not, ask the driver and be certain you understand his answer.

Be able to distinguish between a Transit Authority bus and other operators, such as extra-fare express routes. Some of the outings make use of the expresses, and the operators are named.

Fares On buses, you may use a subway token or ninety cents exact change in nickels, dimes, and quarters (not pennies, half dollars or the ill-fated Susan B. Anthony dollar). Except for pass riders and senior citizens with reduced fare cards, everyone age six or over pays the full fare.

One transfer is free, and while you don't have to make the switch immediately, you must do so at the intersecting point. Transfers are supposed to show the allowable time limits, but not all drivers tear the slip of paper correctly, in which case there is unlimited stopover time for that one day.

Drivers carry no change, so if you find yourself in trouble, be bold and ask your fellow passengers. Most times you will succeed in getting the change you need. The best solution is to carry tokens or a pocket full of correct change.

Equipment The new General Motors buses are comfortable and air-conditioned. The windows, however, are often heavily tinted, which makes seeing inside difficult and looking out like early evening at noontime. Buses delivered since 1984 have less tint. The rear doors are very heavy to open, so if you are slight of build use the front door for exiting.

The older equipment may be in good shape—or be rattle-traps with windows permanently stuck open on cold days and sealed tight in summer. Avoid sitting on the back (hot) seat over the engine after May and before October.

Safety Most people consider buses a safer way than the subway to travel. The driver, being always nearby once you're on the bus helps, although you should do your best to avoid bus stops where there may be few people around.

Long Island Rail Road

INFORMATION: (212) 739-4200, twenty-four hours a day.
OFFICES: Jamaica Station, Jamaica, NY 11435

The Long Island Rail Road is by far the busiest commuter railroad in the United States, and also operates the New York area's best train service (although New Jersey Transit may wish to dispute the statement).

Appendix

The majority of the trains operate from Pennsylvania Station, Manhattan, while others begin at Brooklyn's Flatbush Avenue and Jamaica Station in Queens. A few diesel trains start out at Hunterspoint Avenue and Long Island City, both in Queens.

Tickets and Fares   Purchase your ticket before boarding the train; you'll incur a $1 surcharge if you buy it from the conductor. The Penn Station ticket windows, always open, are located in the very busy main concourse on the lower level of the station near 7th Avenue and 33rd Street. Occasionally the lines are long, especially at rush hours and on summer weekends. Allow ten extra minutes to be safe.

The more adventurous may wish to try one of the ticket vending machines, issuing five types of one-way tickets to all 128 stations on the line. You have a staggering choice of one hundred buttons to push—read the instructions carefully.

There are several different ticket categories depending on your departure time and day of the week. The more expensive, by twenty-five percent, peak-period trains are shown in the shaded areas of the timetables (outbound Monday to Friday from 4 to 7 p.m. and inbound Monday through Friday arriving at the terminal stations from 6 a.m. to 10 a.m.) Off-peak one-way fares are valid at all other times during weekdays and on weekends and holidays, and tickets are valid for ninety days from the date of sale.

Senior citizens (sixty-five and older) and the handicapped, with proper identification, travel for half fare on all trains except the shaded westbound morning trains into New York. Children five to eleven pay half fare. All fares are based on the zones from which and to which you are traveling.

Parlor Cars   Some summer-season weekend trains (Friday out and Sunday or Monday returning) to and from the eastern end of Long Island on the Montauk and Greenport Lines have reserved seat parlor cars. The trains offer two seats on one side and a single seat on the other with an attendant to serve drinks and snacks. The branch timetables indicate which trains carry parlor cars. The additional charge is $12 out to the resorts and $8.75 back.

For parlor car reservations, call (212) 526-6464, weekdays 9 am.–5 p.m, Fridays to 7 p.m. For westbound only reservations call (516) 283-8439 or 283-0312, Saturday 9 a.m.–4:30 p.m. and Sunday 12:30 p.m.–10 p.m.

Timetables and Information   Schedules are available at the racks in Penn Station, with one rack for specific stations and full branch timetables in another. There are eleven color-coded branch line forms, and exact shades may vary from issue to issue.

  Form 1   red — Port Washington Branch
  Form 2   medium blue — Port Jefferson Branch
  Form 3   purple — Ronkonkoma Branch with Greenport Service

Form 4   light green — Oyster Bay Branch
Form 5   mustard — Hempstead Branch
Form 6   brown — Far Rockaway Branch
Form 7   dark green — Babylon Branch
Form 8   orange-red — Long Beach Branch
Form 9   light blue — West Hempstead Branch
Form 10 gray — City Terminal Zone
Form 11 charcoal — Montauk Branch

There is no central departure board for Long Island trains, although one is planned. To learn from what track the train will depart, inquire at the central information booth or wait for the train announcements, usually given with authentic New York accents. The departure gates will list all station stops, the connections, and indicate whether the train is peak or off-peak.

Trains and Equipment   All lines operate multiple-unit electric trains with three and two seating facing both forward and back, with these exceptions: the Oyster Bay Branch shuttle trains are diesel-hauled, as are trains operating beyond Hicksville to Greenport, trains beyond Huntington on the Port Jefferson Branch, and trains running beyond Babylon on the Montauk Branch. Most of the electric equipment is well-maintained. The older diesel fleet is gradually being overhauled, and the old low-back seating is being replaced with more comfortable high-back three- and two-adjoining seats, as found on the electric trains.

Smokers and non-smokers alike will be interested to know that some branch timetables show a train diagram indicating the locations of smoking and non-smoking cars. On most trains, unless there are more than ten cars, only one smoking car is provided.

Bicycles   The LIRR will carry a limited number of bicycles on its trains during off-peak hours. To apply for a $10 Cyc-n-Ride permit, ask for an application at any LIRR station, and allow ten days for processing. The relatively flat world of Long Island can then be your oyster, with the geographical options nearly limitless.

Tours   The LIRR has a varied program of spring, summer, and fall day tours to historic houses, gardens, and inns that are reasonably priced and all-inclusive. For information and reservations, call (212) 526-7782.

Metro-North Commuter Railroad

INFORMATION: (212) 532-4900, twenty-four hours a day
OFFICES: 347 Madison Avenue, New York, NY 10017, (212) 340-3000

Metro-North operates frequent train services from Grand Central Terminal, with many trains stopping at 125th Street and Park Avenue, over three different routes—The Hudson, Harlem, and New Haven Lines. There are local, local-express, and express trains on all three lines.

Tickets and Fares   Purchase your ticket before boarding the train to avoid the extra $1 charge levied by the conductor. Ticket windows are located in Grand Central's main concourse upper level, and they are open from early morning to late at night. The wait in line is rarely more than five minutes.

There are several types of tickets depending on the day and time of travel. Peak-period trains, listed in the shaded areas of the timetables, are more expensive, and run outbound from Grand Central, Monday to Friday between 4 and 7 p.m. and inbound on all morning trains scheduled to arrive at Grand Central before 10 a.m.

Off-peak fares, at a savings of about twenty-five percent off the regular fares, are in effect at all other times during weekdays and on all trains on the weekends and holidays.

Both the Hudson and Harlem Lines offer one-way off-peak fares, valid for three days. The New Haven Line's off-peak fares are on a round-trip basis, priced at one hundred fifty percent of the one-way regular fares, good for one day, up to 3 a.m. the following day, and may be bought up to three days in advance of travel.

Senior citizens, sixty-five and over, and the handicapped, with proper identification, travel at one-half the regular one-way fare at all times except for inbound morning peak-hour trains. Children under twelve travel at half-fare, and those under five are free when accompanied by an adult.

Timetables   These are available at the information booth in Grand Central. Schedules for specific stations and groups of stations are in the racks to the left of the information windows. Complete schedules for all trains and all stations on any one of the three lines are obtainable upon request at the information window, and they are color-coded: Hudson Line schedules are green, the Harlem Line is blue, and the New Haven red. The color-coding extends to the departure signs at the track gates for quick identification.

The main departure board is located over the Metro-North ticket windows, and lists the departure time, train number, and destination, with connections. The track gates have a listing of all stopping stations. Metro-North departures are not announced unless there is a change in the usual departure track.

Trains and Equipment

Hudson Line.   Modern and recently rebuilt electric multiple unit cars run on most trains from Grand Central to the end of the electrified third-rail line at Croton-Harmon, thirty-three miles from Grand Central. This line is a particularly scenic one, for which a Rail Route Guide is provided earlier on in the book.

There is fixed seating, facing forward and back, with three seats on one side of the aisle and two on the other. Most of this equipment is in good repair, although you may have to hunt for a clear window on some of the older cars.

A wide variety of equipment, ranging from the latest diesel rail cars to some of the shabbiest coaches found anywhere in this country, operates from Croton-Harmon to Poughkeepsie, a distance of thirty-nine miles (seventy-one miles from Grand Central). You simply take your chances. Some windows are completely opaque, so get to the train early to find the clearest ones, not always an easy task in the subterranean half-light of Grand Central.

Some trains run through from Grand Central to Poughkeepsie without having to change at Croton-Harmon, and they are shown in the timetable without the small letter *c* before the times for stations from Croton-Harmon to Poughkeepsie. These Poughkeepsie trains, as well, operate with the wide variety of equipment mentioned above.

There is no food service of any kind on Hudson Line trains, and bar service is limited to a few selected afternoon rush-hour departures. However, Grand Central has take-out services galore.

Harlem Line. The latest electric cars operate all trains from Grand Central to Brewster North, a distance of fifty-three miles. Beyond that point for the additional twenty-four miles to Dover Plains (seventy-seven miles from Grand Central), most trains are single diesel rail cars traveling over a single-track rural branch line. The scenery is pleasant most of the way, wooded or suburban with some open country. There is no food service on any Harlem Line train, and bar service is very limited.

New Haven Line. Electric trains, many in need of refurbishing, run on all trains from Grand Central to New Haven, a distance of seventy-two miles, and on all trains on the New Canaan Branch. Older coaches, in varying states of repair, operate only on rush-hour through trains from Grand Central to stations on the Danbury Branch. Diesel rail cars run on other trains on the Danbury Branch, and on all trains on the Waterbury Branch. Occasionally, if the diesel rail cars are in the shop, other less suitable equipment will be substituted.

Many rail fans like the old coaches and elderly diesel engines, but the regular riders generally do not. Unless you fall into the first category, you'll probably be happier traveling on the less venerable equipment.

The New Haven line has bar and snack cars on many of its trains operating to and from Stamford and New Haven and to Danbury during weekday afternoons and evenings.

Bicycles are now allowed on Metro-North trains, except at rush hours. Call for information about obtaining a permit. The New Haven Line is scenic, and a Rail Route Guide has been provided.

184 Appendix

Port Authority Trans-Hudson Corporation

INFORMATION: (212) 466-7649, twenty-four hours a day
OFFICES: One World Trade Center, 62W, New York, NY 10048

The PATH system links midtown and Lower Manhattan via two tunnels to the Hoboken Terminal, Journal Square, Jersey City, and to downtown Newark, New Jersey. The system was built in the early part of this century to connect various rail terminals and other rapid transit lines, and PATH still performs its job admirably.

While the service runs twenty-four hours a day, the four separate weekday routes are combined to two late at night and on weekends. Study the useful PATH Map Guide for details. The Manhattan terminals are at 33rd Street and 6th Avenue, with stops along 6th at 23rd, 14th, and 9th Streets, at Christopher and Greenwich Streets, and in Lower Manhattan at the World Trade Center.

Fares   There are no manned token booths anywhere on the system. Passengers must have exact change (nickels, dimes, and quarters) for the seventy-five cent flat fare, or use a $1 bill in a machine that returns a quarter.

Timetables   The PATH Map Guide, periodically updated, shows routes and frequencies, and is available at most terminal stations. Be sure to look for signs above the train doors that read "HOB" for Hoboken, "JSQ" for Journal Square, "NWK" for Newark, "WTC" for the World Trade Center, and "33" for 33rd Street and 6th Avenue.

Trains and Equipment   Nearly all the equipment looks fairly new, even though many of the cars are twenty years old. All cars are air-conditioned, offer a variety of seating arrangements and large picture windows, and are without graffiti.

Two words of warning. Rush hours on the WTC–NWK and WTC–HOB trains are among the most crowded in the city, and in some cases the conductor's announcements are inaudible. Over the next few years, too, all the PATH cars are being put through a complete overhaul.

The PATH is considered to be quite safe at almost any hour. If you have doubts, ride with the conductor, who usually stands in either the first or last car of the train.

Bicycles am permitted on weekends only with a special permit issued by the Port Authority. However, many cyclists appear to use the system without one.

New Jersey Transit Trains

INFORMATION in New Jersey only: (800) 772-2222; out of state, including New York, (201) 762-5100 6 a.m. to midnight

OFFICES: 95 Orange Street, P.O. Box 720, Newark, NJ 07101

In the last few years, New Jersey Transit has made dramatic improvements on some of its most important rail lines, with new coaches, additional and rehabilitated electrified mileage, increased train service, and the restoration of many of its stations. New Jersey Transit's rail services can be recommended for the casual rider with very few qualifications. Note that there is no food or bar service on any New Jersey Transit trains, and that bicycles are not permitted.

It is well to keep in mind that New Jersey Transit trains use three different terminals for their rail operations: Penn Station, New York, the Hoboken Terminal, and Penn Station, Newark. The lines assigned to each terminal will be included below and repeated in *Getting There and Back* information for each outing.

Tickets and Fares Purchase tickets before boarding the train to avoid paying a $1 surcharge. Ticket windows are open for all but the very earliest and very latest departures at all terminals. The waiting lines generally move quickly.

Fares are on a regular one-way basis or seven-day round-trip excursion, giving a reduction of about one-third off two one-way tickets. The excursion fares are not available on trains arriving at the three terminals in the morning rush hours and on trains leaving the same terminals during the afternoon rush hours, or on some outbound early morning weekday departures. Peak-hour times vary from line to line, so it is best to consult specific timetables, looking at the head of the columns for circled numbers 1, 2, or 3, and then reading the restrictions.

Senior citizens, sixty-two and over, and handicapped persons travel at reduced one-way fares, which are not listed in the timetables, upon presentation of a New Jersey Transit Reduced Fare Card or Medicare Card. Children five to eleven travel at roughly half fare when accompanied by a parent or guardian, and children under four go free. In addition, on weekends and holidays, two children eleven and under travel free with every adult paying the regular one-way or excursion round-trip fare. A Special Excursion Fare ticket, priced at $10, allows unlimited one-day weekend and holiday travel on all New Jersey Transit rail lines.

Terminals, Timetables, Information, and Equipment

PENN STATION, NEW YORK Timetables (red) are available at the information booth in the ticket concourse, in the racks, or from the attendant on duty. There are schedules for the entire line as well as individual cards for specific stations. All departures are announced, sometimes with great style, and posted on the departure boards in the ticket concourse and the main waiting room.

North Jersey Coast Line. This line offers direct service or a change at Newark to Shore Points on the New Jersey coastline as far south as Bay Head Junction, sixty-seven miles from New York. The connecting trains at Newark are indicated in the timetables by the letter *c*. There are trains every day of the week, although the service is greatly reduced on Saturday, Sunday, and holidays. Summer weekends see an expansion of service to the resorts, including the limited-stops "Shore Express."

The equipment is new electric multiple-unit coaches on all trains running from Penn Station to Matawan. On diesel trains originating in Newark and operating beyond Matawan, most of the coaches are in good condition, with a few exceptions, mostly at rush hour, when everything that runs is used.

Northeast Corridor Line. Use this line for direct service to New Brunswick, Princeton Junction (change for Princeton), and Trenton, fifty-seven miles from New York. The line is a full-service operation with frequent trains running every day of the week. Some stations are also served by Amtrak trains at slightly higher fares. The equipment is all electric, and generally in good condition.

NEWARK PENN STATION Timetables (red) are available at the information booth in the main waiting and ticket room. There are schedules for the entire line as well as individual cards for specific stations. Departures are announced and posted in the main waiting-ticket room.

North Jersey Coast Line. Those trains marked with the letter *c* next to the departure and arrival times at New York (Penn Station) originate in Newark, with a connecting train from New York.

Northeast Corridor Line. All trains originate in Penn Station, New York, and stop here.

Raritan Valley Line. All trains originate in Newark, are diesel-hauled, and carry relatively new coaches. The line reaches twenty-nine miles to Raritan, with some rush-hour trains operating to and from High Bridge, the end of the line.

HOBOKEN, NEW JERSEY Timetables (blue) are available at the ticket windows in the main waiting room. Departures are not normally announced, but are posted on the main departure board in the train concourse. The individual track gates give a list of all stops and connections, if any.

The Morris and Essex Line. Trains run to Morristown and Dover (forty-one miles) on the Morristown Line, over the Gladstone Branch (forty-two miles), and over the Montclair Branch (thirteen miles). This heavily used and recently modernized line operates frequent train service during the weekdays, weekends, and holidays. There is reduced Sunday service on the Gladstone Branch, though, and no midday, Saturday, Sunday, or holiday service on the Montclair Branch.

All the equipment is modern electric multiple-unit coaches offering first-rate service. Complete re-electrification in 1984 sent the ancient Lackawanna electrics dating from 1917 to 1930, and featuring rattan seats, ceiling fans, and open windows, out to pasture.

Main Line/Bergen County Line including Port Jervis service. Most trains run to Suffern (thirty miles) with some rush-hour and a couple of off-peak trains offering service to points in lower New York State as far as Port Jervis (eighty-seven miles). On all but several rush-hour trains, change at Suffern. There is fairly frequent service on weekdays, with reduced departures on Saturday, and no Sunday service.

All equipment is diesel-operated with well-maintained locomotive-hauled cars, operating as far as Suffern, except during morning and evening rush hours, when trains run through Suffern to points in New York State. When a change of trains is required, the equipment is usually vintage diesel-rail cars.

Boonton Line. Diesel-hauled weekday rush-hour service only to Dover (thirty-eight mines) and Netcong (forty-eight miles).

Pascack Valley Line. Diesel-hauled weekday rush-hour service only, with one late evening train from Hoboken. The line operates to Spring Valley, New York (thirty-one miles).

Amtrak Trains

INFORMATION AND RESERVATIONS: (212) 736-4545 or (800) USA-RAIL, twenty-four hours a day

CORPORATE ADDRESS: National Railroad Passenger Corporation, 400 N. Capitol Street, N.W., Washington, DC 20001

For purposes of the outings mentioned in this book, Amtrak trains operate north and south along the Northeast Corridor from New York's Penn Station, and north along the Hudson River from Grand Central Terminal. At some stations where local commuter services also operate, passengers cannot use Amtrak trains, even though they may stop there. See the Northeast Corridor and New York State timetables for these restrictions. At stations where passengers may choose between Amtrak and the commuter railroad, Amtrak trains will usually be more expensive, more comfortable, perhaps faster, and may be less frequent.

Tickets and Fares   There are five Amtrak locations in Manhattan (credit cards accepted) and numerous Amtrak-appointed travel agents.

1. Pennsylvania Station between 7th and 8th Avenues and 31st to 33rd Streets. Ticket concourse is open for all trains except in the middle of the night. Allow an extra ten to fifteen minutes at peak times.

2. Grand Central Terminal at Park Avenue and 42nd Street. Ticket windows are up the ramp beneath the clock on the right-hand side, off the main upper-level concourse, and are open for all trains. Allow an extra ten

to fifteen minutes at peak hours. Timetables are available at the information booth in the center of the main upper-level concourse.

3. Lobby of One World Trade Center among the airline counters on the West Street side. Open regular business hours, as are nos. 4 and 5.

4. Amtrak office at 12 West 51st Street, just off 5th Avenue at Rockefeller Center.

5. 1 East 59th Street in an arcade with several airlines.

Buy your tickets before boarding, otherwise you pay a penalty of $3, and you may not be able to take advantage of some of the reduced fares.

There are two individual fares—one-way and round-trip excursion, good for thirty days, but not for trains scheduled to leave Friday and Sunday between 1 and 7 p.m. and during certain holiday periods.

Family Plan Amtrak offers a special fifty percent discount for a spouse and children 12–21 when one adult pays full fare; children two to eleven travel for seventy-five percent less. The Family Plan is available at all times. Senior citizens sixty-five and older with proof of age receive a twenty-five percent discount on round-trip travel, with some holiday restrictions.

Trains and Equipment

FROM PENN STATION   All trains on the Northeast Corridor are modern and electric-locomotive-hauled, with coaches having two reclining seats on each side of the aisle. Most trains, except the Philadelphia "Clockers," carry snack or dinette cars. Extra-fare club cars have spacious two and one reserved seating with an attendant. Meals and snacks are included in the fare. The hourly Metroliner Service trains are available from New York south only, and they are extra-fare and must be reserved in advance.

FROM GRAND CENTRAL   Trains are locomotive-hauled diesel-electric, with coaches and snack or dinette cars, or Turbo Trains with a snack car and a reserved seat Custom Class car available for an extra charge of $6. Custom Class is highly recommended for holiday travel periods.

Departures   All Amtrak trains are announced at both Penn Station and Grand Central. The departure gates have signs listing station stops (not necessarily all stops at Penn Station). At Penn Station, track numbers are posted about ten to fifteen minutes before departure, while at Grand Central, the departure gate is known well in advance.

Bicycles   Bicycles may be carried on a very few trains marked with baggage car symbols. The charge is $10 plus local tax including a mandatory box, and handlebars and pedals must be removed. Be sure to phone in advance to see that a box is available, and arrive at the station about an hour before train departure.

INDEX

Adirondack Trailways, 96
Amtrak, 76, 109–112, 127–129, 143–146, 152, 158, 167, 187–188
Amusements, 24, 45, 49–50, 55, 121
Antiques, shopping for, 40, 65, 69, 88, 91–92, 155
Aquariums, 49–51, 55, 174
Aqueduct, 16
Armory (Flushing), 26
Art exhibits, 64. *See also* Museums.
As-Is Thrift Shop, 40
Asbury Park, 121

Bay Head, 124
Bayard Cutting Arboretum, 72–76
Beaches, 49–52, 55, 119–124, 166
Belmar, 121–123
Bennett House, 63
Bennett Park, 6
Bicycling, 165–166
Bird sanctuary, 10
Block Island, 158, 163–166
 Block Island Conservancy, 165
Boating, 96–97, 170–174
 excursion, 166, 171–173
 race, 171
Bookstores, 69, 93, 155, 171
Borough Hall (Brooklyn Heights), 33, 35–36
Boscobel Restoration, 88–89, 93–94
Bourse (Philadelphia), 125
Bowne House, 24–28
Bowne Street Community Congregational and Reformed Church, 29
Brass Penny Restaurant, 116, 118
Brass Rail, 106
Bridgeport and Port Jefferson Steamboat Company, 68
Bridgeport ferry, 66–68
Brighton Beach, 49–52
Bronx River, 16
Bronx Zoo, 13–14, 17–18
Brooklyn Botanic Gardens, 40–45
Brooklyn Bridge, walking the, 32–34
Brooklyn General Post Office, 33
Brooklyn Heights, 31–40
 Brooklyn Heights Promenade, 35–36
Brooklyn Historical Society, 35

Brooklyn Museum, 40–43
Burial ground, Indian, 10
Buses
 Bronx, 9, 12–13, 14–15, 17, 19–21
 New Jersey, 104, 117
 New Paltz, 96
 Upper Manhattan, 3

Cathedral Church of St. John the Divine, 5
Central Park, 5
Circa Antiques, Ltd., 40
Circa Too, 40
City Hall (Philadelphia), 134–135
City Island, 18–23
 City Island Historical and Nautical Museum, 23
Clam Broth House, 103, 105–106
Clipper Ship Bookshop, 155
Cloisters, The, 3, 6
Cold Spring, Village of, 88–95
Concerts, 13, 64, 75, 82, 94, 150, 157, 166
Coney Island, 49–50, 54–55
Connecticut, 141–174
Connecticut River Steamboat Dock Foundation, 154–155
Crafts, 63
Cruises. *See* Boats, excursion.
C. W. Campion's, 122

Danford's of Bayles Dock, 70
Delicatessens, 51–52, 93
Dreschers, 150
Drifters I, 105
Dyckman House, 3–4, 7

1833 House, 169
Enid A. Haupt Conservatory, 13, 15
Environmental learning center, 13
Esplanade (Brooklyn Heights), 35–36
Essex, 150–157

Ferries, 23, 70–72, 157
 Block Island, 163–164
 Fishers Island, 162–163
 Port Jefferson, 66–68
 Staten Island, 61–62

189

Index

Ferrybank Restaurant, 36
Festivals, 81–82, 169, 171
Fishers Island, 158, 162–163
Fishing, 50, 52–54
Fish Town, 51
Flushing, 24–31
  Flushing Meadow Park, 24, 26
  Flushing Meadow Zoo, 26
  Flushing Town Hall, 27–28
Foffe's, 35
Fordham University, 14
Forno's, 114
Fort Tryon, 6
  Fort Tryon Park, 3, 6
Foundry School Museum, 92
Four Seasons Hotel, 138–139
Franklin Institute Science Museum, 124–125, 133–134
Franklin Plaza Hotel, 139
Fulton Ferry State Park, 37

Gallery (Philadelphia), 125, 135
Gardens, 6, 11–17, 24, 29, 40–45, 64, 70, 72–76. *See also* Parks.
Gateway National Park, 47
Gladstone, 116–119
Golf course, municipal, 10
Goodspeed Opera House, 157
Good Times Bookshop, 69
Grace Episcopal Church, 23
Gramma's Sweet Shop, 69
Grandad's Barn, 22
Griswold Inn, 150–154
Gull, 155

Harbor View Cafe, 37
Helmer's, 106–107
H. H. Richardson Railroad Station, 159
Hikes, 13, 89, 94–95
Historical Museum (Staten Island), 63
Historical Society (Port Jefferson), 70
Hoboken (New Jersey), 102–108
  Hoboken House, 106
  Hoboken Land Building, 105
Holiday Inn (Philadelphia), 140
Horticultural programs, 48, 75
Hotels, 33, 123, 138–140, 164–165. *See also* Inns.
Houses, historic, 3–4, 7–14, 24, 28–29, 34–35, 37–38, 45, 63, 81–88, 93–99, 161, 170
Hudson House, 91
Hudson Palisades, 3

Hudson Rogue Company, 93
Hudson Valley Rail Road Guide, 76–81, 87

Iberia, 114
Independence Hall, 135
Inns, 21, 91, 150–154, 167–169. *See also* Hotels.
Inwood Hill Park, 3
Ironbound, 109, 113–116
Irving's Deli, 52
Islands, 158–166

Jamaica Bay Wildlife Refuge, 42, 46–49
Johnny's Reef Restaurant, 22
Joshua Hempsted House, 161

Kavkas, 52
Kingsland Homestead, 24, 26, 28–29
Korean Church of Queens, 29

Lady Jane's, 107
Lakes, 10
Lake-Tysen House, 63
Lectures, 12, 48, 75, 94, 171
Lefferts Homestead, 45
Le Jardin, 108
Liberty Bell, 135
Liberty Lines, 9, 12, 16–17
Lighthouse, 165
Lisanne, 39
Lobster Box, 22
Long Branch, 121
Long Island Historical Society, 35
Long Island Rail Road, 25, 68, 72, 74, 179–181
Lyndhurst Castle, 81–85

Mallory Building, 172
M & I International Food, 51
Manhattan, Upper, 3–8
Margaret Corbin Plaza, 6
Marie's Forever Old Shop, 92
Mattatuk Museum, 149
Max's, 121
Maxwell House Coffee plant, 105, 107
Metro-North Commuter Railroad, 76, 85, 89, 96, 143–146, 181–183
Milk Farm, 47
Minnieford Yacht Yard, 23
Mohonk Mountain House, 95–99
Mosholu museum, 136–137
Mrs. Stahl's Knishes, 52

Index 191

Museum of American Indian, 5
Museums, 3, 5, 23–24, 26, 30, 40–43, 63–64, 70, 92, 124–125, 130–134, 136–137, 149, 154–156, 166, 172
Mystic, 166–174
  Mystic Marinelife Aquarium, 174
  Mystic Seaport, 170–171, 173
  Mystic Seaport Museum, 166, 168–169

Nathaniel Hempsted (Huguenot) House, 161
Nathan's Famous, 55
National Tennis Center, 26
Nautical Antiques, 22
Newark (New Jersey), 109–116
  Newark Penn Station, 112–113
Newhouse Art Gallery, 59
New Jersey, 100–124
New Jersey Transit, 109–112, 116–117, 120, 127–129, 184–187
New London (Connecticut), 158–162
New York (state), 57–99
New York Aquarium, 49–51, 55
New York Botanical Gardens, 13–17
New York City
  boroughs, 1–56
  Transit Authority, 175–179
  Transit Exhibition, 31–32
New York Sailing School, 23

Offshore Sailing School, 23
Olde Post Inn, 91
Orient Point, 158, 162–163
Our Lady of Lebanon Maronite Church, 35
Out O'Mystic Schooner Cruises, 173

Parks, 3, 5, 9–10, 12–17, 21, 26, 36–37, 42, 45, 47. *See also* Gardens.
PATH. *See* Port Authority Trans-Hudson Corporation.
Pelham Bay Park, 21
Peninsula, the, 114
Penn's Landing, 136–138
Philadelphia, 124–140
  city transportation, 129–130
Philadelphia Museum of Art, 124–125, 130–131
Philipsburg Manor, 81–82, 85–86
Photographic workshops, 12
Plays, 64
Point Pleasant Beach, 124

Port Authority Trans-Hudson Corporation, 103–104, 109–110, 116, 184
Port Jefferson, 66–72
  Port Jefferson Historical Society, 66
Port of History Museum, 137
Pratt House, 156
Prospect Park, 42, 45
  Prospect Park Zoo, 45

Quaker Meeting House (Flushing), 26–28
Queens Botanical Gardens, 24, 29
Queens Museum, 24, 26, 30

Resorts
  mountain, 95–99
  seaside, 119–124
Restaurants, 36–39, 52, 92, 103, 105–108, 116, 118, 121–123, 155
  French, 32, 35, 39, 106
  German, 106–107
  Italian, 35, 37, 106
  Middle Eastern, 32, 38–39
  North African, 38
  Portugese, 114–115
  seafood, 18, 21–22, 70, 105–106, 169
  Spanish, 114–115
Rhode Island, 141–174
Richardson, H. H. Railroad Station, 159
Richmondtown Restoration, 59–65
Ricco's Ristorante, 106
River Cafe, 36–37
River Museum, 155–156
Riverdale Park, 12
Rodman's Hollow, 165
Rodin Museum, 124–125, 132–133
Rogue & Rebelo, 114

Sagres, 114–115
Sailing
  courses, 23
  museum, 136–137, 172
Sailors Snug Harbor, 60
St. George Hotel, 33
Sandpiper Restaurant, 123
Seaman's Inne, 171
Seaport Store, 171
Sheepshead Bay, 49–54
Shops, 22, 39–40, 43, 51, 69, 85, 92–93, 122, 125, 135–136, 155, 171
Shore Line Rail Road Guide, 143–146
Sleepy Hollow Restorations, 81–88
Snuff Mill, 15

Index

Snug Harbor, 64
 Snug Harbor Cultural Center, 59
Southeast Lighthouse, 165
Spring House, 164–165
Spring Lake, 121–123
Staten Island, 59–65
 Staten Island Botanical Gardens, 64
 Staten Island Ferry, 61
 Staten Island Museum, 64
 Staten Island Zoo, 59–60, 65
Station One, 92
Steamboat Cafe, 169
Stephens House, 63
Stevens Institute of Technology, 105, 107
Stillman Building, 172
Subway
 Bronx, 9, 12, 15–17, 19–21
 Brooklyn, 41–42, 45, 51, 54
 Brooklyn Heights, 32
 Flushing, 25–27, 30–31
 Manhattan, Upper, 5
 Staten Island, 65
Sunnyside, 81–84

Tennis, 26
Thwaites Inn, 21
Trains
 Brooklyn, 46–47
 Connecticut-Rhode Island, 143–150, 152, 158, 167
 Flushing, 25–27, 30–31
 Hudson Highlands, 89, 95
 Hudson Valley, 76–81
 New Jersey, 103–104, 109–112, 116–117, 120

New Paltz, 96
Oakdale, 72–74
Philadelphia, 127–129
Port Jefferson, 66–68, 71–72
Staten Island, 64
Tarrytown, 82, 85, 87
tourist, 146–150, 156–157
Trolleys, 113, 136

Valley Railroad, 156–157
Van Cortlandt Manor, 81–82, 86–88
 Van Cortlandt Mansion, 8–11, 14
 Van Cortlandt Park, 9–10
Voorlezer's House, 67
Voyager Cruises, 173

Walking tours, 12, 31–32, 34, 48, 70, 105, 154–155, 165, 170–171
Wanamaker's, John, department store, 135
Warren Hotel, 123
Washington Heights, 5
Waterbury
 branch line train ride, 146–150
Wave Hill Estate, 8–9, 11–12, 14
Weeping Beech Park, 26
Weeping Beech Tree, 24, 29
Whale Oil Row, 161
Whaler's Inn, 167–169
Wildlife refuge, 10, 46–49

Your Country Deli, 93

Zoos, 13–14, 17–18, 24, 45, 59–60, 65

FOR YOUR INFORMATION

The Harvard Common Press is located in Boston, Massachusetts. We specialize in practical guides to small business, careers, travel, family matters, and cooking. We also have an imprint, Gambit books, which includes illustrated children's books and literary titles. If you'd like to see a copy of our complete catalog, which includes our line of travel books, please write to us at: The Harvard Common Press, 535 Albany Street, Boston, Massachusetts 02118. Our books are available from bookstores, or, if you'd like to order directly from us, please send a check for the cost of the book plus $2 postage and handling.

We have listed a few of our titles below that we thought might interest readers of this book.

The Best Things
in New York Are Free
By Marian Hamilton
$10.95, paperback, ISBN 0-916782-75-1
A comprehensive resource book to everything that's free in New York City. Includes all sorts of attractions and activities: museums and historical houses, art galleries, churches, films and concerts, special tours, libraries, parks, cultural societies, and much more, with over 1,000 listings. *560 pages, available August, 1985.*

Best Places to Stay
in New England
By Christina Tree and Bruce Shaw
$9.95, paperback, ISBN 0-916782-74-3
A guide to the best accommodations in New England, including inns, small hotels, motels, resorts, bed & breakfasts, and farms. This is the first guide to group accommodations according to the kind of vacation experience the reader desires. *288 pages, available December, 1985.*

Inside Outlets
The Best Bargain Shopping
in New England
By Naomi R. Rosenberg and Marianne W. Sekulow
$8.95, paperback, ISBN 0-916782-66-2
This handy, informative guide provides a critical, quality-conscious listing of the best in New England's bargain shopping. Special features include at-a-glance price/quality level ratings, shopping "itineraries" for scenic regions, savvy consumer information, and over $100 worth of money-saving coupons from big-name stores. *224 pages, available now.*

*How to Take Great Trips
with Your Kids*
By Sanford and Joan Portnoy
$14.95, cloth, ISBN 0-916782-52-5
$8.95, paperback, ISBN 0-916782-51-4
Taking the kids on a family trip can be easy and fun—but many parents don't know the special techniques that will make it that way. Whether you're driving to Aunt Helen's or flying to Zanzibar, this book offers the ABCs of planning, packing, and en-route problem-solving. *192 pages, available now.*

The Portable Pet
How to Travel Anywhere
with Your Dog or Cat
By Barbara Nicholas
$10.95, cloth, ISBN 0-916782-50-6
$5.95, paperback, ISBN 0-916782-49-2
Every year thousands of Americans choose to travel with their pets, yet a maze of requirements and regulations confronts such travelers. Now the answers can be found in this lively and pragmatic guide to travel with dogs and cats. *96 pages, available now.*

THE CAREFREE GETAWAY GUIDE FOR NEW YORKERS